D0323513

## ALSO BY CHARLES ROWAN BEYE

*Odysseus: A Life*

*Ancient Epic Poetry: Homer, Apollonius, Virgil*

*Epic and Romance in the "Argonautica" of Apollonius*

*Ancient Greek Literature and Society*

*Alcestis by Euripides: A Translation with Commentary*

*The "Iliad," the "Odyssey," and the Epic Tradition*

# MY HUSBAND
## AND MY WIVES

# MY HUSBAND AND MY WIVES

---

## A Gay Man's Odyssey

## CHARLES ROWAN BEYE

Farrar, Straus and Giroux

New York

Farrar, Straus and Giroux
18 West 18th Street, New York 10011

Copyright © 2012 by Charles Rowan Beye
Distributed in Canada by D&M Publishers, Inc.
Printed in the United States of America
First edition, 2012

Library of Congress Cataloging-in-Publication Data
Beye, Charles Rowan.
    My husband and my wives : a gay man's odyssey / Charles Rowan Beye. — 1st ed.
      p.   cm.
    ISBN 978-0-374-29871-5 (alk. paper)
    1. Beye, Charles Rowan.   2. Gay men—United States—Biography.   3. College
teachers—United States—Biography.   I. Title.

HQ75.8.B49A3 2012
306.76'620092—dc23

                                                                    2011050217

Designed by Jonathan D. Lippincott

www.fsgbooks.com

1   3   5   7   9   10   8   6   4   2

# Contents

# Author's Note

I am grateful to Richard Barsam and Jane Scovell for separately bringing this memoir to the attention of Jonathan Galassi, and to that gentleman for his acute and sympathetic editing. Several friends who read the manuscript gave me suggestions for the prose or reminded me when my memory had gone awry; I must thank Mort Berman, Lindley Boegehold, Casey Cameron, Henry Chalfant, Nick Dubrule, my cousins Jane and Jeremy Hamilton, Chris Holownia, Sally McElroy, Scott Perry, Bill and Judy Plott, Willard Spiegelman, Ann Rosener, and James Tatum. My friend Stephen Pascal and my daughter Helen Tomilson did close reading and provided commentary that was miraculous. My husband, Richard, who has heard during the past twenty-two years every anecdote of my life more often than he could possibly want, provided a very useful corrective.

This book is dedicated to the many people named or described in its pages who are no longer with us to tell their versions of what I describe herein. To them and to those who still walk this earth, I give my devoted thanks for making me the person I am.

# MY HUSBAND
## AND MY WIVES

# Introduction

In May 2005, the woman I had married on the sixteenth of June, 1956, lay dying in an assisted living facility about ten blocks from my home. We had been divorced since 1976, and after some years of embarrassed, frosty encounters, we were once again able to speak with honesty and affection to one another, at least when discussing our four children and their progeny. The children were in town, staying with me, going over to talk with their mother, who went in and out of consciousness as the pain, and the opiates, and her disinclination to eat or drink dictated. I should have written "with us," since the household included Richard, my partner of fifteen years, whom I was to marry in a church ceremony three years later in 2008. He had long since become a kind of stepfather in the family. At the time he was coming home from teaching to do a lot of the housework so I could tend to whatever the children needed.

Whenever any one of them came home from visiting their mother to get some rest, the inevitable was, "Dad, you really should go to see Mom, to say goodbye, or something."

And I would resist, arguing that she was lying helpless in bed with no control over those who came to her, that she and I had too many bad memories, that the deathbed setting would be a temptation to try to "make things right," and that would be too lopsided, wrong, if not cruel. Better to stay away. But they persisted. On the night of May 8 they stood together in the doorway to her bedroom, where she lay between oblivion and consciousness, themselves going back and forth about the impending visit that some of them were determined to force me to make the following day. Finally it was agreed that they would argue me down when they returned home that evening.

Two hours later she died, and when they reported to me the scene of that evening, I knew in a flash that she had said to herself, *I want out of here. No visit from Charlie.*

What would I have said to her? Or, she, poor thing, to me? The kaleidoscope of emotions that color any recollection—hurt, pride, joy, sorrow, embarrassment, shame, passion, one could go on and on—render any seemingly assured remark highly suspect. One wants to sort out the details of the past, but often it is like going through yesterday's wardrobe, surprised by the irremediable damage and wastage of so much lying in those drawers next to undeniable treasures. It is not what one had suspected.

That scene comes to mind maybe because I am writing a memoir that is in one way or another addressed to her. It is the story of a male who grows up to be gay, complicated by the fact that at age twenty-one he got married—yes, to a woman, and yes, it was a highly pleasurable relationship and the sex was good. She was my wife for five years until her tragic, premature death. Almost immediately I went on to marry a second woman, with whom I had what I remember as a delirious sexual relationship and who bore me four wonderful children, two boys and two girls. Throughout all the years of this surprising turn in sexual affections I never stopped having the strongest possible desire for males of almost any age, a desire I tried to realize whenever I could. Now that the whole thing is nearly over—I'm more than eighty—I ask myself, *What was that all about?*

The burden of parenting eventually killed the marriage. At least that's how I think of it; she would have said it was because I was gay. Obviously I was, as they say, sexually conflicted. Heterosexuality did eventually lose its charm for me, true. My wife and I grew estranged. I tried sex with a third woman, in an odd little inn in Arles, of all places. We were traveling with my children, all in their early teens, which more or less killed the chance for the passion to grow into what might have made for a real affair. That brief episode stifled the impulse with women for me, except for those every-now-and-then grim attempts to "make our marriage work," and at the end, as we moved to the final stages of divorce, some bizarre couplings, ferocious, really.

After twenty years we were divorced, and I moved to Cambridge, Massachusetts, the home of eternal youth. Thereafter I had four young male lovers in succession, real affairs of the heart, the first real relationships with males I had ever known. All this practice in carnality and connubiality culminated in a long-term relationship and subsequent marriage to a male, a fellow student of the classics, almost my coeval, who I hope will be there to close my eyes in death.

It all seemed so easy when I first contemplated a memoir. Some of my young gay friends have urged me to write about my high school years, since I grew up in a world they can only imagine. Some older gays, however, are not so sympathetic. You had it too easy in high school, they declare. Where's the pain? Have you repressed it? Or they ask: What were your real motives in marrying? Once for the lark of it, yes. But twice? The boys you had sex with in high school were straight? Weren't you just a teeny bit predatory? Aren't we almost talking a kind of rape, maybe? Or what kind of a sex life were you having, giving satisfaction and getting none in return? What does that say about your mentality? I have a woman friend who calls those high school blow jobs abuse. ("Those boys were abusing you. Did they care about your satisfaction? No. That's clear sexual abuse.") But she's a professor and in the academy sex is all about power. And, of course, there is always the question: What about you and those students you were involved with, Professor? An old friend of mine, with whom I had a brief affair when he was just about to graduate from college, has always told me that he considered our relationship to be the foundation of his adult happiness, the key to understanding human intimacy and sustaining a good marriage. He was surprised recently to be told by a therapist that he must consider my overtures and his yielding as the sexual abuse of a youth by an older male. I was thirty-five to his twenty-three.

I could be writing another kind of memoir. The WASP story, for instance. There is a lot of talk about the white Anglo-Saxon Protestant heritage in this memoir that my name does not suggest. I am named after my father's mentor, Charles James Rowan, the chief of staff in the Department of Surgery at the State University of Iowa, a kindly old Roman Catholic of Irish descent who agreed to stand sponsor at my Episcopalian christening when he didn't find anything in the language of *The Book of Common Prayer* that was theologically offensive. Beye was the surname of Wilhelm Friedrich Beye, who came to the United States from Halle an der Weser in the 1850s as a fifteen-year-old boy, enlisted in the Union Army from Illinois when he was nineteen, and several years later met and married a Bostonian, Nellie Christabel Lombard. She was descended from people who came on the first and second ships to Massachusetts, principally Thomas Lombard, who settled in Dorchester in 1630. The Beyes raised their family in Oak Park, Illinois. Their son, Howard Lombard Beye, my father, married Ruth Elizabeth Ketcham, also of Oak Park, a woman who could claim a genealogy also studded with dates and place-names that resonate with the earliest history of the English settlers in the New World. That was why, I suppose, my mother made such a thing about the WASP ethnicity; old Wilhelm, even if he changed his name to William and had a school in Oak Park named after him, the William Beye Elementary School, must have spoken with an accent. Sad that she never lived to meet my second wife. This was a woman who could trace her ancestry back to the ship that arrived just after the one bearing Thomas. Her parents lived in a farmhouse in New Hampshire that her forebears had occupied for seven generations. She herself couldn't have cared less, nor could my children, for whom the business of "background" and "heritage" is meaningless.

Mine was a midwestern upbringing in the world of manners that Mother must have taken from Edith Wharton novels; perhaps she took her cue from fantasies she had about her Bostonian mother-in-law. There was a touch of Chekhov, too, the "Cherry Orchard" years when the money and servants went and we sold the big house, where we also led a kind of "Three Sisters" existence except that at least three of us escaped the boredom of Iowa for the excitements of Manhattan. My youngest sister, who lived all her seventy-five years in Iowa City, used to intone grimly, "You crossed the river." I suppose she meant the Mississippi, but it felt more like a sinister threat. The River Styx, maybe?

The current popularity of physical or mental trauma in memoirs might have led me to concentrate on the four-year-old Charlie who fell off a balcony onto some stairs, damaging his lower back so thoroughly that he first wore a corset and then a brace until he was eighteen, by which time his posture had developed correctly. The pain, however, continued intermittently well into my thirties, when finally new advances in therapeutic techniques of exercise radically reduced it. This could have been balanced by a focus on the six-year-old Charlie whose father died in an automobile accident, and who then experienced what Russell Baker, whose fate was the same, has declared was having the rug permanently pulled out from under him. The loss of physical agility, the loss of father, compounded by the loss of material wealth, made me overreact to betrayal. Paradoxically, despite my refusal to trust, I want to believe.

No, the real story is being gay. I always remember that Arthur

Ashe used to say that every day when he woke up his first thought was: *I am black.* When I was sixteen I discovered that I was the Other. Pretentious academic claptrap, of course, although there is an instructive truth to it. Cocksucker, fairy, queer, homosexual— what was it I discovered? These terms come loaded with perspectives; I can't bring myself to use any one of them to describe this, my primal scene, as it were. I will try to be neutral and say that I discovered that I was a male who had a sexual interest in other males situated in a society, a world of people, who felt differently. I had to learn codes, identities, relationships, modes of behavior that had never been part of my instruction. I had to confront the world absolutely alone. I think of the black youngster who comes home sobbing to tell his mother that some other little children kicked him and called him "nigger," and his mother puts her arms around the boy to comfort him and explain how monstrous white people so often are. I can see that same scenario played out in Germany in the 1930s when the race laws went into effect. But these youngsters had adults who helped them understand hatred and prejudice and condemnation. The gay child walks into his home, the only place where the human race can expect sanctuary, to find that the larger societal prejudices are just as vivid there. He is alone.

Who was I? The first time I heard "cocksucker" shouted at me, I was shocked. It was so dramatic and reckless a word, the idea of defining me somehow by the use I made of my mouth on someone else's penis. It was something I did, not somebody I was. It lacked the distance, using the French sense of the word, that "queer" or "fairy," for instance, possessed. Were we talking about the act, or a depraved person? It was never clear to me or to those who used the term. They tried to define me with the words, and I resisted. Then we graduated to "homosexual." That made the matter much clearer; my sexual orientation (not that I understood the term in 1946) was a condition like my damaged back. There were two sets of name-callers, those who were heterosexual and defining me, and those who were homosexual and defining me. And then I became "gay"; this was in the seventies, as I remember. It was a relief not to have an affliction any longer and not to be described by acts that carried the speaker's condemnation in the definition, but "gay" was not exactly right for me either. I didn't think I could live up to it, nor was I sure that I wanted to. It was what they used to call a "lifestyle," and made me feel just as much the country rube that coming from Iowa had branded me in Manhattan. It wasn't quite clear what "gay" implied and what were my responsibilities to the title. I'd never been to Fire Island; Provincetown bored me; San Francisco's Castro overwhelmed and alienated me. The bar scene for someone over twenty, well, it was not for me, at least. I loved opera off and on, but rarely noticed vocal technique. Judy Garland and Barbra Streisand—could not stand either one of them. True enough, once I had my own house, I took to decorating it nonstop, and if push comes to shove I can talk about hairstyling with at least a semblance of enthusiasm—lucky too, because one of my sons married a stylist at Vidal Sassoon.

When I used to find myself in a gay ghetto I always felt like one of those women in a Helen Hokinson cartoon—the heavyset body, bad hairdo, shapeless dress, bulky thick purse, sensible shoes with thick legs thrust into them; in short, a matron from the Midwest. Just not enough chic for a gay ghetto, that's my problem. I don't see myself in Lycra on Rollerblades flashing through South Beach; I have been there, seen the gorgeous young men wheeling down Collins Avenue, and I always say to myself, *I just can't do gay.*

I may not wake up every morning to the thought that I am gay, but I know that I am something else than the other guys on the block. Straight men I pass on the street, straight men with whom I talk at work or at the gym, every day, everywhere, seem to me to be different; I may not be able to define it, but I know it, always. Or is it that I have accepted the verdict leveled at me from my early teens, that I am different? On the other hand, because I have tried so hard to resist gayness, to refuse a category, I have alienated myself from a lot of the gay population. Well, where am I, then? If I were to talk like the academic I once was, I might say this is about negotiating difference.

This is a personal memoir, but much of what I describe is commonplace experience for homosexual males. I have written for a general audience because everyone has gay people in their lives even if they do not know this. There are gay friends, relatives, students, employees, even spouses whom the straight world does not identify as such, though now, of course, less so than a half century ago. I would be gratified if the reader took from this book a better understanding of the obstacles and shoals the gay male must navigate just to grow up and assume the responsibilities of adulthood.

Readers must know that I mention the sex act frequently and perhaps with more detail than they would like. Sexual activity per se usually doesn't amount to a hill of beans and is not worth talking about, but when it happens in a repressive, hostile, and dangerous environment, then it becomes worth mentioning, not for the act itself but for what it means, like two people exchanging eye contact, or maybe a crust of bread, maybe just a murmured phrase beneath the cruel gaze of their Nazi captors as one has seen so often in those decades-old gritty black-and-white films. The act, whatever it is, becomes worth noting. Sexual acts that I describe are here to show me coming to understand myself as a sexual person, but more than that they demonstrate the chance to exist for a moment, express oneself, know that life is worth living, that there is hope and freedom and dignity perhaps in some world where the Church, where evil homophobic do-gooders, where desperate cruel and empty people with no real life or dreams or hope for themselves find their pleasure in inflicting cruelties on defenseless victims, are momentarily silenced. That is why in this memoir when I often record encounters between myself and some other man, it is not to titillate my reader, nor for the erotics of the memory, but to remind myself of the many wonderful males, straight and gay, I met this way, and to keep alive the fact that even in the darkest hours of my youth and later in other repressed times, there were extraordinary moments of self-expression, joy, and happiness. I mention a sex act only because it reflects in some way on the psychology or life circumstances of one of the two people involved. When old King Nestor in the *Iliad* calls out to the Achaean troops to "go to bed with the wife of a Trojan in revenge for Helen and to make them cry," he is talking about violence, destruction of property, assault on manliness, he is not really talking about sex at all. If he cared the least bit about women he would know he was talking about rape as well.

I was not cruelly used as a teenager, and only once driven to contemplate suicide, and that was by something my mother said to me, not by a bullying classmate. I never stifled my desire for other males, I never deceived a woman about who I was, never used marriage as a cover. There were plenty of miseries that came my way, but where do they not? As it says in *Ecclesiastes*, "The heart of the wise is in the house of mourning; but the heart of fools is in the house of mirth." I would hate to be other than I am, that is, gay, even though it has caused me conflict and misery, because fundamentally I like being me. I value the perspective on life that gayness affords me, the interactions it creates for me with both men and women. Experts deride as simpleminded the slogan "Men are from Mars, women are from Venus," and maybe it is nothing more than acculturation, but I do sense it in my relations with men and women from the peculiar perspective of my gender sensitivity. I am a male, of course, but though I sense the commonality of that line of guys at the urinals in the interstate rest stops, I sense that I am not one of them, no way.

It is distressing to hear talk of searching for the gene that determines homosexual behavior in the human male or female with the correlative idea that it would then be possible to eliminate this trait in human reproduction. The twentieth century's history of "cleansing" populations comes to mind. Nowadays, when gays seem to be better accepted in the United States, they would do well to keep somewhere in the back of their minds the experience of the assimilated Jews of Germany, who thought they were safe until it was too late. One should never underestimate the power of the Abrahamic religions to fuel a hatred of gays.

# ONE

# *1930–1945*

*Ruth Beye with her baby boy, Charles, July 1930* (Courtesy of the author)

I was born March 19, 1930, the fifth child, second boy, of six children carried to term. (There were six miscarriages.) An older sister often reminds me resentfully of hearing our father on the phone shouting in joy, "It's a boy, thank God, it's a boy, it's a boy." My father is more myth to me than flesh-and-blood reality. Since at the time of his death I was a small boy whose life was spent in the nursery, I had seen little of him. In fact, my memory of Daddy is little more than the sight of his body in the coffin that the servants took us to view. It reposed in the front hall of our home, since our father, being an atheist, was given a nonreligious funeral there. Although he died only a few days after his fiftieth birthday, he was already head of surgery at the State University of Iowa Hospital, and a distinguished thoracic surgeon. Whatever else I know of him comes largely from Mother, who loved nothing more than to reminisce over cocktails at the end of the day, even if, in the loneliness of her widowhood, her companion was just her teenage son.

Over the years I was to learn that my father was an admirer of Theodore Roosevelt, that he too spent his summer holidays hunting and fishing. I well remember my mother showing me the box in which he kept the trout flies he had made; it was like viewing the crown jewels. He was an acolyte at the altar of the white Anglo-Saxon Protestant hegemony in the United States, fearful and disgusted, if my mother is to be believed, at the invasion of these shores by the Irish and Italian Catholic immigrants, and determined to match their prodigious birth rate with his own efforts, however my mother might have felt about it. (That she did not like children all that much she managed to convey to us in her magisterial indirection.) Needless to say, he was equally affronted by Jews, not because they were superstitious and feckless, as he imagined the Catholics to be, but because he considered them so extremely sharp and grasping. When a parent dies young, there are so many questions a son has not had answered. What, I often wonder, had my father, who was a doctor in the U.S. Army in the First World War, thought about shooting at German soldiers, who must have included his blood relatives, or at least the descendants of fellow townsmen of his father, Wilhelm? How could it be, as Mother often told me, that he was planning a year's sabbatical in Germany for the academic year 1937–38, so as to get to know the Germans better, when as a reader of newspapers he must have noticed the dire turn of events since Hitler's accession to power in 1933? How was it that he admired so very much the Viennese Jew who headed the Orthopedic Surgery Department while always pleased that he and my mother found accommodations in hotels that stated "Gentiles Only"? Again, if I can go by Mother's testimony, this orthopedic surgeon was to be valued because he was a repository of European tradition and learning, but, more than that, because he was a Jew, one of a people who, in my father's opinion, had a more profound sense of high culture, were more refined, than the rest of mankind.

I have always thought that I would not have liked my father very much, but then I remember a favorite family anecdote about Daddy. It happened that when his first four children were very young, he entertained the Roman Catholic priest who had been the chaplain in his unit at the front. This very jolly young man and my father enjoyed sitting about, drinking wine and reminiscing. During his stay, the family dog, Jiggs, died, and, of course, the children were inconsolable. My father hired a carpenter to make the dog a wooden coffin; then my father and his friend contrived that the latter would don his robes of priestly office to lead a procession down to the back of the garden where a grave had been dug. In the presence of the children and the household staff something appropriate was said, and Daddy took the shovel to fling in the first load of earth, and signaled to the grieving little tykes waiting with their toy shovels to take their turn. Mother loved to tell this story, laughing all the while at the kitchen staff, all of them first-generation Irish or German Catholics, who marveled that someone so atheistic and impious as Dr. Beye could yet manage to hold a kind of Catholic burial, including even a priest, for his dog.

My small hometown was distinctive in being both the commercial center for the surrounding farms and the site of the State University of Iowa, which even in the thirties was renowned for its departments of art, theater, creative writing, and music. On Saturday nights there were pickup trucks parked in rows outside J. C. Penney on College Street, where farmers in clean overalls with their wives, dressed in homemade cotton dresses, were shopping. Over at the university another, different crowd was gathering for a performance of the symphony orchestra or on their way to the university theater to see a play. The streets, which were paved in brick, were shaded over in summertime by giant American elms that gave the effect of so many naves of Gothic cathedrals. Where the town ended began open fields as far as the eye could see. This was not the Iowa City of today; large-scale construction after the war turned a village into a city, brought housing developments to the surrounding farmlands, and the tragic invasion of Dutch Elm disease took out the shade. But I don't really see those changes. Maybe I have just looked at too many Grant Wood paintings. He was, after all, a resident of the town.

We lived in a large house, large enough to be renovated into apartments in later years. The property stretched from the street back as much as the length of an average city block, with a steep terraced hill in the front, climbing beyond the house to a level where there was a formal lawn surrounded by flower beds. Then the property sloped gently down to the back boundary, beyond which were open hilly fields and one could see miles into the distance. As a small child my existence was confined to the nursery on the top floor, where I was given meals, and my bedroom on the second floor, and the back, or "servants'," staircase down to the side door, which we children were meant to use. Apart from a swing that stood on the crest of the land, a sandbox underneath a shady tree on the gentle slope rising to it, and the flat lawn for croquet by the kitchen door, we children were sent to play way out in back of the house beyond the formal lawn, and beyond the formal garden, where there was a miniature house built for us. Beyond that, past a cherry orchard, there was a two-story small barn, the upstairs loft of which had been converted into a "clubhouse," and to the side of it was a chicken coop. We were seriously discouraged from entering the kitchen or pantry except by invitation. There were four or five women who worked for my parents doing all the household chores and we were not to get in their way. The living room, front hall, and vestibule that led to the front door were also out of bounds. There was one man who did the gardening, the heavy lifting, and drove my father to work (since, if Mother is to be believed, my father did not think a surgeon should strain his hands before morning surgery by handling the wheel of a car). The gardener would sometimes help us with our little garden, but we were reminded that he was also busy, and not to be bothered. Only the upstairs maids, who had also functioned as our nursemaids when we were smaller, were part of our world.

Once when friends asked my second wife and me why we did not let our children come down the front stairs or enter the living room in our baronial house in Brookline, we discovered to our amusement that we both had instinctively and tacitly (one of those ça va sans dire things) thought that this was the way of the world between parents and children; even in our modern glass box of a house in California, where many of the dividing walls did not go to the ceiling, where there was what they used to call "flow," we just did not encourage the little tots to go into the living room. I notice that to this day my instinct upon entering our living room is to make sure that the pillows are all plumped up and in their proper place, that the books and magazines are properly arranged, as well as the photographs in their framed stands on any coffee table or end table. In my childhood home, while the adults were eating in the dining room, someone was in the living room rearranging the pillows and emptying the ashtrays so that the room was more or less pristine when anyone entered it. Because I was crippled I was allowed to sit reading in the living room during the day; my reading chair was next to a large mahogany library table, upon the highly polished surface of which all the current magazines were neatly arranged. Always neatly arranged; I don't remember seeing them scattered.

When my father died, Mother decided to eat meals with the children, and thus I left the easy comfort of the nursery and descended into the formal dining room. Breakfast especially was meant to be a family occasion. We had always to be punctual. ("Be considerate of the servants, Charles.") About six-thirty in the morning a maid went through the corridors awakening us with chimes, so there was no excuse for tardiness. At breakfast time we stood behind our chairs until Mother entered, then my brother held her chair for her, and when she was seated the rest of us sat down, she unfolded her napkin, and she rang a small silver bell to indicate to the kitchen help that they could bring out the meal. We were required to make conversation, and if we brought up unsuitable subjects—the tedious retelling of something we had read or a joke we had heard, the whiny account of an argument with a sibling— Mother remonstrated with us and insisted upon stimulating or genuinely amusing talk. Wit and rapid delivery were key. It is a marvel that we children did not all end up stuttering, but, instead, all six of us were wonderful conversationalists in adulthood, witty, informative, and fun to talk with. My second wife, an unusually taciturn lady, whose family gatherings were a torture of stammering, silences, and meandering lines of thought, used to marvel at my siblings on display. Her family hid behind silence and impassivity. Mother taught us to hide behind brilliance. It was a godsend to me in the ordeal that was to begin in my sixteenth year.

What I have just described is life lived as theater: the living rooms continually returned to the state in which they must be when the curtain goes up, the gathering at the table required to "make conversation" rather than simply speak. There was a kind of audience, the help who glided silently in and out of the rooms, before whom we were enjoined never to say anything embarrassing or revealing. Mother also taught us that creating whatever reality we wanted meant ignoring what didn't fit. The most dramatic demonstration of this came in a horrible and unforgettable incident at breakfast when our aged serving woman was suddenly struck with a seizure of some sort while passing toast on a silver salver. She shuddered slightly and staggered, emitting a kind of groaning noise, as the toast fell from the tipped platter. I was terrified, but such was my mother's insistent pleasant conversation, holding us all in her gaze, that I did not turn around to face the woman. None of us rose to assist her and she finally made her exit. For the briefest moment Mother's voice slowed, then she resumed what she had to say as though there had been nothing unusual to witness in the room.

Born in 1892, Mother was an Edwardian belle, who came out in Chicago in 1910. She had an exaggerated notion of what it meant to be a doctor, even so distinguished a surgeon as my father, as one could tell when she would remind us children that the husbands of our Oak Park aunts were "in business." The tone of her voice made you know that this was a terrible taint, although in fact they were all heirs to family fortunes, and what was odder still, her own father had been, as I have been told, a businessman. One has to imagine that she was moving up, which might account for her extraordinary acuity when it came to categorizing people socially and culturally, as well as the wit with which she laced her anecdotes. I was surprised to be told at one of my high school reunions by at least three members of my class that they had the strongest memories from the time they were small children of my mother as the funniest person they had ever known.

Equally surprising was the observation by several classmates that one of the truly outstanding events of the years they spent in the lower grades was "the annual picnic at Charlie's house." This was my mother's doing. Once a year she had me invite the entire class of twenty-five children, and various teachers as chaperones, to walk through the streets of Iowa City from the school to our house up into the backyards to the formal lawn, where servants had laid out tables of all kinds of food, drink, and sweets. There were always a clown, jugglers, a magician, pony rides, balloons. In small-town Iowa in the economic depression of the thirties this was an extraordinary event, and I can see why it stayed in the memories of so many youngsters. It was my day; I was required to play host, it was my responsibility to see that everyone had a good time, that events and the dispersing of food went smoothly. Mother was "good with people," even if her manner could sometimes be frosty, and I have to believe that she wanted her children early on to learn that form of social command.

The society of Iowa City in the thirties and forties had the businessmen, bankers, and lawyers as the pinnacle of the "town" and the professors and university administrators as the pinnacle of the "gown." Doctors bridged whatever social gap existed because they were sometimes part of the faculty of the State University of Iowa Medical School but also served the townspeople. In the late thirties my mother had been approached by some of the town worthies, who asked her to run for the school board—from on high, one might say; that is to say, as the widow of the great surgeon, with an independent income, the big house on the hill, and no connection to the town's business interests, she was free of the suspicions that had attached to recent candidates or members of the board. Although she was very short and always reminded me of Elsa Maxwell, she had an air of invincible rectitude not unlike that of Queen Mary. I imagine that she campaigned standing still, upright, a wax figure, a small smile and nothing more indicating that she was in communication. When her opponents were quick to point out that not all of her six children went to public school, one would think that her campaign was doomed. But never underestimate the Queen Mary factor. She did win, and her older daughters were soon to be joined in the public schools by my little sister and myself, while my brother stayed in the local private school to realize his dream of being a football star.

Mother was elected president of the board and remained in that position for many years until, again at the request of various factions, she stepped down to run for mayor of Iowa City, a doomed proposition for a Republican in so liberal a university town. In all those years she was a font of amusing anecdotes about the workings of the school system. She took the matter very seriously, worked closely with the superintendent, and was constantly well informed, but she could be funny about it all. Her descriptions of board meetings delivered at our dining table the next day were often cruel, but there was no question that she knew her subject. Her conversation displayed all the ugly tribal prejudices of her era, as everyone in her stories was identified as "Irish," or "Italian," or "a Jew," or "Catholic" or "lower class," with the frequent use of "you know" (as in, "He's Irish, you know"), which presumed a commonplace understanding of this category of person. Only the upper-middle-class WASPs were left unidentified; they were the norm, the standard by which everyone else was implicitly judged, from which all others had fallen short. She was never angry, never sneering, she was only concerned that I understood that there was a vast chasm of behavior and understanding between the Americans who could claim English descent and Anglican religion and the other groups, who were dubious in one way or another. Their probity, their drinking habits, or their religious beliefs were often the object of her notice. Germans in the United States were, like the English, "the backbone of the nation," my father's favorite phrase as quoted by Mother, whereas those in Europe who were fighting us in the war were inherently evil for being German. In the same way, when our Jewish orthopedic surgeon friend secured the safe exit of his entire family from Vienna after the Anschluss, my mother immediately offered to house some of them until they got themselves established in this country. Mother was breathless in her admiration of their upper-class, elegant manners, although dismayed and annoyed by what she sensed was their condescension to her overly relaxed manner in dealing with the help.

I have gone on at some length here because I was deeply influenced by her. As I became sexually aware it became increasingly obvious that I was deviating from a standard, failing to fit into any category or type I had heard my mother enumerate, and thus fell prey to a growing concern with my own identity. In the dilemma of my life as a sixteen-year-old in danger of becoming a complete social pariah, I was saved by her idea of staged living, by her high standard for conversation and her great wit, by her insistent artificiality in social situations, by her constant dissecting of the social scene and her acute distinctions between people.

Mother's breakfast-time practice of polite conversation was augmented by a daily review of the latest developments of the major campaigns of World War II. To this day I remember most of Operation Torch, the Allied invasion of North Africa on November 8, 1942. After the invasion of Italy, the prosaic analysis that she took from nighttime radio broadcasts was often punctuated by emotional eruptions of anguish over the treasures of art and architecture that were being threatened in the fight up the Italian peninsula. In June 1944 she awakened us all from our beds to shout out exuberantly the news of the Normandy invasion.

In the fall of 1942 when I was twelve I enrolled in the public junior high school, a giant brick Victorian pile that had formerly held the high school, now relocated in a dazzling new building, thanks to the WPA, on the very eastern edge of town. At first junior high seemed exotic. Instead of walking silently on beige cork floors, our feet drummed on the old wood darkened by fifty years of varnish that creaked as we walked. Instead of sitting at round tables with movable chairs, we sat at desks mounted on ornate wrought-iron stands bolted to the floor; the wooden writing surfaces, also darkened with varnish like the floorboards, were carved with the initials of generations of students. In my naïveté I assumed this represented the last word in educational chic.

My previous school was a research lab, so to speak, for the State University of Iowa School of Education where young people engaged in research and development were the teachers, but here I encountered older, more maternal or paternal figures, whose years at their calling had carved them into distinctive personalities. Their individuality made them unpredictable and more interesting. Needless to say, they were overwhelmingly welcoming to me, the son of the president of the school board.

Equally welcoming was a small band of boys with whom I proceeded to walk to school each day. Remarkably enough, there was none of the new-boy negotiation one reads about as an almost universal experience. I have to think that this was due to the fact that I was so unlikely a figure in their daily lives that they did not have to consider assimilating me as one of them. To begin with, I was physically handicapped and did not play sports, and in fact had only the dimmest idea of any of the games that engage the hearts and souls of boys. Then I had a kind of glamour. I was the son of the great doctor, we had lots more money than most people, I lived in a large house up on a hill, and because I had spent most of my life sitting in a chair reading, I spoke with a vocabulary and manner that was entirely unlike their own. If I believe what everybody used to tell me at school reunions, I was even at this age flamboyant and witty; luckily this amused rather than repelled the young fellows with whom I walked; luckily too the daily walking and bonding more or less neutered us all, at least as far as I was concerned.

One boy, Bob, became my particular friend. He was a lean, quiet boy, tall and muscular, too thin, really, who struggled hard to be a first-rate athlete—indeed, he became a high school baseball coach. We spent hours together talking, me doing most of it, while he listened. I remember him scratching behind his ear just before he would begin to speak, I remember his soft and low chuckling at some of my crazier pronouncements. I never watched him play; we never talked of sports. He accepted that. It never occurred to me that it should have been otherwise. He was the first real friend I made away from the set of youngsters who were my classmates from the private school.

My first experience of dinner at Bob's house was so exotic that I was atingle for hours. We ate in the kitchen, out-of-bounds for me at home. Bob's father sat at the table in his undershirt. I was relatively unfamiliar with the behavior of adult males, but I was quite sure that underclothing of any kind was not the garment of choice in most places, certainly not in my mother's house. Bob's mother stood at the stove cooking and serving the food, never really sitting down at the table with us, more or less taking bites and tastes from the plates she passed on. Everything set on the table, such as milk, remained in the bottle or carton in which it had entered the house instead of being transferred to pitchers or salvers for the presentation. There was an overhead light instead of candles. These were the Depression years and several of Bob's relatives lived in the small house with them and sat at their table. I remember the silent men, somewhat beaten, their drab women,

Bob eating quietly while his mother and I made the conversation, cracked the jokes, laughing loudly, inspiring a wan smile in some of the others from time to time. Occasionally Bob and his sister got into a fight. Their shouts and shrieks filled the room; no one stopped them and so they continued until they grew tired.

When I began junior high school I also entered puberty, which meant that I spent hours of my time masturbating, sometimes, if my memory is anywhere near correct, as often as ten times a day. I discovered this delightful occupation on my own, I was proud to acknowledge, especially when my friend Bob told me that he only learned when his uncle told him what to do. I had no close male relatives (my brother had gone east to college, not that I can imagine sufficient intimacy between the two of us to acknowledge the penis), but I had an insistent libido. Masturbation for young males is as much about mechanics as pleasure. In those early days of my new maturity I was confronted by another one of the crowd with whom I walked to school. He asked me if I could now ejaculate, admitting shyly at the same time that he could not, although in his jeans and T-shirt he seemed to me the quintessential boy. When I said yes, it was only minutes later that he had persuaded me to demonstrate my new skill, and as the jism squirted powerfully from my penis he gasped in awe. I was very proud indeed: maybe I could not play sports, but I had a handle, so to speak, on a very basic game that all men want to play well. When I tell women friends this anecdote they have a hard time understanding that for men orgasm is a function as much as an expression of desire. The commonplace practice of boys at camp or young soldiers standing in a row jerking off to compete in ejaculating is a response to the former; women only know the latter.

My first experience of sexual relations falls somewhere in both of these two categories, I imagine. At this distance in time I only dimly recall the moment. A youngster named Buddy and I were alone at his house. We must have been at some function because I picture Buddy in his gabardine pants, wing-tip shoes, dress shirt, and tie. If you can, try to recall Andy Hardy and you will get the idea. We were standing in the garage, where Buddy's father carried out his hobbies of woodworking and car repair. Buddy had gone into a drawer of tools and fished out some magazines, which he evidently knew were there. The one he opened for our inspection showed a series of naked women facing the camera with their legs spread or being mounted by naked men, the typical porno shots of the time. I don't remember being amazed, horrified, repulsed, or attracted by the photos. What I do remember was the bulge in Buddy's pants. Somehow I stepped back from viewing the magazine, which gave me the perspective to notice the distinct articulation of Buddy's member. Without thinking, I moved to unzip the fly of his pants, and gently maneuvered his erection through the opening of his underwear. Dropping to my knees, I took Buddy in my mouth and stayed there, moving my head until I felt him come. And then I stood again, bent my head slightly to the side, and spat the contents of my mouth onto the concrete floor of the garage. We both stared at the small pool shimmering in the light from the work lamps nearby. Buddy put his penis away, zipped up his fly, put the magazine back into the drawer, and we both left the place. Neither of us said a word. I guess I went home. I have no further recollection of the incident, nor do I remember in the rest of the years of my schooling speaking with Buddy. He was never part of my crowd; I think he went to parochial school and I do not know how I came to be with him that day. Something about those gabardine pants and wing-tip shoes makes me remember him as what we would now call a nerd.

By eighth grade we were pairing off into couples, "going steady." Few of us had any real understanding of the boy-girl phenomenon. A girl named Rosie had taken upon herself the role of social arbiter of the class, and she was unofficially establishing couples. I was assigned Betty Lou, a very well developed girl with a loud voice, a habit of cracking gum, and an aggressive friendliness, a very good female equivalent of me, come to think of it; Rosie clearly had talent for what she was doing. Betty Lou, who lived near the school, used to sit with me on the school steps in the gloaming and we necked. I kissed her, she let me put my hands on her breasts through her blouse. I even invited Betty Lou to my house, and she appropriately enough appalled my mother, especially when she told her that her own mother was a scrub aide in surgery at the hospital and had "worshipped" my father.

In my second and last year at junior high school I guess Mother took it into her head to be more aggressive in giving me an all-masculine environment. At any rate, she suddenly announced that instead of freshman year at high school I would go away to Andover, Massachusetts, to attend Phillips Academy, the renowned prep school there. When I consider the present-day orientation and preparation leading up to the decision to send a child away to school, and then the actual journey to arrive on opening day, I am astounded at my robust cheer at what I went through. First off, her decision to send me to Andover did not include any discussion of the matter with me, either over going far away from home or the particular institution where I was to be enrolled. The sight of me sitting reading in a silent room perfectly ordered, smelling of fresh-cut flowers, which in fact I had somewhat earlier helped my mother arrange, might have put her in mind of the story of Ferdinand the Bull. Or maybe it was the tableau that presented itself to her eyes as she sought me out one day when I was up in the nursery. I was seated at one of my sisters' four dollhouses rearranging the furniture while dreaming up domestic drama. As usual I was ignoring the elaborate electric train set with its many switches, main lines, off lines, mountains, valleys, lakes, and bridges. It was not that I did not like electric trains, but their potential was easily exhausted, whereas interior decoration and drawing room comedy offered endless variations. One sight of that, I fear, and it was Andover for me.

The next thing I knew, a huge wardrobe trunk had been delivered to my bedroom, the kind that people in thirties films used to maneuver around in their stateroom on transatlantic voyages. Before the war I had more than once crossed half the continent on trains when my little sister and I traveled with the help from Iowa City to Montreal, where a car picked us up for the ride to join our family at the summer place in Vermont. This trip I would be alone, and somehow that grand trunk suggested a kind of ominous permanence. Suddenly it was the day of my departure; at four in the morning it was just turning light as I waved goodbye to Mother and boarded the *Zephyr,* an art deco masterpiece of stainless steel that took me to Chicago. From the LaSalle Street Station I found my way onto the Parmelee Transfer, a bus that brought me to Union Station and the *New England States,* a deluxe all-Pullman train on which I slept overnight. The following morning in Boston's South Station I looked at my now quite tattered set of instructions and took a taxi to North Station, where I boarded a commuter train to the town of Andover. There I engaged another taxi to take me up to the school, where I found Rockwell House, my dorm, and someone to sign me in. Finally I was lying exhausted on the bed in my room listening to the voices of other boys and their parents coming through the window.

The account of this journey sometimes horrifies people. Contemporary helicopter parents, certainly, cannot imagine it. But in wartime things were different. The only distress I remember was the embarrassment of arriving not dressed in a jacket and tie, attire no one in Iowa would consider for a boy on a two-day train trip. At the same moment, when I realized that all the other boys seemed to be accompanied by parents, I froze with the sense of being an outsider. I have to think that Mother did not come with me because wartime travel was so much controlled and limited; and I can now see that most of the boys came from New York and Boston, from rich eastern families whose parents no doubt were cheating on the gas rationing in order to drive their boys to New

England prep schools. Still, I was alone and I was betrayed. Perhaps I should imagine that this was yet another maneuver in my mother's never-ending struggle to make a man of me. (My husband, Richard, thinks that I am being charitable.) It did succeed in reinforcing the idea that you can count on no one. That, I guess, is what being a man is all about, or was in the mind of an Edwardian woman. Years before, I had tripped at school, and, although I was unaware of it, broken my ankle. When I hobbled home for lunch, sobbing in pain, Mother seemed indifferent and sent me back to school. When I struggled home again at three, the pain and swelling were enough to induce her to take me to the hospital. Cruel and inhuman treatment? Monstrous indifference? Incapacity to deal with another's suffering? Determination to make a little lad into a stoic? Whatever her motive, the experience was good training for the ordeal of my sixteenth year.

The year at Andover actually went well enough. The teachers were excellent, and I regretted later that I had not attacked my assignments with more passion. My housemaster complained that I was a dilettante. Testament to the truth of this proposition was my indifference to consulting a dictionary for the meaning of that word. Most of the time, like any other fourteen-year-old, I was just hanging out with the guys. My schoolmates were a congenial lot, but I was not part of their athletic program, which is the true glue of teenage male relationships. I was placed in the dorm for the maturer beginning students where we each had our own room. This was a lucky stroke, as it gave me the privacy to experiment sexually that year without shame or fear. I cannot believe how innocent I was, how readily I took to sex, and for how long I let the Andover experience form the pattern for it.

Uninteresting as descriptions of sexual intercourse can be, I shall describe my relations with my two partners that year because they changed me forever. A month after my arrival found me in the bathroom near my room waiting for the one available shower.

It was afternoon, I was excused from athletics, of course, and had decided to profit from the absence of my dorm mates, since two of the three showers were broken in our wing. Unaccountably, another boy had arrived there first. Warren was his name. He was a short, wiry, muscular blond, with a hard, determined face. "Out in a minute," he said, peering around the shower curtain. Seconds later he spoke again, this time without showing himself, to invite me in. Absolutely innocent of any preconception, Your Honor, I took the towel off my waist and entered. The space was small, scarcely big enough for one boy. When I adjusted to the steam of the shower I saw that Warren sported a major erection. Almost instantly I grew hard myself.

"Always get a hard-on around now. Every afternoon," Warren announced. "What about you? Why are you hard?"

Could I ever have been so simpleminded? "Because you are, Warren."

I agreed when he asked if he could fuck me in the ass, but the pain of entry was far too much. "Let me suck you," I suggested, sinking to my knees before getting his assent. I think that this startled him; I sensed uncertainty. But blow him I did, then and at least once a week thereafter throughout the course of the first year.

Two weeks later another boy, Butler, and I found ourselves at loose ends in the dorm when our English class had been canceled. We gravitated into my room, sex being perhaps already in our subconscious even if we did not recognize the desire. Thinking of Warren, I proposed fucking Butler, who cheerfully lowered his pants, bent over, and submitted to my greasing him up. But the pain of entry instantly made him straighten up and reject me. Butler asked to fuck me, and I agreed, forgetting in my excitement the pain Warren had caused. Somehow now the pain seemed easier to take; maybe it was the grease and my extreme arousal, or perhaps Butler was not so well endowed as Warren. As Butler had his way with me I discovered that extraordinarily pleasant sensation of the thrust, moreover the bliss of sensing the spent prick up one's bum. English class was canceled again the following day. Butler and I fairly ran back to my dorm room for another session. This time, needless to say, it was far easier and far more agreeable.

Butler and I had a real relationship that year. We seemed to gravitate on Saturday afternoon into my room and go to bed together naked. This meant that there was much more contact between us than I had with Warren. Butler would hug me, sometimes kiss me, rub his body against mine, but he would not bring me to orgasm, although he tolerated me jerking off. We would lie about, talking, until we were aroused enough to go at it again. Sometimes I played games with him, refusing his advances until he was beside himself with sexual excitement. Butler was a tall, gangly boy, not too bright, but affectionate like a golden retriever. He was constantly horny. Some evenings just before lights-out he would get permission from the hall monitor to come down to my room, ostensibly for consultation about our English assignments. He arrived in his pajamas clutching the textbook to his crotch behind which he had hidden the tube of Vaseline and his erection. Because the doors would not lock and there were boys in the hall getting ready for bed, our drill was quick and efficient: down with my pajama bottoms, bend over the bed, off with the Vaseline cap, a swift swipe of grease with his finger, penetration, thrust, thrust, spasm, sigh of contentment, withdrawal. "Thanks. See ya," and he was out the door, leaving me to lie in bed, glowing in my lower torso and ready to finger the instrument of my joy, as the porn romances would have it. Butler and I made plans to room together in our sophomore year. It would have been a disaster. He would have enjoyed the available sex and homework assistance, but anyone as sexy as Butler would soon have discovered girls. I would have fallen in love with him, but by then he would have considered our sex as somewhere between desperate measures and outright perversion.

Blowing Warren never got beyond minimal physical contact. Butler and I were friends, we wandered around the grounds together, we studied together, we went with other friends to the ice-cream parlor. Warren was friendly enough when we met for an encounter, but there was none of the extension of personality that marks friendship. But one evening he came to my room and threw himself on my bed. This was uncharacteristically demonstrative for Warren, almost a provocation. By now I was fully adept at anal intercourse and so I unzipped his fly, brought him out, got on top of him, and sat down. He went wild with excitement. "Why haven't we done this before?" he asked hoarsely, thrusting up and down energetically. He was off a second later. The next day after my shower I walked into his room clutching my towel around my waist, threw it aside, and lay down on his bed. Without a word he stripped, lay down, and entered me. For the next four or five days he was either in my room or I in his. One day we got it on in the morning and again in the evening. This made him very angry, as he growled at me when we were doing calisthenics together in the exercise room. By now he was furious with himself and with me. At the time I could not understand why, but now I think that he sensed he was growing too excited by what we were doing. The next time he walked into my room, he moved toward me, then stopped, and an ugly look crossed his face. He yelled at me, saying I stank, that I was too dirty to get near, and with that he walked out of the door and out of my life.

Although I got along well enough with the boys at Andover, I certainly did not like an all-male environment. They were a boisterous lot, the boys of Rockwell House, sometimes erupting from their rooms in flights of enthusiasm and jollity, running up and down the corridors bellowing at full voice, playing tricks on each other that verged on physical mayhem. Having been raised among women, I was put off by teenage male high jinks. When I went home for Christmas I began a campaign to convince my mother to let me come back home to City High.

The Christmas visit itself convinced me that Iowa City was the best place of all. My mother had encouraged me to host a dance during the holidays. I called it The Caribou Stomp, don't ask me why. Invitations were printed up and sent. It was to be formal, there would be the forties equivalent of a disc jockey putting on and taking off the 78 rpm shellac records every three or so minutes. I had dance cards printed as well. It was certainly flamboyant, maybe pretentious, with maybe even a hint of the ridiculous, veering toward camp. Who knows what goes on in the brain of a fourteen-year-old about to blossom? The dance was a great success. All the many friends I had made in junior high school were there, as well as the old friends from my earlier school days. It was a moment in my life that I would never visit again. Yes, there have been other gatherings, other outpourings of affection over the years, but never again would I know the pleasure of blending into the crowd, of being at one with my peers and colleagues. Within a short time I would come to know affection, when affection was there, blended with amusement, or condescension, or acceptance, or forgiveness—take all the vocabulary for the attitudes with which one views a freak, an anomaly. In every other gathering in later years I had to hold the crowd at bay; whether dancing, dining, toasting, laughing, telling stories, flirting, charming, I was always cornered.

# TWO

# SEX, LIES, AND HUMILIATION

*Charles Rowan Beye, Class of 1948, Iowa City Public High School (Kadgihn Studio, Iowa City, Iowa)*

By the time I came home in June after my Andover year, President Franklin Delano Roosevelt had died in April and the Germans had surrendered in May. These were dramatic changes— Mr. Roosevelt had been president almost my entire short life—but nothing compared to the personal upheaval I was about to undergo in the following months. At the moment I was just happy to be back with my friends, most of all Bob, whom I had met when I started in junior high school. Now he and I started a summer job working with the public school maintenance crew refinishing floors. Despite my mother's support for the highest ethical standard in the school board's dealings, she was not above a little nepotism, although her capacity for ignoring conflicts and unpleasantness did not desert her here. She managed to describe the job as something the school Buildings and Grounds Department had brought up all on their own.

While I thought everything was the same, I was radically changed, although at first I was completely unaware. It is hard at this distance to imagine my naïveté, my innocence. The reason I did not register that I had an unusual sexual interest that was a crime or a sin in the eyes of most people was that I had lived a sheltered life. Up to this point I had never heard anyone talk about sexual matters, period. Hard to believe, but true. Boy-girl relations were founded on the Judy Garland–Mickey Rooney paradigm, at least in my blinkered sense of things. I remember once a girl in my sixth-grade class talking about seeing what must have been a spent condom floating in her parents' toilet bowl, about which she was snickering with classmates. They did not enlighten me and I did not ask. I was probably not particularly dim-witted; in my earliest years I lived in the nursery, the lone male among women; later my father was dead and my brother was either off at football practice or had headed east to college. I didn't play sports, so the only male who crossed my path with any regularity was our gardener. Neither of the two boys with whom I'd had sex at Andover remarked on its being unusual or perverse. They simply accepted it and enjoyed it, except when Warren had had enough. In his angry rejection of me, however, he never said anything like "freak."

Over the course of the summer I had three important experiences. The first occurred on a night when I invited Bob for a sleepover and he brought his friend Billy along, another neighborhood kid, who had transferred from parochial school. The little cottage out near the cherry orchard had two beds in it, and we arranged a mattress for Billy on the floor. After a bit of conversation Bob dropped off to sleep. Billy climbed up to my bed so we could go on talking without waking Bob. The next minute we were fingering each other. My experience at Andover made me ready for something more erotic, so I asked Billy to suck me off. I thought he would refuse but then ask me to do him the favor. Instead, he laughed at this as though it were a joke, so I laughed too. Then he climbed down to go to sleep. Moments later he knocked on the wood frame of my bed. I thought he wanted to masturbate and wanted to assure himself that I was asleep, so I kept still, curious to hear him. I heard nothing.

It's a long story, my relationship with Billy, but I think it all began that evening. When the outcry over my behavior became the talk of the town, Billy was in the forefront of angry denunciations and threats, sometimes even with a band of his former classmates from the parochial school. Years later when the dust had settled, so to speak, and we must have been seniors in high school and he was more or less a friend, he invited me for a sleepover when his parents were out of town. Odd that I went, odd that he asked me. In any event, there were a couple of other guys as well, old friends from parochial school days, and the four of us sat in our underwear in Billy's bedroom playing poker until finally we went off to bed. Which room the other two went to I do not remember, but I chastely slept the night with Billy, who rolled himself in and around me, in the deep sleep of someone drugged. I saw him thereafter at all the high school reunions, and he was always especially cordial, almost sentimentally friendly.

Do I say to myself rhetorically, *Go figure?* No, I say, after thinking about this for years, that on the fatal night in the playhouse Billy had knocked on my bed because he had suddenly figured out—he was a little slow on the uptake—that an invitation to a blow job could go either way. His reputation in high school was of a horny young devil (women at the reunions were always remembering his unwanted attentions), and I think if he and I had made out that night, he never would have erupted into the angry censor of the next few years. The jury is still out in my memory chamber as to why we four were playing poker in our underwear the night of Billy's sleepover. From other experiences I had in those days I would have said the boys thought they would get some action but were too nervous to ask for it; by then I had moved along enough in my relationships with other boys to wait for a definite hint, if not an outright request.

The moment of crisis occurred in the summer months of 1945 when I propositioned two boys, which set off the incendiary gossip that destroyed my reputation. They were neither of them boys I knew, other than by sight as classmates. The one, Joey, was finishing at the urinal in the men's room of the town recreation center when we stared into each other's face and in this locale, reminiscent as it was of the bathroom where I had first encountered Warren, I was inspired to suggest what I did. It was late afternoon, we were both of us on our way home from our summer jobs, and needed to pee. The recreation center was open but deserted at this hour. Joey was quickly satisfied, and left with no more words than a quick goodbye. The other, Tom, I encountered walking on the street near my home on his way to his own in a section of town that lay beyond geographically and at an even greater distance socially. Something about Tom and me in our walk and talk inspired me to allude gingerly and obliquely to sex between boys. He responded alertly enough that I invited him to come with me into the grounds behind my house, past the cherry orchard to the clubhouse at the top of the small barn. On the way I made a quick detour into the house for some Vaseline, because Tom had implied something more complicated than the quick exchange with Joey. Tom and I went about the business with scarcely a word exchanged between us, although the silence was certainly not threatening. Afterward I led him back down to the street, and we parted with a brief smile.

One day Tom called to ask if he and Joey could stop by together. This was out of the blue, but by chance I was free to say yes. How do I account for the fact that I was alone at home that evening? My little sister must have been at camp, my other siblings had all moved on in life, and my mother, very much a social person, was no doubt out. The boys came by with only one thing in mind, and I invited them for the same reason. Within minutes we were naked on my bed, Tom penetrating me from behind, Joey in my mouth. This produced a new charge of sexual excitement for me until I heard one of them say to the other with a snicker, "Hey, this is better than the whores down in Davenport." The other laughed in response as I froze. Every illusion I'd had died instantly as my basic paranoia and distrust took over. Rigid with fear, I brought them to their climaxes. Their comradely salutes upon departure did not reassure me; trembling, I took a shower, masturbating mechanically to rid the pressure of arousal, and sat in my towel in the darkness of my anxiety and confusion, searching for a vision of what the future would bring.

It brought a lot of misery. The news of my queerness spread through the low-life teenage males of the town, and slowly infected the town athletes. I could sense Bob and the other males of my circle of friends politely withdrawing psychologically, although they had to maintain proximity because of my great popularity with the girls. These boys were forced into polite behavior, but there were other boys for whom I was a vocal object of derision, boys to whom I was personally unknown, boys from parochial school, for instance, or the boys who worked or farmed and did not play sports, and therefore, as things go in public high schools, did not sit at the "good" tables in the cafeteria. The onslaught came from all sides and intensified when school began in the fall, as I took to riding a city bus out to the high school, jammed in with a million other kids, where crowding encouraged the cowardly anonymity of an ugly shout. "Cocksucker!" I must have heard the word a million times that year, on the bus, in the school halls, in the downtown streets, over the phone, driving in my car. It made my heart stand still, or so I thought, every time. But I would not visibly acknowledge it. If I had to go downtown, I walked past the guys standing in front of the pool hall, and hoped for the best. Sometimes I did not get a rise, other times I did, but I smiled at the guys nonetheless, since most of the time only one had shouted the ugliness aloud, they had not all spoken, and I was, as a matter of public performance, their friend and they, mine. That was how I maneuvered all the dangerous places that horrible school year of 1945–46, as I went from fifteen to sixteen.

What had been a private transaction at Andover grew promiscuous and out of control. For instance, I can recall times when a carload of boys pulled over to the curb as I walked along a sidewalk and one or more would shout out the window, asking for,

sometimes demanding, a blow job. It was an ugly demonstration
of power that instinct told me had to be blunted instantly. I did
not hesitate, but took control by stepping briskly into the car, as
though it were all my idea, and off we drove to a secluded spot,
where I could have them off one by one as the others stood outside the car smoking.

The wrenching agony of fear was worst when I had to respond
to an anonymous call. The voice on the phone said, "Be there in
ten minutes," and there was the click as the connection ended. I
was afraid not to go out to stand on the designated street corner
near my home to wait for whoever it was who had called, for fear
of some scandal that might be visited on my mother. They came
by and picked me up, always with the merest muttered greeting. It
was like a gangster film in which I was the man picked up by the
toughs who goes along in silence to the place where they are going
to kill him, and he knows that they are going to kill him, and they
know that he knows, and there is this chilling complicity. Except
that here it was all about blow jobs, and I was hoping that these
boys were out for pleasure and were not hostile. My goal was to
make the occupants of the car, one of whom, to my mind, had just
assaulted me on the telephone, not harm me in any way, whether
physically or verbally. And as we drove along I made conversation.
I did all the things that I knew you are supposed to. I asked the
boys about their sports, their jobs, I was giddy with goodwill and
chatter. Most of these boys had rarely, if ever, encountered witty
banter. It is not something males are ever good at or even know
they like, particularly working-class kids. And thus I began to dis-
arm the boys of the town.

These strange, tense expeditions happened a lot in that school
year. In every instance, boys whose initial stance was hostile,
whether for reasons of class, homophobia, or a combination, were
tamed—I thought of them as unpredictable ferocious animals—to
the extent that there was a goodwill when I left that car that had

not been there when I'd entered. I exercised rigid control over my feelings, as well as forcing myself to the most powerful exertions of social interaction in which I had been taught as a child. In that car I was an object of fear, of curiosity, of gratification, but my capacity for hypnotizing conversation, the celebrated social skills of Mother's drawing room, gave me dominance. Not once, not twice, but every time. How I remember the tension headaches!

That year and the two thereafter provided me with many surprises. There was the boy in my sophomore botany class who, while passing out lab materials, whispered, "After school, top-floor can." I met him that day and many others, a nice quiet kid who discovered a source of sexual gratification. There was the one and only black kid, whom I ran into as we were trying to find a way to scale a wall to get into a state basketball tournament for free. When we failed at that we turned to something else, which developed into a habit, about twice a week for the next several years, because racial mores prohibited his going near white girls. He was a star athlete in our school, whose years with me, as he once told me with a chuckle when we were in our fifties and having dinner, required a real adjustment to women as they came into his life. There was the carload of three athletes who sought me out one night, one of whom was so entranced by the experience that, without ever telling his buddies, he was with me twice a week for the next few years. Our relationship in fact continued into the years of his early marriage, when he was a college student and his wife was working. Conveniently enough they lived in student housing, where I would visit him, and because for the first time we could lie down in bed, I sometimes entered him from behind, an experience we never acknowledged. Another athlete, a university school track star, sought me out, and in the course of our meetings described some anal stimulation he claimed to have "learned about in Algiers." That led to his lying back on the car seat with his legs in the air while I pumped into him, furiously trying to finish while he kept shouting, "Hurry up, this hurts." But, as the expression goes, practice makes perfect, although it was not for at least a couple of years that he was able to admit it, moodily confessing that he had "some kind of problem with men." As in, maybe, he liked to get laid? Once, in an evening of sheer delight while we lay on a blanket in a secluded meadow and practiced a variety of treats, he took me in his mouth, but when I came he spat the liquid out and said quietly, "Not for me."

Males react differently to anal intercourse and to fellatio. The ancient Greeks celebrated male-male relationships, preferably a man in his thirties with a teen; they coined the word "pederasty," although they did not mean ugly exploitation and misuse of pre-teen male children. In this relationship they valorized anal intercourse. Fellatio was for female prostitutes. The same could be said of contemporary Arab culture, where males have offered to enter me when I requested sex, but generally balked at my wanting to fellate them. Once in a bath in Tangiers a married man in his late thirties who had been my guide to the city that day, and who had accepted my invitation to him and his wife to a restaurant in the evening, allowed me to use my mouth on him, but told me with amusement that he had not had such an experience since he was a youngster. In Afghanistan there is the well-attested and commonplace Pashtun custom of dressing up beautiful young boys and using them as the equivalent of female lovers; no doubt this centers on anal intercourse as well. Males have inhibitions about the masculine performance of fellatio; I remember a fellow countryman of my Turkish brother-in-law asking me for sex, and when I refused to let him penetrate me but offered my mouth, he declined.

In U.S. prisons, where straight males are often forced to perform as the passive partner in anal intercourse, one does not hear of them doing fellatio. Males who patronize transvestites in the areas of prostitution in our major cities pay for blow jobs, usually understanding quite well that the people offering their services are males in drag, but they would not seek out a self-identified male doing the same thing. Nowadays in the United States one hears that teenage girls will fellate their boyfriends. That must eliminate gay boys from the action, poor guys, although contemporary straight teens, now that they have learned the concept "gay" and no doubt think "gay" and "straight" are opposites, probably refrain from even a tiny dose of gay sex, thinking that gayness is catching.

In retrospect I feel fortunate that I lived at a time when I could enjoy relationships, however limited they may have been, with so many great guys. I grew up in circumstances where I had little access to male company. As it is, males in our culture are notorious for their repression in expressing their feelings, or any other intimacy. A chance blow job is not a moment for "sharing," as Oprah would no doubt put it. But the repeated experience of sexual intercourse, however it is framed, with the attendant moments of before-and-after sitting about, usually in a parked car, is a psychically intimate experience. I think of a fraternity boy at the university with whom I met often, always in my car, where we graduated from the simplest oral-genital transaction to the exposure and manipulation of his naked chest, and his fondling me, albeit through clothing, and finally to long, wet kisses before, during, and after his orgasm. Our last encounter was when a friend hailed me from a parked car in downtown Iowa City, where he was sitting with his girlfriend and, lo and behold, this same guy, his fraternity buddy. Of course, I did not acknowledge that I knew him; it was obvious that my high school friend had summoned me over to exhibit one of the wits of his hometown. What was ironic was that I had a far more superficial relationship with my high school friend whom I had known for years than I had established with the other fellow.

There are those who pity me for coming late to the full realization of the various attitudes and experiences of homosexual lovemaking. I concede their point, but I must insist that when my straight partner was a totally agreeable fellow I was strenuously aroused by the correlation of anticipation, by the delight of feeling in control with males whom our culture has designated as in control, modulating their rising passion, practicing the slightest retard, feeling my own surge of power as they surrendered all control at orgasm. Once, when I was in my late forties, because of an amusing mistaken exchange of instructions and telephone numbers with friends abroad I found myself in the hotel room of a major American professional athlete. It was clear that he knew I was gay, and that it would be acceptable to act on the fact; there was no doubt that he was gorgeous, if a giant, at least a foot taller than I. His twenty-five-year-old brown body, which was perfectly sculpted, made me think of nothing so much as the Riace bronzes in Reggio Calabria. To have this huge creature thrusting into me, groaning and shouting in a deep baritone, thrilled me, particularly the moment when he erupted into paroxysms of ecstasy, when it seemed that he had lost all control and I was dominating him. Afterward in our mutual postcoital repose I looked up at the ceiling over his shoulder, realizing that I could not move out from under him without his permission, which made me consider for the first time what women experience as the norm. He was a witty, intelligent man with whom I had a memorable half day, more treasured because coincidental and unexpected. I can't believe there would have been the commonality between the two of us, separated as we were by age, race, education, interests, if we had not chanced upon sexual intimacy. Clearly he and I both would have liked to spend more time together, but he was only passing through on his way home to his family.

My sophomore year in high school did not improve as it continued. With the end of winter came another of Mother's bombshell announcements, this time that she had put our house on the market and we were moving. The house she had chosen was a compact fake colonial two-story, four-bedroom dwelling with the conventional one and a half baths, living room, dining room, and kitchen, set on what real estate agents would call a "decent-sized" lot. It was one of four or five homes built in the postwar development of a forested spit of land adjoining an established neighborhood, a great place for a man with two kids who had just made tenure at the university, someone on the way up. Did she feel as I did that coming from our large house on the hill we would be more or less camping out? She did not comment, but then Mother was not the kind of person to dwell on the apparatus that formed the sets for her life's performance, nor verbalize her concerns; if I had been less the self-engrossed teenager I might have noticed what she had been experiencing: the servant class had decamped, and managing so large a house without servants was becoming intolerable. I did indeed feel guilty at my impotence watching her struggle to take the spent coal (called "clinkers") out of the giant furnace, a task which the fragile vertebrae of my lower back made a physical impossibility. In our old house there was a lot of enforced walking about: the kitchen had the stove, the pantry had the refrigerator and sink for washing dishes; there were only two telephones, one in the lower back hall, one in my mother's bedroom, and the recent war prohibited additional service. With no one in the kitchen always available to pick up after the first few rings, running "to get the phone" was, I am sure, one of her nightmares. I imagine our aged gardener must have come to shovel the myriad walks, stairs, and driveways that ran about the property.

I often wonder what giving up that house meant to her. It was the locus of her married life, where she raised a family and entertained on a grand scale. The new house was more the setting for the life of Mr. and Mrs. Cleaver. At age fifty-five she was going to learn again those cooking skills she had once acquired at Fanny Farmer's Boston Cooking School. Her new kitchen, with its vinyl floor and Formica table and counters, was also the room in which we would be eating, since there was not only nobody around to cook the food, there was no one to serve it—and come to think of it, no one to make the beds and dust the floors. Since she was a tight-lipped adherent to the code of "Never complain, never explain," I have to imagine that wartime wage inflation made the cost of a staff more than she could afford, if indeed she had found anyone in the forties who still wanted to go into domestic service. Our meals resembled what one ate at a club: a lamb chop, a steak, roast beef, calf liver, roast chicken, with a rotating selection of vegetables and a salad. I'm sure the stiff drinks she tossed down beforehand made the routine meals and unforgiving setting palatable enough.

She was not opposed to youngsters taking a drink or two. I well remember her ordering me a bourbon old-fashioned in the restaurant of the Palmer House on a shopping expedition to Chicago, and growing angry when the waiter brought up the state liquor laws. Her improbable denunciation of the poor man, claiming that he was like a Communist stooge forcing some state law between a mother and her son, led to his surrender and the arrival of the drink. Still, Mother was no fool about drinking; I remember her drawing my attention to a friend of my sister who controlled the pain of his wartime injuries with heavy drinking, using him as a lesson for me in accepting the pain I endured in my back rather than surrendering to addiction. Still, she was willing to serve me a cocktail in the late afternoon before she set out to make the dinner. Because they unlocked our tongues into a semblance of friendly conversation, I always enjoyed our afternoon cocktails, although they began when I was only sixteen and we had just settled into our new house. They became a ritual, developed, I am sure, as an unconscious response to the impasse in our relationship at which we soon very dramatically arrived.

Any honest emotional bond between my mother and me died within a twenty-four-hour period in late April, a month after my sixteenth birthday, when in fact my world came apart completely. Every detail of the gruesome experience remains with me. One day, I was sunning myself on a blanket while reading a book when Mother returned home, came to the porch, and summoned me in. The tone of her voice was a premonition; the look on her face made me steady myself to keep from fainting.

"I have just been talking with Father Putnam," she began in the coldest, most serious voice I think I had ever heard her use. "He has told me awful things—"

Waves of reaction crashed into my brain with howling sounds. I was desperately attempting to gain a purchase as the ground shifted, swayed, opened under me. Aristotle defined that moment in tragedy when the character realizes everything as anagnorisis. The moment, for instance, when Oedipus realizes that he is not the successful king of Thebes so much as he is the murderer of his father and the bed partner of his mother, the taboo figure created by a destiny that mocked his pathetic attempts to escape his fate. This was that moment for me. I think of the scene in the MGM film *Marie Antoinette* when Norma Shearer as the doomed queen is shown in close-up after the lackey has looked at the coin in his hand and realized that Robert Morley is Louis XVI in disguise. They are in their coach at Varennes trying to flee France, and at that moment reality shatters the delusion. I think of the second act of Verdi's *Macbeth* after the king has seen the ghost of Banquo, as the guests begin to depart the banquet hall in horror, and the king and Lady Macbeth add their voices to the choral song as they realize that their dream is a delusion, their murdering Banquo to get on with their life won't succeed. I do not know how much I must credit to innocence and naïveté, how much to denial, but whereas I had been blind before, suddenly in a flash I saw it all. The jeers of the students, the cruel barbs I could somehow let pass me by. They did not describe for me my condition, my situation. But that cold, precise voice coming from those almost pursed lips: "That your name is written on lavatory walls. That you are doing terrible things. I don't understand what he is talking about." That hit home. She shivered, shook herself as though to dislodge the incubus: "Horrible, terrible." I began to cry. Everything was being taken from me. I had no foundation any longer. I felt myself sinking into some limbo where I was alone and without shape or form. "You must go talk with Father Putnam. I will send you to a psychiatrist." I sobbed harder. Now it turned out I was crazy!

There I sat in the living room, by the picture window, the sun cloaking me in warmth . . . but no, that was not it at all, no, it was the sun like a naked bulb over the culprit's head as he is worked over by some detectives attached to the precinct. And there across from me, somewhat by contrast harder to see—or was I blinded by my shame and guilt?—stood Mother. And then she was gone. Without extending a hand toward me, without any further remarks, she left the room. We were never to speak of this again in the eight years that remained of her life. In fact, we never had another honest conversation.

How strange and sad it is that for the next sixty years I never questioned her response. That she did not sit by me, put her arm around me, tell me she loved me, cry with me over my sorrows, did not seem unusual to me then. Intellectually I have been convinced that the "normal" parent would have; otherwise I still don't get it. Father Putnam, our Episcopal priest, changed for me into a monster of betrayal. Why did he not come to me first, talk with me, who was his acolyte at Holy Communion almost every Sunday, who was so often the crucifer at the later service, who was president of the St. Vincent's Guild, the association of altar boys, at the church? How, I have often asked myself, could this brash young priest, new to the parish, have gone up to a woman on the street as indeed he had and delivered such information? How could he have been so blind to the limitations of understanding in a woman who was so obviously a product of a Victorian-Edwardian upbringing? One wonders at the fact that he went on to become the bishop of Oklahoma and was much praised by the people there at his death. At the risk of judging, which the Lord says is a dubious practice, I say that the swine had much to answer for when he met his Maker.

At Mother's request—"hysterical demand" perhaps is better— I went to see him. He urged that we descend to our knees and recite the prayer of general confession together. When we got to the words, "We acknowledge and bewail our manifold sins and wickedness," and I realized that he wanted us to have in mind the behavior that he had brought to my mother's attention, I could not, would not submit to such self-condemnation. If nothing else, I knew in my heart and would go to the stake in my belief that I was without blame or sin for wanting sex with another male, of this I remained convinced, and I rose and walked out the door and I never entered a church again as a communicant.

I set off for the appointment with the psychiatrist the following day in complete terror. His office was in the psychiatric hospital, not too distant a walk from our home. It was not quite twenty-four hours since Mother had accosted me. Since then she had spoken to me in measured somber tones of trivial matters upon the occasions that brought us together. I truly felt that I was going to go mad, such was the turmoil of emotions that I could no longer identify, sort out, or manage. Most of all I was trying to resist being suffused with guilt and shame. The absolute joy and excitement of sucking cocks, of taking cock up my ass, had suddenly become dirty, degraded. God, Church, priest, Mother all called me dirty. I kept hearing Mother's "your name on lavatory walls." In my mind I saw the words *Charlie sucks cock* as I had never seen them before. The mechanism of denial that had protected me up to this point failed, when, as it were, my mother, our priest, and the institution of God's Church stood beside me in the smelly men's room looking at the grimy off-white tile wall with the pen marks on it: *Charlie sucks cock.* I had never felt so depleted; I wanted to kill myself. Before meeting with Father Putnam I had gone to the library just across the street from the Episcopal church to look up something on mushrooms, on poisons, but I was so sunk into depression that I could not even read what I was looking at. Now I struggled to walk smartly down the sidewalk that took me to the office of Dr. Miller. He, as fate would have it, looked very much like my late father: gray at the temples, a mustache, steely eyes, a severe compression of his lips when in repose. I quailed.

"What is your problem?" he began quietly and soberly. I began to snivel, and, through my coughs, stammering, and sniffs managed to mention as abstractly as possible my sexual interests.

"But, I mean, what is it exactly that you do with these boys?"

"What is it that you are doing, Charlie?" he said again when I could not speak, and I heard an empathetic tone in his voice.

"Fooling around," I mumbled in reply.

"Fooling around? How?"

"With the other boys," I whispered.

"How? What do you do?"

"Just fooling around."

"Yes, but what exactly? You take hold of them?"

"Yes," was all I could muster.

"Take hold of the penis?"

"Yes."

"Put it in your mouth?"

And so it went, detail by detail. Slowly he drew from me explicit detailed statements about the sexual acts. The transformation in my feelings was swift. Whereas before I had been trapped, cornered, cowering before the onslaught of my mother and Father Putnam telling me that what I did was evil, suddenly I was the author of my acts as I spoke them. They were mine, and nobody could take them away from me, alter them, give them another meaning. The sentiment may not have lasted long, but its immediate liberating effect stayed with me for a long time, really forever.

There was silence when I finished my rather slim litany of the sexual behavior and positions I had so far managed. Dr. Miller puffed on his pipe, another maddening similarity to my late father.

"The problem is . . ." he said at last, taking the pipe from his mouth and looking me directly in the eyes, "the problem is that you need to be more discreet. You know, you are a little too emphatic, too obvious. Keep a lower profile; that's what I would recommend. People tend to talk, you know."

Benediction. We said little more; I departed and walked slowly home. My chest, which had felt in the last twenty-four hours as though it had been shut, turned in, hardened almost to the point of denying my breathing, suddenly opened. I was too exhausted to be happy, too apprehensive of Mother. But Dr. Miller had called me whole, had called me sane, had called me normal. It was not the substance, but the style. "Need to be more discreet." The words stayed with me like the kindly squeeze of a hand on the shoulder.

The gay community has its stories of the ugly sessions between hapless youth and ponderous shrink as the latter tries to wrench the psyche of the former around to some kind of "normal" behavior, whether through words, shock therapy, or some other kind of demeaning resistance to what is obviously a natural instinct. I was so very, very lucky. In those three days I had confirmation of some basic truths: first, that I could never count on my mother's emotional support; second, that I knew in my heart and soul that if there is a god, he, she, or it would want me to be as I was; and, third, that an adult, a doctor charged with healing the sick in spirit and soul, a man whom fate had made resemble my father, had let me know that there was nothing wrong with anything I had been doing.

Another profound change in the emotional landscape was that I was no longer dishonest. Perhaps my mother would never bring up my sexual orientation again, but she would know what it meant for me to stand next to a good-looking male, what it might mean to see me coming out of my bedroom in the company of one, or going off to the movies; most of all she would not be urging pretty young girls on me as date material. What I learned years later was that she sometimes talked to my older siblings about my gayness, that she confided in her favorite sister-in-law, who also had a gay son, that she discussed me with the psychiatrist more than once, but she never said another word to me. Paradoxically, a profound truth underlaid our dishonest relationship, however much unspoken. Once in the more enlightened 1970s I had a young boyfriend who, shortly after we began our relationship, announced that he intended to tell his parents that he was gay. The old fogy in me counseled caution and silence, whereupon he said, and I shall never forget: "I don't want either of them to die without knowing me as I truly am."

And I think of all the men and women who have lived their lives entirely as a lie with the people meant to be most profoundly intimate with them. Nothing could be sadder. I have friends who cry at the mention of their dead parents and don't know why, but I am sure that they ache over the basic lie of their relationship. I was also lucky that I never had to experience the long, drawn-out trauma of resistance to and then surrender to the process of "coming out." Whether they liked it or not, everyone in my hometown had to recognize me as a "queer," "cocksucker," "homosexual," "different," whatever.

Ironically enough, my school friends forced what might be called an entente cordiale, whether or not they really knew what they were doing. It is the gang—that is, the clique of "nice kids"—I am talking about. Who was this group? They were the ones who ruled the roost in the school, the ones who were never without a date at the school parties, the boys and girls who held all the elective offices, the youngsters with smooth skin and minimal pimples, the students with high grades, warm and winning personalities, the ones who were in some aggressive pursuit of their ideals and dreams. The gang was invited to some girl's home for an outdoor badminton game followed by something to eat in the cellar recreation room. I was invited as usual. Why? Well, because, as I said, the girls all seemed to adore me. Probably the truer answer is that no one could figure out how to drop me. I was too suitable, desirable, attractive—I had the use of a car, was good-looking, a super dancer, and had lots of pocket money. There was just this one teeny-weeny dubious aspect. We ended playing badminton illuminated by the headlights of the cars parked in a circle. Then it was time to eat and the girls filed in and down the stairs. This was 1946 and the girls were supposed to cook, boys were supposed to stand around talking sports. I sensed danger out there alone with the boys and began to sidle toward the house to take cover helping to get the meal. No luck. I was cut off as the boys encircled me. This was a setup. I froze.

"Listen, you cocksucker." That was Bill, Bob's best friend, the boy whose knock I had not responded to the previous summer when he slept over.

"Okay, stop, Bill." That was Bob. I was identifying voices. Partly my terror and anxiety had somehow temporarily blinded me, and the night was washing the light from the sky as well. Bill's voice, indignant. "Me stop?" I saw him whirl on me. "He should stop, the son of a bitch." Then they were all talking at once, and I was crying. The girls must have known what was going on, because they did not call us in to eat. Every one of those boys had a complaint against me. They could not stop using the term "blow job." I whined and sniveled more. They wanted to "help" me, that was the thrust of this horrible gathering. I, like a dog who will lie down on its back spreading its legs so other dogs can sniff its crotch, yielded to their solicitude. It made me hate them, but it made me safe. If you think about it, it was a kind of odd coming-out party. Now all my old friends of junior high days who had angrily talked about me among themselves and practiced eyes-averted denial when they were with me, now they had finally laid cocksucking on the table, so to speak. I promised to reform, they promised to help me, not that they had anything concrete on offer. Never again did we mention it. Several of them now felt free in the months and years ahead to have sex with me. I continued to have sex with whom I chose, and they maintained a friendly stance. Oh, the joy of things unspoken!

Of course, when I married, and I took my wives back to high school reunions, it was as though it had all never happened. Then, when the marriages ended, the high school reunion crowd all had a story to tell me about a gay son of some friend of theirs. About twenty years ago I brought Richard, the Staten Island native, to give him a sample of "real America," and the reunion banquet speaker had trouble when introducing the spouses because she could not get beyond "friend" to designate him, and I insisted out loud on "lover" or "boyfriend." (I don't know what she would have done with "husband.") The whole room had a laugh over that, and one woman said later, "You know, when all this business about 'gay' came about, gee, it was nothing to us kids from City High. We all knew about that starting in the forties, maybe not the name, but what it was all about. All due to you, Charlie." Coincidentally, not long ago I was introduced to a young fellow in New York City who remarked that his father had grown up in Iowa City. Further conversation revealed that the young man was gay, the son of someone I dimly remembered as a jock classmate. He told me that when he nervously confessed to his father that he was gay, the older man took it in stride, simply observing that he had known about such things since his high school acquaintance with a gay boy.

Suddenly now it was summer again, and I was free of having to hold the psychic carapace in place throughout the school day. Bob and I were back working on the school maintenance crew, he pleasant but distant, which I realized was how it had to be. He was a true friend, however, because he had done me the favor of neutralizing his friend Billy, who ceased to be a menace. They were off to their summer athletics programs, so Bob's complete absence from my life was not so hurtful as it might have been. He lived for baseball in the summer and basketball in the winter. I can only imagine how the boys in the locker rooms must have talked about me, although I am sure that none of those who had been intimate with me ever acknowledged that fact. Some evenings I would be part of a group of boys and girls who set off in two or three cars for the public swimming pool in the town fifteen miles to the east of us. There we would be a bit later, we boys, naked in the changing room, laughing and talking together with the inevitable snapping of towels, and among them would be one or two or three naked bodies or parts I had seen on other occasions and in other settings.

The odd feature of that summer was the new gang of boys that I picked up with, a crowd that was alien to everything I had ever known before. These were the boys or really in many instances young men of my high school who could be called the "bad boys" or "rough kids" or "losers," depending on the degree of the speaker's contempt. From shooting hoops in impromptu neighborhood games they often had a tenuous friendship with some of the "good boys," but never, never with any of the "good girls." These boys did not do athletics, they all had jobs, many worked as mechanics or filling station attendants; their hands were often greasy, their fingernails were a mess, their hair needed serious trimming. They drove older-model four-door sedans that they kept in perfect repair, some restructured after their own designs, usually with powerful noises coming from the exhaust pipes. They lived in the "wrong" parts of town, some of them lived in trailers, often alone with their mothers; fathers were often absent, off on a job, in the military, or simply drunk. Some of them had been in the reformatory for juveniles, some of them had been kept back several grades.

Joey, my first local fuck when I returned from Andover, had graduated into membership in this gang, and some time or another when he and I were making out in the school parking lot, one of his buddies came by for a little action. Before long I knew them all.

I remember afternoons of great fun with this gang. We would get into a flock of cars and race off to one of the little towns that stood out in the majestic desolation of big sky and endless cornfields, towns with names like Lone Tree or What Cheer. There was always a speakeasy in such a town. Iowa had remained a "dry" state when Prohibition ended; you had to get your wine and spirits in state liquor stores, and other than beer there was no drinking in bars or restaurants. Little towns with no-account populations fell off the radar of the Liquor Commission police or the bars bribed them. The places we went to were always dark. There were folks sitting at the bar, others clustered around the two or three pool tables, while the tables set up in the gloom of the cavernous space accommodated men who sometimes sat alone. The talk in the bar was frugal, bitter, and harsh; they were minimalists, those people, the bartender, the men and women getting a drink in the middle of the afternoon. It had the mood and ambience of *The Last Picture Show* or *Paper Moon*. In 1946–47 the condition or at least the mood of the Great Depression had not left pockets of the rural Midwest. My translation into this world was no less than Dorothy's experience of Oz in reverse. The adults, with their pinched faces and thin-lipped mouths and their sparse fatal talk, were dramatically unlike the teachers in my high school, with their constant good cheer, their obsessive uplifting effacement of the bitterness of life. Odd folks they were, too. Farmhands on an afternoon off, women looking for some fun, or wanting to earn a little money giving someone else a little fun, people who had strayed from a traveling circus, salesmen, hitchhikers who had been dropped off somewhere in the vicinity, often demobilized soldiers trying to get back to the big transcontinental highways and on to their homes.

My "bad boy" friends were equally refreshing. With no standing in the school, often ashamed of their homes or their family situations, determined to fail in class so they could drop out at the first
opportunity, they were cynical, funny, harsh, and abrupt, talking of
things I had never considered. They took me on as a mascot. They
were highly amused at my jokes and anecdotes, they loved my
accent, my large vocabulary, my sissy, dainty, pretentious manner.
They taught me pool, they taught me how to drive a truck, they
taught me how to take a crap in a field when nowhere else was
available, how to wipe myself with leaves. They explained to me as
best they could the innards of a car, showed me how to change a
tire, gave me new and unusual illustrations of life, what to do when
the police are after you, for instance, or what to do with your dick
if you are facing a wide-open pussy in front of you. They didn't exactly ruffle my hair and give me a smile whenever I rode along in
one of their cars, but they were enormously protective of me, and
so friendly, happy to know, I suppose, that if they suddenly felt
horny there was someone at hand to give them a blow job. From
time to time when they offered lifts to the hitchhiking servicemen
they urged them to take advantage of me in the car for some relaxing fun. In the bars where we became—what shall I say?—
occasional regulars they presented me as their friend who liked to
suck cock, and there was never anyone who seemed to find this
remarkable or reprehensible. They all liked my style as well. I felt
the welcoming wide embrace and learned to take a certain amount
of teasing from my guys and their bar friends, teasing that was
based on my sexual interests, but it always seemed affectionate.
Afternoons with these boys made me feel "special" rather than
"queer," as the one who had a difference that could be useful and
pleasing to my friends, a difference that could be amusing as all
differences are, but not to be disparaged.

My other great talent highly valued in that long hot Iowa summer was dancing. Iowa City maintained a recreation center for the

teenagers and young adults, where we could congregate on Friday and Saturday nights for dancing or Ping-Pong, where the beverage of choice was Coca-Cola. All so innocent and dear, and all so long ago! And all so sweaty, I might add, when dancing in a room with temperatures at least in the high eighties and humidity to match left us all awash in our bodily fluids. The brace that held my spine so it would grow straight could be removed from time to time with no damage. The pain of excessive articulation of my hips and pelvis was a trade-off for the joy of dancing. Years later, when I was out dancing among a group of African Americans, a friend remarked that I was the only white guy he had ever seen who knew how to throw his crotch around. From my experience of teaching white boys to dance, I would have to agree that they were all afraid to acknowledge their crotch and swing it. These things go in phases, of course; one remembers the tight jeans of the sixties worn without underwear so that their owner could put everything he had on display. Nowadays it is depressing to see that males are so alarmed at the notion of exposure that they wear baggy pants down to their knees on the court and in the pool, a costume that ludicrously mimics the billows and flairs of a woman's skirt, effectively obscuring any hint of masculine sexuality from waist to knee.

Dancing in the forties was mostly the foxtrot or jitterbugging. Girls favored the former if they liked their partner enough to want to be close; boys, who might well have yearned for the proximity of the foxtrot, were usually so awkward that they chose to jitterbug, to avoid unseemly stumbling. Most boys, in fact, stood at the periphery with their hands in their pockets—controlling their erections, probably—and made dumb jokes. I danced every dance, every style. This was my high school moment; I was a wonderful dancer and everyone knew it. There wasn't a girl in that recreation center who did not yearn to dance with me; I heard it again and again through the years when my classmates reminisced at the reunions. And to make it Andy Hardy perfect I had my driver's license and my mother's car almost every weekend night. The difference was that after squiring the girls home I often parked in a shady grove with the other male of our double date.

Memories of my sophomore year naturally brought up anxieties as I started back to school for my junior year, but it was all so different almost immediately. I was old news now, the shock value was gone, the jeer factor useless. Teenagers are a fickle lot. To use contemporary slang, I was "so last year." I did not, however, disappear into the faceless mass. The school administration embarked on two radical efforts at social remodeling. One was to organize a series of girl-bid dances in the gym, an obvious attempt to minimize the notorious power to create wallflowers that males traditionally possess. The other was to establish two lunch-hour periods a week during which there would be dancing in the large open foyer of the school. The motive here, it seems, was to keep the kids from spending their lunch hour smoking and God knows what else in the parking lot. Since everyone lunched at the same time, there would be no unseemly music disrupting studies. The right to choose partners immediately flowed from the one event to the other, and I was besieged on every side. In retrospect it surprises me how many girls wanted to invite me to the girl-bid dances. Yes, I was good-looking, a wonderful dancer, had a car, and I was witty, but I was not the slightest bit a studly emotional thrill and they all knew that. As for the lunchtime dances, I was on my feet for every number. I could not get enough of dancing, ever, and it's true even today. I particularly liked partnering girls who were not only skillful but exhibitionists as well, so that we could let ourselves get carried away. I was also happy, very happy, indeed, to note the circle of boys, the wannabe dancers with the wooden feet, who stared hungrily at the seeming seduction that dancing can imply.

One social triumph led to another. I joined the drama club at the suggestion of some of my more demonstrative dance partners, where my major role that year was as the evil genius in a kind of made-for-kids Restoration drama where I teetered about in fake eighteenth-century boots with high heels and fought a duel with one of the school's true hotties, an assessment I was lucky enough to confirm from personal experience before the year was out. I also took up debate and participated in the tournaments in which our coach entered us throughout the Midwest. The debate society was a very serious group of students who never in any way acknowledged that they might have heard of the scandalous doings of their newest member. After a meet, their enthusiastic approval was registered by a restrained "Well done," voiced together with a pat on the back.

The national debate organization had set "Socialized Medicine: Good or Bad?" for the topic in the school academic year 1946–47. For this they sent out a large booklet containing materials for study so that the debaters would be well prepared on the subject. It led me to a surprising minor career for the rest of my high school years: the writing of term papers for students at the State University of Iowa. I say minor career, but in fact it was a major intellectual stimulus for a teenage boy. It all began when I encountered a former City High student bemoaning the assignment that confronted her for a longish paper on socialized medicine. "Gee, I could write that for you, Dottie," were the first words out of my mouth, and history was made. She got an A for my ten-page effort; I got ten dollars at a dollar a page. It was not long before her friends sought me out, and I set up a system: supply the topic, the relevant books from the university library, give me a week, and you would have your paper. My second masterpiece was "The Annexation of Bosnia-Herzegovina and the First World War," another A. The requests came thick and fast. My sainted mother, president of the school board, was sufficiently insouciant to write endless classroom excuses so that I could stay home to sit at the card table I had set up in the living room to manage my term-paper factory.

I branched out, buying back used papers, as it were, at half price, and retyping them for someone else's submission. I naturally charged less for these, seventy-five cents a page, as I remember, but there was little to fear. This was the era of the GI invasion of the university; general education humanities courses could have an enrollment of up to a thousand, and tired graders could only remember so much. I am sure the Declaration of Independence would have slipped through. What interested me in reviewing the grades of papers sold and bought back several times was the range. I grew to believe that teachers tend to dole out the grades that they fancy the student deserves rather than what the specific work suggests. Nothing in my later teaching career has made me think otherwise, for which reason I always tell youngsters go for the A's at the start, then sit on your ass, and the A's will keep rolling in. I am always amused at horrified responses to my term-paper-writing anecdote, which stress my years as a university professor, as though a seventeen-year-old boy is thinking of academic values. Those who question my willingness to practice something dishonest, if not illegal, forget that a homosexual in the forties was liable to a prison sentence if caught by the police *in flagrante*. Thus, for someone outside the law, the practice of paper-writing might be considered no more than a logical extension. I quickly learned how little the teaching faculty valued the papers as a genuine form of dialogue, and grew indifferent. But it did influence me in making term-paper assignments throughout my career, where I have tried as far as possible to tailor the topics precisely to the terms and values of discussion employed in the class.

My term-paper-writing business would never have gotten off the ground if I had not started the first semester of my junior year with a course in typing. I was not the least bit prescient, but anxious to round out my social life, such as it was. "Everybody" took typing, not just the girls who were looking at a secretarial career. This was because the teacher, a young, truly beautiful, terribly lax disciplinarian and high grader, made the hour so much fun. Why

she was never fired, I cannot imagine. The classroom was filled
with the hubbub one associated with the lunch hour, and that was
because everyone who sat at the best tables in the cafeteria was
also in Typing I. Not to mention Typing II. It was an ideal locale in
which to solidify my acceptance among my classmates, although I
don't remember being that calculating about it. No one could leave
for fifty minutes; conversation flowed back and forth all around
the room over the list of assignments we were sharing. Boys who
had only known me when they made their nervous drives at night
to take me to a dark place for their satisfaction had to interact day
after day and discover that there was no complication, shame, or
tension in having a verbal relationship with me. Of course, all my
girlfriends were in the room as well, making for an enormously
positive Charlie experience for everyone.

I came to be known as more than a resource for term papers.
Perhaps as a hint of my future career as an academic I taught a
few boys how to dance and how to drive. The first category of student came about out of the sheer desperation of a classmate who
was determined to make it with the girls through dancing. He had
calculated the risk, he told me later, of spending hours in my
arms, bodies pressed together, as he with furrowed brow counted
out the side of the foxtrot square and tried to yield to my insistent
swing and flow and dip, the fluid movements of the experienced
dancer. That we got erections in the contact is what one would
expect from teenage boys, especially when one of them is tinged
with so erotic a coloration. That he learned to dance well and that
we had sex were both true, and it gave him sufficient satisfaction
that he told a friend or two. The first boy I agreed to teach to drive
looked at my car with such wistful yearning that I could not resist
humoring him. I chose the back road in the city park where he
would meet no other car, and over the next half hour he shifted,
stalled, shifted, jammed on brakes, accelerated too fast, too slow,
and stalled, while he puffed in serious concentration. When the

lesson was ended, he leaned back, exhausted, and I, thinking of the number of boys who had assumed exactly that pose in this very car, could not resist placing my hand on his crotch, which he must have expected, since I could feel him springing into action.

It was in the spring of my junior year, two years more or less since I had discovered sex, that I started a relationship with a man who reciprocated in every way. Leonard was an older man, a veteran of twenty-eight, who took me to his apartment and made love to me. It was true lovemaking, since he was more interested in bringing me to orgasm in every way imaginable than in his own pleasure. His passionate kisses were the first I had ever known apart from a couple of kids who got carried away in the moment. He was handsome, warm, and very funny, as we lay in bed talking, particularly about his war experiences in India and Burma. He made me smile inside, all through my body, and I could feel myself warming into affection and love, until he delivered the chilling news that he was married. I suddenly looked around the bedroom of the apartment to which he had brought me, and sure enough there were photographs of the happy couple everywhere. It was two o'clock in the afternoon and he, the student on the GI Bill, was getting fucked by a high school teenager while his wife worked in the university law school administration to help pay the rent. Scandalized, I kept a smile on my face, but wanted to get out of his apartment as soon as I could. My ears were ringing in shock all the way home: I might have left the Episcopal Church, but the teachings of the Church were still very much with me.

Thank God I had Dr. Miller to talk to. His advice about Leonard, the married man, was that I was not to make moral judgments about him and his wife, that I knew nothing about their relationship, that I should concentrate upon what was happening between me and Leonard. So I went back to that apartment often in the next few years, even staying with him in a hotel when he moved away with his wife and children. Leonard was a perfect lover; it is clear that he was saving himself for no one else but his wife and me. Every time that we were together I was treated to pleasuring and loving attention as never before. But Leonard sternly insisted that we would not fall in love or become emotional, and so I had the experience of unfailing attention, scrupulous lovemaking, without any love whatsoever. Sometimes it seemed as hard for him as it was for me. Because my childhood home had not been graced with a loving couple as parents, my mother being a widow, I could cope with lovelessness, although I was growing impatient with sex without feeling and playing the game of love without its content.

My discontent was reinforced by an encounter I had with a varsity university swimmer whom I had met at the home of a high school chum he was dating. He called me one evening requesting a meeting and I went to it assuming he and my friend were having "love problems" and he wanted my advice about her. To my amusement, he blushed deeply and hemmed and hawed his way through a strained revelation of his desire to have sex with me. But my smile turned to surprise when he disrobed, leaned back in the car, lifted his long swimmer's legs to brace his feet against the car roof, and invited me to enter him. His grimace and groan made me wonder if he was a virgin at this sort of thing, but he was persistent that night. We continued this way for a year, more or less, taking turns pleasuring each other one way or the other, although he laughingly refused to kiss. ("That's not what I do," implying he had had same-sex intercourse for years.) Then one day he told me, as though he had just thought of it, that he was a candidate for a government position that would require his being investigated and our continued relationship seemed to him a risk. Since he, like Leonard, had been so resolute against any emotional investment, we had our pleasure that day and I never saw him again, only occasionally hearing about him from my school friend as he advanced through life's stages of career, marriage, children. She's dead now, so I will never get the denouement.

My introduction to romance was as flamboyant and memorable as a teenager could want, especially one who had been yearning so much for passionate attachment or its simulacrum when seeking sex. It all began in chemistry class in the spring of 1947 when my lab partner, the son of a Puerto Rican mother and a North American father, sighed in nostalgia for the island where he had lived as a child. His mother had left his father and was living in her family home in Río Piedras. His reminiscences were so compelling that I took them home to Mother, who, since she knew and admired his mother, who had once upon a time taught Spanish in the school system, eventually offered to pay both our flights to Puerto Rico if his mother, Carmen, would put me up for the summer and show me around. Carmen and I recognized we were soul mates from the moment we met at the airport. My lab mate had the Anglo-Saxon reserve and dour nature of his father; poor guy, he had no doubt steeled himself against the intimacy that inevitably develops in travel. After all, it was not your ordinary boy he was traveling with. But Carmen, this vibrant, beautiful woman in her late thirties, bored with living under her father's roof, and looking for adventure, was all drama and vitality and crazy emotion, everything I had always thought a Caribbean woman would be like (not exactly Carmen Miranda, but going in that direction.)

She had been told I liked theater and the arts, so she produced a twenty-one-year-old drama student from the university in Río Piedras. He was dark, handsome, with a pencil mustache, attentive dark eyes, and a smile that revealed white, white teeth. As they say in romance literature, I almost swooned. Miguel took me on a tour of the university theater, guiding me along with a little pat here and a little pressure there to the arm and shoulder, gestures that by the afternoon seemed positively erotic. The next day on a tour of old San Juan we stopped at a friend's apartment, where Miguel, as I by now had expected, took me to bed.

For the very first time in my life, after four years of sexual

experience, I was in the arms of a man who was making passionate and slowly fulfilled love with me. Still, it was not reciprocal.
Miguel was a type of Latin who thinks of himself as entirely straight,
who treats a gay man well, gives him love, courtesy, understanding,
excitement, but scrupulously observes limits. He enters his gay
partner, he accepts blow jobs, but he will only help his partner get
off with the friction of their two bodies. This did not matter; I was
awash with romantic feeling. Carmen, who was living the affair
vicariously, drove us out to places in the country down by the
beach where we could dance together. Since in those days young
peasant women were kept at home, males dancing together was a
normal enough sight, and Carmen sat with us enjoying her drink,
providing a kind of heterosexual context for what might otherwise
have had too much of a homoerotic aura. How can I describe the
sheer intoxication that began in the Cuba libres I drank at our table and continued on the wooden floor down near the resounding
surf under rustling palm trees that shrouded the moon's strong
rays in the dancing rhythms that animated our bodies pressed close
enough to sense the half-tumescent masculine energy that had
vitalized our day? Whew, the memory demands the prose. The
overwriting will nudge the reader to think of the summer as the
theatrics of Carmen and Miguel, who, it is clear to me in retrospect, were filling an otherwise boring summer with first-rate romantic drama, produced and directed by Carmen and starring
Miguel, as a kind of young Adolphe Menjou, exerting his sexual
charm over an innocent from Iowa in the ingenue role.

First love usually has no compromises; I doubt that I have ever
been happier in my life than in Puerto Rico during the summer of
1947. What no doubt made that happiness complete was Carmen's
approval. This was the first adult I had known apart from Dr. Miller
who considered me normal. But Carmen also considered our lovemaking desirable, something to be envied, gloried in. She did
everything in her power to foster the affair; she smiled widely and

rolled her eyes with joy when I described my time with Miguel. We talked together of how handsome he was, what a natural lover he was. In the meantime my lab partner spent the evenings chastely talking with a sixteen-year-old girl he had met. Naturally they were always in the presence of her sharp-eyed aunt. His only liberty with this extraordinary beauty was to walk with her before supper in the plaza, a female relative always sidling along like a sinister shadow. He was forever complaining about the meager pickings, and I was meant to sympathize. As for my large-scale romance that was being conducted from the house in which we were staying and abetted by his very own mother, he never mentioned it. He talked of Miguel as my casual friend. The intimacy that arose from our sharing a bedroom would have been too compromised if he had had to acknowledge what I was doing with my body. I remember a furious argument he had with his grandfather's cook, who was cackling with glee over having watched Miguel and me fucking one day as she peeked through a shutter. It was in Spanish but they did not realize that this gringo was sufficiently quick-witted to have picked up enough of the language to get the point. My lab mate was angrily insisting she lied. He could not accept the notion that the pristine heterosexuality of the room in which he disrobed and slept had been violated by his roommate using his own bed for sex with another man.

I came home a different man, if nothing else, a week late for the start of classes. Imagine the distress of our new high school principal when the son of the president of the school board made his late entrance. He must have heard about me, my antics in the school parking lot, certainly. Now here I was, a week late, dressed in shorts (unheard-of as street clothing for males in the forties), sandals (ditto, worn only by Jewish refugees on the university faculty, but at least with socks!), tanned (farmers in Iowa got bright red in the face; everybody else stayed indoors), with one ear pierced for a circle of gold (Carmen had persuaded me to do it).

I was certainly oblivious to any dismay I caused. For the first time I felt absolutely comfortable with myself even in a setting where trouble always lurked. That there had been a sea change expressed by this moment of return was underscored when my mother persuaded my brother, back from the wars and at medical school, to pierce my other ear for the sake of symmetry.

It is odd that I never caught on to cruising for gays. I still did not really understand that such a category existed. Homosexuality was a term that I knew, of course. When I went weekly to the university film series there must have been gays in the audience, there must have been gays at least once in a while in the university men's rooms that I must have occasionally needed to use. Once, as I was examining a flyer on a bulletin board while walking across the university campus at night, a man came out of nowhere and stood near me so insistently that I recognized it as a sexual gesture. We went into the building and up into his office and had sex. Why did I not absorb this event? Was I ignorant of the cruising glance? Incapable of recognizing it? Were the gay university students afraid of picking up a high school student? Did I look too young, vulnerable, and innocent? Photographs of the time seem to show me that way. The students were also much older as a group than college students nowadays, since they were mostly veterans in their mid-twenties. It is a mystery to me why I never met a bunch of gays then. Years and years later my nephew discovered himself to be gay as a young teenager in a remote midwestern community, and he has since told me that one of the things that sustained him was reading the *Village Voice* and knowing that he was not alone, that there was a whole community and culture out there to which he belonged.

One evening on the street I ran into a friend of my older sister, one of the many who was a regular at our dinner table when they were in class together at the university. He was another wounded veteran, and back then he had seemed so formidable, an older, big, gruff guy who exhibited a toughness that repelled me, although it clearly excited my sister, who must have staked him out as potential date material. Here he was on the street, suddenly looking at me in an entirely different way, appraising me. "Well, well, well, little Charlie has grown up!" he said in an insinuating voice— nowadays I would say in a very campy way. He invited me to his apartment and the door was scarcely shut before he began making advances. And then we were naked in bed. He lay on his back, holding his legs up and apart so that I could enter him. As I pumped away into this big, tough, gruff man, examining his graying hair, the scars across his chest and down his side, still livid and puffy, my ideas of masculinity were confounded. This was a homosexual? Afterward he was funny and mocking and then he wanted more. "Oh, do I like 'em big like you, sweetheart," he kept murmuring. Even though I knew what he meant, I felt so small next to the hugeness of his war memories, his body, and personality. Much, much later he took me out for an ice-cream cone, and it was as if again he were the older man and I my sister's little brother. As I watched him stand at the counter and order the cones, and looked at the big body in cast-off military clothing, I felt so distant. It was so confusing. I could not understand that he and I belonged to the same tribe.

In the summer of 1948, when I had graduated from high school and was getting a head start taking summer courses at the university, I encountered a man who changed the course of my life. We met in a way that was classic for gay males at the time. Not at the church supper or side by side at a concert, but in the bushes outside the university library, where I had followed him after catching him looking at me as I sat studying, following his gaze as he moved to the exit. Dan was another veteran, studying for want of something better to do. Shrapnel ended his dream of being a dancer, but he was determined on going to New York. We spent the summer evenings making love in his apartment and talking about Manhattan. I was determined to go too, and when I tried the idea out on Mother, she not only did not resist but surprisingly enough offered me an astounding $400, an enormous sum in those days when a workingman might live on less than $2,000 a year. As I have reasoned it out over the years, she had moved finally to accept the idea that I was homosexual, but the idea, the mental image, really, of me having physical relations with another guy—that was too much. I think Mother took the measure of my relationship with Dan and wanted me out of her life.

Well, of course the drama played out as youthful romance must. He changed his mind, stayed at the university, eventually stopped communication, while I sat in my lodging in a rooming house at 115 West Eighty-fourth Street, and cried. I had gotten myself a job as an office boy at Producers Representatives in the RKO Building for $27.10 a week after taxes, paid $9 a week for my room, ate a lunch daily at the counter in Woolworth's Dime Store; 55 cents would get me their lunch plate special—brisket or some gray piece of beef, covered with gravy, mashed potatoes, green beans, with a cup of coffee. I usually ran out of money on Thursday night, sometimes with enough left for an evening meal. I skipped Friday lunch waiting for the secretary to hand out the pay envelopes at the end of the day.

I had two sisters in New York. Holly, eight years older than I, was a serious lefty, and like so many of that era considered homosexuality an expression of bourgeois decadence. Her husband, David, like most artists of the period who hung out at the Cedar Street Tavern, did not "believe in" homosexuality, as though it were a religious stance. Marvelous Barbara at twenty-two was more fun, and her first project was to take me to MacDougal Street in the Village to visit the gay bars. Queer bars, I guess they called them back then. Barbara was the only family member who openly acknowledged that I was actively in pursuit of a sex life with other males. Odd as it may seem, she had to explain to me what such a bar was as she took me inside and sat there through my first half hour.

I took up the culture of gay bars very timidly. The conversation, the presentation of personality, the attitude, were all so stylized, so aggressive, so intense that I was at first speechless, frozen into a seat at the bar, unable to do more than order a beer, which at age eighteen had just become my legal right. But, if I may pretend to objective analysis, I was quite a handsome kid and, what is more, new to the scene, always a treat to a bar's habitués. One thing I realized soon enough: I was not in Iowa anymore. These men were older, many of them Europeans, men who had escaped from Hitler, others American-born, who had escaped from the wrath and fury of small hometowns. For the first time in my life I did not need to proposition anyone. I was in demand, and, as an object of so much lust, was able to demand as much satisfaction as I gave. At first I was in ecstasy. I thought that at last I would find the means to do the queer equivalent of sitting in the drugstore like Mickey and Judy drinking a soda using our two straws. But after a month or so I was not making any progress in that direction. These men did not want a relationship, they did not even seem to want straightforward sexual satisfaction. They wanted games, poses, positions, erotic logistics, sex as a work of art, perhaps. I found it boring, even though I was only eighteen and hormonally alive; it left me with a barren feeling that made me feel so lonely. I guess I just wanted sex without having to be clever.

I missed the simple virility of my high school friends pumping their orgasms into me while we huddled in the backseat of my car. One night I was walking disconsolately away from MacDougal Street when I caught the eye of a man glancing my way while he was in conversation with another fellow. He quickly came over to my side to introduce himself and ask if I needed a ride anywhere. He was a curly-haired man, short, stocky, and swarthy, and his companion was a taller, muscular black man. With the recklessness of the young I accepted a ride to my rooming house with both of them. As we pulled up before my address, he asked if he could come in, telling the other fellow to explain to his wife that he was "hung up at the gym." It turned out he was a boxing manager, a "deeze and doze" James Cagney tough guy such as I knew only from the movies. He never explained himself but clearly enough he went for wrestling around naked in bed with a young guy, getting blown, jerking the other fellow off. I liked his smell, liked his muscles, his roughness, directness, humor. Of course, it was a moment in the night, but I could not stop to think of the difference with the sex I had been having all that fall. I know it is perverse, but there is a certain kind of "guy-guy" who turns me on; I leave it to the shrinks.

By chance, during roughly the same time, I took to spending Friday evenings in a midtown bar featuring a Dixieland jazz band with a beautiful woman friend of mine from work. The money I spent on beers guaranteed that I would go hungry after Thursday noon, but I reckoned the music and camaraderie were worth it. Shortly thereafter the bar became our place for a pickup routine that with an essential variation was a staple of a host of comic films of the time, the ones in which some beautiful woman is out on the town with her plain-Jane girlfriend and they bump into a handsome guy, more often than not a sailor, and his ordinary friend searching for fun and romance. The narrative arc has the two lookers falling for each other, with their sidekick friends turning to each other as consolation prizes. We played that film routine one Friday night after another. The bar was frequented by the military and by college students. My woman friend was a real beauty who easily attracted first-class sailors or university students to her side, which left their buddies to talk with me. As the night wore on and libidos raged, the good-looking guy would confess that he and his friend had not thought to get themselves a room for the night, whereupon my friend would invite the guy home, which left his friend out of luck until he reluctantly accepted an invitation from me. On the surface of it the invitation produced no particular hesitation. Strange men sleeping in the same bed was not the aberration then that it would be now; the Depression and the war had made doubling up a commonplace. Two men lying side by side in their underwear, however, can go just about anywhere they want to take it. Most nights I lucked out; otherwise I practiced discretion. Mostly it was lopsided sex, me giving, them taking, but I liked the companionship in it.

I met and hooked up with plenty of gay men here and there on the sidewalks of New York, but as far as negotiating the bars and the gay scene, I seemed to be a failure. As luck would have it, a case of gonorrhea forced me back to Iowa, back where I knew doctors who would give me discreet treatment, and where I could go back to the university. There were plenty of sympathetic doctors and clinics in New York, obviously, so I must have wanted to go home. The noble experiment was over. "Noble" I say with irony, thinking of all the brilliant gay youngsters who came to the city and stayed to make a name for themselves. Was I a simpleminded wimp or was this the way it was supposed to be? To this day I cannot decide.

Back home the doctor who treated me required that I give up sex for six months, and so I turned all my energies to study. At this point my intellectual self had been formed from my extensive reading as an invalided youth, the many classic films I saw in the MoMA film series shown at the State University of Iowa throughout my earlier teen years, and the rigor and discipline of researching and writing on all conceivable subjects for college-level term papers. I enrolled in Intensive Ancient Greek, which with doubled class hours and extended assignments brought the student enough mastery to move into second-year coursework after one term. And why Greek? I had hated Latin in high school, although I did well enough in it. The previous summer, however, in shopping at registration for courses I discovered something worth only two credits called The Love Poems of Horace and Catullus. It sounded like an easy A, and I enrolled. The instructor that summer was intellectually seductive enough that I followed him into Intensive Greek and thereafter into courses in the literature of Greek, and from there I went on to be a classics major. That was the summer term of 1949. Almost half a century later I was to retire from my endowed chair as Distinguished Professor of Classics at the City University of New York, author of six or seven books and maybe fifty articles, mostly on the subject of ancient Greek literature or the civilization. I had found my life's work; what is more, I had found in me a passion, an obsession, really, that for years rivaled what riveted me to another human being. I guess I might say that it was the Great Love Affair of my life. And, having sympathetically listened to so many young people flounder about trying to figure out what interests them, I am deeply grateful that I found a life's calling, and so early on. Perhaps it made me narrow in some ways, because it wasn't until I retired that I really started to study other matters in some detail, European history or economics, for example. But for decades my absorption in the study of antiquity, particularly ancient Greek literature, gave me real coherence and purpose.

I ran across Dottie, my initial term-paper client, who introduced me to a male couple. Dottie's friends were the first two men whom I had ever encountered who were committed to each other and obviously in love. Somehow I had lived in this small town all my life and never fully recognized that there must be a pool of potential lovers on the one hand and a place where they congregated on the other. These sweet guys recognized me for the naïf I was, and promised to take me to the gay bar that sat on the street bordering the campus. For over two years I had been a regular at the bar next door, owned and run by a father of a high school friend, but somehow never noticed that a very different clientele was patronizing its neighbor. I suppose they wouldn't serve minors, so I never entered. It wasn't exactly a gay bar, but rather the bar where the university's students of drama, writing, and music congregated, which tended to include the gay population as well. So it was a bar in which one could wave one's hands, flit about, in general behave as differently as possible from the patrons of the bar next door, where townies like myself and the fraternity and athletic crowd hung out.

Thus began the second phase of my life in a gay bar. I guess I went to the Uptowner, as it was called, almost every night of the week, and usually came away with someone to sleep with. Not for the night, surely, because I was living at home while attending university, but for a few hours in a dormitory room or rooming house. These were fellow students, for the most part, Iowa boys, with all the virtues of small-town rural life, that is, basically friendly, not aggressive, easygoing. Just the same, they had an edge, they were wounded people with all the tendencies to lash out, nurse grievances, and feel inferior that came from the knowledge that they were freaks and pariahs in the minds of the larger population, sinners, of course, to the Christian community, which would generally include their parents and other family members.

I found them so different from the men I had met in the gay bars of Manhattan, who were mostly older, more experienced, for whom the mere act of homosexual intercourse was no longer a psychic challenge. The Iowa boys, by contrast, were at the very beginning of their careers as homosexual men and as such working to shape what they perceived to be their identity. At this stage their sexuality was the all-powerful defining aspect of their sense of self. Simply acting on it consumed them utterly, because it made them; it had to be that way if they were to develop any self-respect, perhaps only dimly understood. I think that the hostility and opposition that they sensed everywhere, and often enough confronted more dramatically, made them fight back as hard as they could with the self, their identity they were shaping, which meant in this environment a life lived by thoughts of homosexual sex and its enactment. Most of them did not think beyond the orgasm to the possibility of a relationship with the man who had helped them to it. They needed first to be comfortable acting out their erotic selves and at the moment it took all their time.

I have always believed that their capacity for focusing on the sex act per se was encouraged by the fact that their partner was another male, equally focused. My prejudice is that women are instinctively attuned to creating relationships out of any sexual encounter; heterosexual males are encouraged or forced to think beyond the immediate sexual act because their partners are female. It's the tired old "commitment" discussion yet again. I know that theories of biological destiny are out of fashion, but there we are. Women are stuck with what comes out of their womb and they jolly well want someone around who will look after them. In the same sense the human race needs to produce new generations and so society invents systems that force people into raising children like a church that calls divorce a sin, like a religion that stones adulterers to death. In a sense, males who attach themselves to a woman have no choice. Left to himself, a male can have an orgasm and get on with his day without thinking; young males more often than not include masturbation as much a part of the morning's ritual as shaving or brushing their teeth. It is all over in a matter of seconds. Two males working at it together can still complete their mission in minutes and be back on the road or into the office or whatever in no time. Who even remembers? The stupendous incidence of promiscuity among gay males relative to straight males derives in my estimation from what I claim is a biological truth rather than the gay male's incapacity to make moral judgments.

The fall term of my junior year at the university I had sex with more good-looking, clean-cut, nice young men than ever before or since. But we did not do repeats. And I learned very quickly from my mistake one evening of trying to make the first night a necking session so as to "get to know" him. When I met that particular guy the subsequent evening, he turned away from me, and it was only from friends that I learned how disgusted he was that we had not gone the whole way as we should have when we were together the first time. Years of hanging out with the girls in high school, sharing in their fantasies of love and romance, had conditioned me to believe in certain silly courtship rituals that had absolutely no place in gay life, and indeed seemed to most guys as completely ludicrous. What a fool I was! How obtuse. And yet I had met Dottie's friends, a loving committed male couple. The succeeding months into the winter and thereafter left me alternately depressed at not having a relationship and hopeful that there were the ingredients for one out there somewhere.

As the year went by I grew more and more disenchanted with my experience of the gay bar. It is a prejudice that has stayed with me for life. Consider for instance the musical *Falsettos*, in which a man leaves his wife for another man. Consciously or unconsciously the relationships between the bereft wife and her second husband and that of the two lesbian neighbors are so much deeper than that of the two gay males, who cannot finally give each other much of anything. It struck me as significant that the scene supposedly depicting the gay couple's relationship was on a squash court, a scene of high and aggressive competition—the truth of male-male relationships I was to learn very well later on in my life. Gore Vidal's first novel, *The City and the Pillar,* describes a young gay male in love with his teenage straight friend. In adulthood they meet again and the gay makes a pass, only to be spurned, which causes him to kill the unfortunate straight. Vidal later rewrote this novel when gayness became more acceptable, changing the ending from killing to anal rape. One understands male prisoners using anal intercourse as an instrument of control or revenge, but it is distressing to find a gay novelist treating what should be for him, and indeed for his gay character, a principal vehicle of the expression of love in a similar fashion. These examples describe the absolute separation of sex from love that is the dreadful psychic fallout from being told from pubescence on that homoeroticism is evil, self-destructive, or socially corrupt. One can love, or one can have sex. One cannot find it in the same person. It is like those men who have been so denatured by the teachings of the Catholic Church that they can only have good sex—that is, fun, recreational sex, by definition sinful—with prostitutes and not with their wives. But the climate that produced that mind-set does indeed seem to have undergone radical change. I noted in the last years of my teaching career that young gay males were dating, often restraining themselves from having sex on the first few evenings out together. Nowadays the gay world is clothed in increasing respectability, if one can use such a word anymore. It is an idea that numbers of gays deplore; still, it ought to make testing relationships a lot easier for young males.

Simultaneous with my bar life I kept on studying ancient Greek literature, which was helping me forge an aesthetic, ethical, and moral system to take the place of the Christianity I had discarded. The Judeo-Christian religions offer a god who takes a personal interest in humans, rewarding those who please him by their good works, punishing those who disobey him. There are rules to be kept or broken, and when broken, the active contravention of the law of this god is called sin and is punished. The Bible stories narrate that mankind sinned by disobeying God and eating the apple, and successive generations are born with sin. God so loved the world that He gave His only son Jesus, who came into this world to free man from this original sin. After death there is heaven for those who have led a good life, hell for those who have disobeyed the laws of their god. Roman Catholicism has a system of priests who stand for the god figure who can offer the truly repentant absolution from the sins they have committed. I had cast off this system of belief because I refused to accept the idea that homosexual lovemaking was in contravention of the laws of God and was a sin. That was the start and I proceeded to dismantle the rest as so much superstition, retaining only the Christian ethic based on love with which I had been raised. In fact I think it is not a bad idea to repeat to myself: "May the spirit of love and truth and peace make its home in your heart now and forever more."

Studying the culture of the ancient Greeks brought to me the vital information that in most of their societies it was socially desirable for a male of twenty to forty to take a mid- to late-teenage boy as his lover. Homosexual physical love is a topic of their literature, their art, their laws, and in the fabricated conversations that survive in the writing of Plato and Xenophon. A man was not a real man unless he had a young boyfriend. Nothing could have given me more support than knowing that the culture that is held to be the very basis of Western civilization valorized male-male erotic relationships as essential for the good society.

In their religious thinking the ancient Greeks had no such personal god as the ancient Hebrew texts describe. Nor did they have a system of belief, a dogma that establishes what is right and what is wrong. The literature is the best expression of their beliefs. In the *Iliad* when Achilles says to Priam, "There are two jars before the door of the house of Zeus, one filled with good, one with evil, and Zeus takes from the jar of evil and sprinkles it upon mankind, and sometimes adds from the jar of good," the narrator is providing a picture of a god who is indifferent to humankind and afflicts them or rewards them in an arbitrary way that has nothing to do with them. The story of Oedipus is of a man who at birth is prophesied to marry his mother and kill his father. His parents send him to be exposed on the hills, a shepherd finds the infant, and out of kindness gives him to someone who takes him to a faraway city. The boy grows up to manhood and sets out to travel, then meets an old man at a crossroads whose carriage bars his passage and in a fit of temper kills him. Journeying on to the city, he meets the widowed queen and marries her, only to discover years later, after she has borne him three children, that he is the long-lost son of his wife and the man he had killed on the road. This story is about deep and impossible evil that a man was born to commit, and nothing can prevent it from happening, no matter how hard the participants try. Through no fault of his own and despite strenuous efforts, Oedipus grows up to do what he was born to do. Instead of trying to justify evil with a system of sin and punishment, the ancient Greeks accepted misfortune as the luck of the draw. It made complete sense to me—how could it not?—having fallen from a balcony at four, having lost my father at six, watching my mother's way of life disappear while at the same time discovering my community turning on me as an object of scorn and derision, living in an age when the newsreels projected death and destruction and the industrial annihilation of an entire people. Somehow the Christian notion that one gets what one deserves was too odious.

The *Iliad* is many things, but one central strand is the story of a young man who discovers as we all must that he is doomed to die, and that fact cancels out any eternal value in living, so that whatever we do in life is all we have and our only definition. In this sense life is tragic; aware, intelligent people live with the knowledge that they are doomed, but act as positively as they can because they want to make each act of life have meaning. This can go in strange ways, of course. One thinks of Aeschylus's conception of Clytemnestra, who kills her husband Agamemnon because he as a general ordered the death of their daughter to propitiate the gods for his military expedition, and she as a mother of that daughter makes killing her husband a way to redeem and valorize motherhood and womanhood. Socrates, Plato, and Aristotle were stressing a common cultural belief when they asserted that man aims at the good, man is a heroic and noble creation. Ancient Greek statuary also attests to that belief; it was amplified and reshaped in the

Italian Renaissance of the fifteenth century. Nothing would have been more repellent to the ancient Greeks than the notion of some Christian sects that man is depraved. That belief is as far different from the tragic sense of life as one can go. It is important to remember that Clytemnestra, Oedipus, and all the others did the best they could, just as much as we latter-day human beings need to remember that important truth about ourselves.

# THREE

# *"LET'S GET MARRIED"*

*Mary Powers, the new Mrs. Charles R. Beye, standing in St. John's Episcopal Church, Ames, Iowa, with her husband after the ceremony, July 1, 1951* (Courtesy of the author)

One early morning—Wednesday, March 28, 1951, to be exact, nine days after my twenty-first birthday—I was returning books to the university library, when my friend Betsy Fontana came into my line of vision. After one of her exaggerated and giggly smooching kisses, she introduced me to the woman with her.

"This, Mary, my dear, is Charlie Beye, the biggest fag in Iowa City."

I protested, although Mary seemed to take it as no more than Betsy's normal flamboyance. We stood chatting, compulsive talkers all, until we remembered we were in a library. I was off on a walk around town with a wad of cash in my pocket, paying bills for my mother; it is hard to remember now a time when shopkeepers appreciated cash in the till and there were no credit cards. Mary offered to accompany me, claiming, as I was to learn was typical of her, that she had "nothing to do." Betsy trotted off to class, and we began our ascent from the library near the river up the hill to the town itself on the far side of the campus where the shops were located. We never stopped talking even to get our breath as we moved along placidly on our walk, but raced from topic to topic, oh, Lord, there was no stopping us. First it was Homer and Greek tragedy. Mary had read the *Iliad* and *Odyssey* closely, although, as she claimed, she was much too immersed in English literature to find time to learn Greek. Still she knew the poems well; I was impressed. I, on the other hand, had nothing to say about English literature, having shunted it aside in my intense pursuit of the ancient stuff. Ah, well, we turned to Tolstoy, a favorite of both of us, whom I had read in high school before I got caught up in classics, so we could argue over the philosophical bits in *War and Peace* and whether they were all that necessary and proclaim our love of Anna Karenina. And, oh, joy, we both had read lots and lots of Proust in high school as well; it took me all of my senior year. I was intoxicated by the endless stream of words pouring from both our mouths, spurred on to more and more outrageous word choices in response to Mary's vocabulary. At last, an hour later, all bills had been paid, and I had something left over to allow me to invite Mary for toast and tea at Whetstone Drugstore where back in the day one could get refreshments. It was now nine o'clock. I had known her for one hour; I was enchanted. We stopped talking to tend to the tea, and I looked across the booth at her and recollected what I had noticed on our walk. She was short, fleshy, there were pleasing curves to her hips—pear-shaped, they used to call it—in symmetry with her round full breasts that her sweater revealed. Her skin tones had a definite copper cast, which went with her thick strawberry blond hair, worn shoulder-length. She wore lipstick, and eye shadow, and penciled her eyebrows. She was definitely not an Iowa City High School girl.

"This has been great," I said. "I think we should get married."

Mary did not hesitate at the suggestion but had a question in reply. "Have you ever slept with a woman?"

"Well, no. I haven't."

Still unperturbed, Mary contemplated the toast on her plate before saying, "Well, that would be basic in any marriage."

"Then we shall have to do so, and the sooner the better," I solemnly decreed. "In fact, perhaps a week from this coming Friday."

The last part of this lunatic conversation was predicated on the coincidence that I was going to be sleeping alone in our house on that Friday night. My mother was about to move us into a small apartment, for which she had discarded a great quantity of household furnishings. This stuff was stacked in the garage, about to be sold in an auction on the lawn in front of our house. Friday night I would be a guard; the double bed on which I was to sleep in the empty house would be moved out to the auction on Saturday morning. My reader cannot possibly find this course of action any stranger or more inexplicable than its author does!

The walk that ended in Whetstone Drugstore cannot be explained. Most of the time Mary and I talked about emotional depression, as I remember. I told her of my experiences growing up gay, an abbreviated version of what is contained in the previous pages. She herself had known hostility, had her own tales of classmates' negative reaction to her sexual freedom in another small-town Iowa high school. Things hadn't improved any, she told me, when she arrived at the university, where she made the mistake of thinking she could combine sex and friendship. If I was the town's notorious cocksucker, she had to contend with her reputation as an easy lay. We both knew a lot about the same things, hurt, for instance, and social confusion, and sexual curiosity. We were also both able to put our experiences into a humorous perspective. We were so much alike; the thought of it threw me into a state of intense excitement.

Marriage? How did the idea pop into my head? The small-town mores of my day dictated that no two people could live together unless they were married. I must have proposed marriage as the obvious status of intimacy. It is a commentary upon the sexless home of my childhood that I never stopped to consider the sexual component, until Mary laughingly asked whether I had slept with a woman. It is a commentary upon Mary that she did not immediately reject the idea of marriage to a gay male. She was spontaneous, reckless, devoid of calculation. The very moment was telling. Mary was a juvenile diabetic who needed daily injections of insulin to maintain her metabolic functions. There she was sitting in the drugstore with me smoking a cigarette, drinking coffee, and eating sugared cinnamon buttered toast. These were so many no-no's, as I was to discover later, to which she was quite indifferent. Mary was up for experience; she exuded the perfume of transgression and it intoxicated me. I think that she was equally attracted to me, that she was willing to give the idea of marriage, ludicrous, crazy as it was, a try, so long as I passed a test in the basics. While sex was not at all central to her idea of friendship, Mary was not about to let go of it.

No amount of psychiatric discussion has ever gotten me any closer to why I did what I did, for which I had no regrets and pretty nearly total satisfaction during the four and a half years that remained of Mary's life. Of course, cynics will always argue that any relationship cut short like that will look good. Think of Alfredo and Violetta in *La Traviata*, or, more to the point, gorgeous Robert Taylor and Greta Garbo in *Camille*. If Mary felt doomed, perhaps she communicated that desperate feeling at some level. It was all of a piece with the ancient Greek tragic sense of life. Well, I am sentimental, I know it, and perhaps I do glamorize the memory.

Oddly enough, I was not the slightest bit apprehensive about having sex with Mary. Once she had agreed to consider marriage, we began to act like any couple going steady, lots of necking, lots of kissing. At first it felt strange to me, touching her or holding her. Mary was small, and soft, and slightly fleshy. Boys were tall, hard, and muscular. Swelling, warm, sweet-smelling breasts had to be won through the challenge of the fortification of a brassiere. How much easier to dip one's hand into a pair of jockey shorts. At this stage I equated breasts with pricks. These were the two appendages of gender that stuck out. My naturally strong libido responded to her flesh, considerably encouraged by her demonstrative affection and attractiveness. Mary was not embarrassed to put her hand on me, to rub my groin and arouse me. Somewhere in the mysteries of my sexual education at home I had learned that women were not aroused by the sight of men, nor were they willing to respond to men's aggressive actions, but rather waited, quite passively, for the male's arrival and entry. Mary was not like this; she was ready to ensure that her male's equipment was ready for action. It was almost two weeks since we made this assignation, and I was certainly ready. Like an athlete in training I had kept myself from any contact with a male, had kept my hand off my dick. Friday night Mother was safely packed off to her new apartment. I had bought condoms and put beer in the refrigerator.

I was what I think is nowadays called "highly sexed," and rather than feel terrified, I was keen on the experiment, and as we entered the house and ascended the stairs I could sense the familiar twist and tightening of my undershorts as the blood began its journey. Mary had been relatively promiscuous since losing her virginity at sixteen and approached a new sexual encounter as simply part of a larger repertoire of interaction that she saw developing between two people who had already amply demonstrated a great gift for conversing on a very wide range of subjects with considerable rhetorical skill. The charge in that was certainly as strong as the physical attraction of two young naked people. I was not the least nonplussed by the demands of fitting on a condom, since the married man with whom I had been sleeping two years earlier had insisted upon condoms until he felt sure that I was clean. It seemed ridiculous at the time, but on this particular night I was thankful for the experience.

The first great discovery of heterosexual intercourse for a veteran of the active role in homosexual anal intercourse was delight at the easy entry. I mounted, slid in, and there I was enveloped in Mary's warm and moist interior. Later I was to be delighted that the vagina could accommodate a somewhat limp penis after its orgasm, allowing for some tentative thrusts to start toward a new crescendo. As I began to develop my rhythm, I was delighted to look down at her face, watching her breasts bobbing below me, feeling them crushed against my chest. The missionary position allowed me to feel my control of her body through my legs and pelvis. It was my show, I was a god and emperor and king, after all those years on my knees staring at a guy's pubic hair as I went up and down on him, or if I was penetrating my partner more often than not confronting his shoulder blades, or when face-to-face having to manage the logistics of balance and stance, not to mention the need to have a harder-than-rock phallus for the penetration of the slightly off-kilter orifice. Oh, joy, oh, rapture, oh, bliss. It was a revelation to me, Mary's continuing surge of sexual desire, matching my own, which until then I did not know I possessed, sharing as we did a reaction to orgasm by slowly moving gently, gently together to produce another. We could make love all night.

For the first time in my life I understood that a woman is a mystery. By this I mean I had complete familiarity with a male's erotic responses because I myself was a male. A commonplace response of hitchhikers whom I had picked up on the transcontinental highway on their way home after demobilization was that I was better than any prostitute they had experienced in Paris or Hong Kong or wherever. It always seemed natural to me, because I was alert to every nuance of their mounting excitement since I knew it from my own experience. No matter how often a male may make love to a woman, if he takes their lovemaking seriously and tries to comprehend it, he will discover that he can never finally sense her response to his presence or to his actions because there is no true analogue to his own bodily responses, not even massaging the clitoris. More than anything else this was the great discovery for me.

I had been raised in a house of women, habituated to talk with them easily. My closest school chums were all women. I felt entirely comfortable with women. God knows I certainly knew the rhythm and frequency of the female menstrual cycle from early on. One of my long-standing anecdotes at the right sort of social gathering was describing my mother's often-repeated request that I walk down to Pearson's Drugstore to purchase Kotex for my many bleeding sisters, and my reluctance as a youth to expose myself to the snickers at my frequent appearance there on that mission, not to mention my wonderment at why they couldn't get their own sanitary napkins; I mean, why me? Now for the first time I discovered at the deepest physical level my alienation from women whom I would never really know at all. Not for me Joan Crawford imitations or drag parties. Women were women and men were men. In bed with Mary I forgot myself: I was a conventional male person and in the process my penis took over from my mouth as the focus point. I think of the psychoanalyst Karen Horney's remarks about male performance anxiety connected with the idea of the penis as a tool, and the fact that women can produce offspring without experiencing orgasm, but that men must perform to function biologically. What is, of course, interesting in this distinction is that I had spent years bringing males to orgasm, experiencing this orgasm orally, controlling it in doing so; my mouth was my instrument. The shared experience of mating as I had sex with Mary, both of us excited together, both facing one another, moving together in response to my thrusting; it was so different from "giving" another guy an orgasmic experience, from the first stirrings through to the ecstatic convulsions, my action, his passivity—no performance anxiety for him, which is perhaps the fundamental allure of fellatio.

I did not see Mary again until Monday. After my morning's work on Saturday I returned to assist Mother at her auction, then went with her to the new apartment to settle in. Monday, Mary and I met again at the drugstore, where she told me that she had spent Saturday night with her casual boyfriend. "I just wanted to be sure that I knew what I was doing," she said with a laugh. "Yes, you and I had a great night of sex, but, you know, 'forsaking all others,' as the marriage service says. I just wanted to comparison-shop."

I smiled, but I was scandalized; obviously the irony of my

adhering to the double standard for males and females did not strike me. Immediately I felt vulnerable, although it was clear that whatever-his-name-was had not proved to be a serious rival. Within a week or so I met the guy when he went out for the evening with Mary and me. As we were driving her back to her dorm I felt him put his arm down upon mine, which was resting on the seat behind her, and his hand pressuring me. Once I bade her good night, Harvey and I drove to his apartment. On the way he introduced the idea of our forming a ménage à trois, for which he had pedantically worked out the logistics. All that was needed, he concluded, was a demonstration of his capacity for homosexual sex. Harvey was the stereotypical ambitious, overachieving New York Jew, an exotic in Iowa, a commonplace in the East. Our time in bed was going to be an experiment. His two roommates, also Jews from New York, greeted us solemnly, then nervously and abruptly withdrew to their rooms, obviously aware of his great experiment. Harvey undressed, revealing a powerful, excited member attached to a well-formed hairy torso. I was immediately overpowered with the kind of desire I would never know with Mary. For the next several hours we tried it all. Harvey, the intrepid explorer, put his member wherever I directed, and, sometimes grimacing with pain, offered his every orifice for penetration, following my example, but it was finally clear that for Harvey, as the expression goes, "Once is curiosity, twice would be perversion." "That's what I thought would happen," said Mary.

Did I love her? people always ask me. I don't know; I am not sure what love is. I liked her immensely, I valued her, I did not swoon over her. I suppose I did not love her in any conventional sense of the word. I certainly did not lust after her. Seeing her nude standing before me did not give me the charge a naked male would produce. We were married July 1, 1951; she died a little over four years later. We never had a devastating quarrel, although once I made Mary so angry that she left our bed in our one-room apartment and slept the night in the bathtub. We yelled and screamed and pouted on many occasions. Our sexual marathons gradually became less frequent and less intense, and finally the sex became more a placid release three times a week. We spent that final Sunday afternoon in bed making love four hours before she died. But in all those days of our life together we never stopped the conversations.

Our courtship lasted three months. I went up to Ames to meet her parents, Carl and Ruth Powers, and to ask for her hand in marriage, that old expression, but we felt old-fashioned to be getting married. It was not a sacrament, a ceremony, no, we saw it as a party event, a drama, a symbol of our relationship to act out. The wedding photos reveal a very young couple, handsome, shy, naïve. My heart goes out to all that innocence as though I, the old man viewing them, had never been part of it. But then, everyone in the scenes seems so young, even my mother, who was only fifty-eight at that moment, just five years older than my eldest child today. My best man seems to be no more than fourteen, although of course he was my contemporary in college. We met through gay circles, I chose him as best man on impulse, really, because I was in another life from my adolescence, and a male from my high school class would carry associations I did not want then. Well, that's what I would have said, perhaps did say, but the fact of the matter is that I had no close male friends from the high school days. He and I and Mary and her attendant drove up from Iowa City the day before the wedding, the ride broken by a longish boozy lunch in a restaurant on the banks of the Cedar River lazily flowing on its long journey to the Mississippi. That night we were nervous and had what we wanted, sandwiches, nothing more, made by Mary's mother. Afterward we two men bade the ladies good night and went to the local hotel to spend the night. After a few drinks in the bar downstairs we decided to turn in. I was nervous; so was he. This was going to be a performance, and we wanted to do our best.

We sat on the edge of our beds in our underpants to discuss it, and as so often happens in scenes such as these the inherent physical attraction of two males almost nude with the added titillation of mounded flesh seen through white cotton fabric caused them to disrobe completely and act on their desire. And that, I suppose, could be called my bachelor party.

I kissed most of the boys goodbye in the two months leading up to the wedding. For example, my former dueling partner in the high school play, now a university student, to whom I had given considerable help with his term papers in exchange for sexual favors, dropped by my mother's apartment one day when she was out. He no doubt imagined that he could get a paper from me as he had before, but this time without having to put out. As I sat on the floor next to him poring over the papers and notes he had brought with him, his thighs, his shoulders and chest, his breath and smell deranged my thoughts. I ran my hand up his leg. Minutes later we were naked on my bed, a threatening headache was gone, and I felt a kind of peace of fulfillment that told me something true about myself that I was willing to accept but not to articulate. I said goodbye to my married friend, who encouraged me to try it straight for a bit—to "get the hang of it." I said goodbye to the big college athlete who took it up the ass and tried to deny it meant anything; yet when we met for the last time, the two of us sitting naked on his bed, he staring moodily at the floor while I looked out the window, he asked, "But what about me?" I didn't know, nor do I know now how he worked out his life. The star high school athlete, my weekly companion of so many years, now a married man, I could not let go. He continued to see me from time to time; in fact, on the very day a year later when Mary and I were leaving Iowa City for Cambridge, Massachusetts, and graduate school, he came by when she was at work "just to say goodbye," and sat across from me staring me in the eye, slowly unzipping his fly, knowing that I could not resist.

After we married, Mary and I moved into a one-room apartment with a tiny kitchen and bath. The bed slid back under a compartment filled with bedding, sticking out just enough to form a sofa by day. Otherwise there was a desk, a so-called comfy chair, and a chest of drawers. We were thrilled, and set about to invite everyone we knew to dine off our grand silverware, needless to say a wedding present, which stood in full array on the card table we set up when dinner was served. Neither of us knew how to cook, nor to keep house, for that matter. Clothes washing was very much hit or miss, not least because the public laundry was a significant walk away, shopping we got to only when the fridge was totally bare, cleaning we thought much too arduous because our wedding-present vacuum cleaner was really too big to maneuver around so small an area.

We ate chicken à la king, the one recipe Mary had learned for her high school pajama-party suppers. It featured chunks of chicken in a white sauce colored with bits of pimiento, served on waffles. The waffles were the essential ingredient because it gave us the chance to show off our waffle iron. We seemed to have eaten a lot of waffles, plain for breakfast, under the sauce for dinner. There was quite a collection of place mats and tablecloths for these events, which was lucky because Mary tended to shove unwashed linens under the bed. She was not prompt nor terribly responsible in most things. For instance, she never wrote a single thank-you note, although her mother begged her almost every day as Mary's silence grew more and more embarrassing. ("Oh, God, Mary, at least my bridge club. Please, please.") Our refrigerator was never too full, but there was always an opened jar of pimientos with a growth of mold filling the upper portion. I was alternately mystified and angered by this behavior, mystified because I could not imagine defying the "rules" so brazenly, angered because her indifference to process and procedure guaranteed to me the frightening collapse of order. I was a very fearful person; Mary was not.

Mary's strongly transgressive spirit was a counterpart to my breaking the rules in my sexual behavior. But I had a well-developed instinct for hypocrisy that compromised my freedom. I think of the night Mary and I went to her friend Harvey's for dinner, and while we and other friends sat at the kitchen table, one of the couples who lived in the house came home and, after saluting us all, went into their bedroom, which was behind the kitchen, where they began to fuck, not ostentatiously loudly, but not silently either. My shock was great; I could scarcely contain myself. Yet if I had been more honest I might have recollected an occasion of only perhaps a half year earlier when I joined three males in their apartment and took them one by one into the bedroom without closing the door while the other two sat talking in the living room.

I had never known anyone like Mary. She was a "girly" girl—makeup, fingernail polish, attention to clothes, shoes, hair—and we could have girl talk, which I loved, and we learned to cook together. At the same time she was quite a slob. Just when she should have been concentrating on turning herself into a femme fatale, she would be thinking too much. She liked to play with language, always did the crossword, loved puns, was conscious of the prose she read and wrote. I loved her for her belly, which was a round mass in the center of her pear-shaped body, just like the bellies of Renaissance Flemish nudes. Maybe that is why she always seemed stylized when nude, if not in fact stylish. Mary developed diabetes when she had scarlet fever as a child, which destroyed the insulin-making part of her pancreas. She was thereafter a "flawed" person, in the sense that she had to make herself complete with insulin injections, that she was liable to insulin shock if she did not manage her intake of glucose. We had this in common, that we were obviously imperfect, vulnerable, flawed people. What kind of premonitions did she have? Why did she agree to marry me? Impulsive? Adventurer? Life was going nowhere? Like the Methodists she believed in their mantra, "Do no harm." That made her a tender person. She had a tenderness in sex that I associate with women, and that translates into something like love—not dependency, but a force for cherishing. Mary was cozy; I think of her drinking tea in her bathrobe, neat with the sash tied, or carelessly sitting in it reading with the front open and her breasts spilling out. Mary was a woman in the house reading, a Degas woman in the tub raising her arm to wash it with a sponge, she was the woman with me in an enclosed space, in bed with me talking, offering her body in which one could sink slightly, so unlike the muscle-and-bone resistance of the male body.

Matters that I had been schooled to concern myself with simply did not exist for Mary. Two months after we were married, for instance, she decided to drop out of school. She was in her fifth year as it was, progress hindered by her habit of getting A's in the courses that interested her and F's in those that did not. "I have a husband," she announced breezily to her horrified parents, "and he will take care of me, so why do I need a degree?" She preferred, when not working her half-day job at the hospital, to pad around our teeny space in her rather dirty green corduroy bathrobe. Saturdays she taught me to leave our bed out so that it filled our only room. There we lay reading, eating apples, spilling cigarette ash over the sheets, fucking at random intervals, and chatting comfortably with one another. You could say she had no ambition, vision. Not true, of course. Never had I encountered anyone who lived for the day so defiantly as she. She took my hand in hers and we embarked on life as a dream. It didn't last, at least not for her, and when she was gone the dream was too.

If she was in many ways a real slob, she never left the house without looking grand. She had a considerable wardrobe. I remember the first time I paid attention as she was taking off a gray tailored suit worn over a blouse with a white background upon which were gray and yellow flowers. Gray suede pumps were an obvious complement to this ensemble, but it was the gray silk brassiere trimmed in a yellow ribbon, and gray underpants, that got to me. "I dress to undress," she explained with a smile. She almost always wore heels; one of life's great pleasures was watching her lift up those marvelous legs to pull on her nylons, with her hands covered with cotton mitts to avoid snags, then attach the garters and adjust the garter belt and stockings. I know perfectly well the theory that these are symbols of bondage, just as high heels keep women from moving freely. Too bad; they excited me just as panty hose repels me. I used to love to buy her lingerie. Dressing and undressing my woman was my new erotic sport. I can't imagine getting too excited about a guy dressing or undressing; with men it's not the clothes, it's the man's body underneath.

In August 1952 we arrived in Cambridge, where I was about to embark on a PhD degree program in classical philology at Harvard. This was certainly one of the most dismal episodes of my life, made palatable only by Mary's never-ending emotional support of me, along with the infusion of her knowledge. And, of course, she paid the rent with her office job, this same woman who had announced that she had a husband to support her! Most of all, Mary liberated my thinking. I was deep into the study of antiquity, mainly reading ancient texts in Greek and Latin. Trying to master the language of each text through the methods of philology required a careful examination of the etymology and usage of each word in a stately procession through the text. Mary had been schooled in critical theory in the English Department and comparative literature courses. She read to interpret texts. Her questions about the material I was studying challenged me to answers I could not find, and in turn raised further questions that forced me to see ancient literature in another way. My teachers had done things differently. Mary taught me about style, narrative, structure, form, imagery, all the ingredients that make a verbal construct a work of art. She was so bright.

Her other immediate intellectual gift to me was placing the

literature of antiquity in a broader context. I had been so narrowly focused—necessarily, since Greek and Roman literatures are so vast—that I was quite ignorant of everything else. For the first time I was hearing about Pound, Eliot, Auden, and the other figures of twentieth-century modernism, not to mention the myriad writers of the English tradition who hardly appeared in the wretched courses that passed for English in my high school. My only contact with the aesthetic and ideology of the twentieth century had been through the foreign films that I had been assiduously watching for the past five or six years at the university art museum. Suddenly an entire world began to take shape for me. The education at home was by far the stronger influence.

Our social life as a married couple first began in Cambridge with our next-door neighbors, who introduced us to friends from their church circle who had no connection with Harvard. We were not the least bit religious, but it was refreshing to meet people who did not have attitude. I mean that there was something about Harvard that worked insidiously to compel one to want to live up to being there all the time.

What began to strike my consciousness was the simple and ironic truth that after seven or eight years of living in a community that knew, whether they liked it or not, that I was gay, I now had to conceal this. I went into the closet, as they say nowadays. Obviously a young married couple moving to a new community will not make friends and find a social circle by advertising the peculiar sexual habit of the husband. Still, it felt odd, this dissimulation. It was not that I wanted to parade the fact of a sexual attraction to males, but for the first time since I was sixteen, those around me did not know me. My homosexuality was common knowledge in Iowa City, for better or for worse. Here I was voluntarily, deliberately concealing a truth about myself, and I often therefore spoke in a way that was dishonest. That could not help but make me feel compromised and corrupted; I wanted to be myself, but I resisted the urge to confess to this truth when I found myself growing close to anyone male or female, if for no other reason than it would not have been fair to Mary.

As I have said, homosexuality is found everywhere in ancient Greece. How ironic that in the classics profession in those days the fact was glossed over and students were uncomfortable with it, whereas I who had lived it could not mention it. From this time forward I was at war with myself, struggling to prevent any inadvertent revelation, and at the same time, working to create a dishonest false public image. It was instinctive and thus unconscious; the humiliation and degradation only registered with me years later when, on a day I will never forget, I was on the crosstown Eighty-sixth Street bus in Manhattan and I idly looked from the window to see a young heterosexual couple freely embracing, kissing, and laughing while looking into each other's eyes, and a hitherto stifled rage welled up and poured into my brain, almost sending me reeling into a faint. Oh, the anger! Now I understood those madmen who get up and spray a crowd with their gun, or bomb a building. I rode the bus across to Park Avenue in a stupor, walked down to Eighty-fourth to the Catholic Church of St. Ignatius Loyola, which I entered to sit quietly in a pew and suck up the peace of God which passeth all understanding.

The other graduate students lived in some monastic setup, but I had a wife, an apartment reeking of domesticity, and the capacity and desire to entertain just as real grown-ups did. Mary lost no time in establishing a kind of salon to which members of the seminars I attended would gravitate after class for the usual postmortems far into the night. One constant visitor was William Musgrave Calder III, still an undergraduate when he introduced himself to me in Henry Joel Cadbury's class in New Testament Greek. He talked like a ninety-year-old aristocrat banker even then, so it became easy to play son to his father when in a short time he had taken over the direction of my professional life, such as it was, when he sensed that I was demoralized and floundering. When first I met Bill, I could not resist bringing him home to tea almost as a specimen for Mary's inspection. She adored him at once, for his quirky language, for his drollery, for the sheer eccentricity of his vast learning (his enemies said he should have been a librarian), and he became a fixture in our lives. He it was who suggested to me—forced me into?—every seminar I took, got me to introduce myself to the man who eventually directed my dissertation. Oddly enough, for one so devoted to antiquity, he had never learned the rudiments of the ancient Greek language properly and needed instruction. In the summer of 1955 I offered him just that, leading him through the grammar and then the text of Plato's *Apology*, the standard fare back in those days. It has been something of a joke over the years that he introduces me as a former teacher. When he was at Columbia he used to get me invited to their Seminar in Classical Civilization, where I heard some great talks, gave one myself at his suggestion, a lecture that became an article and then a book. My debt to Calder is huge.

Mary's gatherings, however, went well beyond the offerings of the Classics Department. Other evenings she would entertain women and sometimes their men friends whom she met through her office or on the streets. Mary was a great socializer; she also enjoyed the company of her own sex. This may seem obvious enough except that in the Cambridge of the early fifties there was a distinct trend among women to spend their time exclusively with men so as to lose the taint of their despised femininity. The first stirring of women's liberation was producing a generation of females whose hatred of their own sex seemed a desperate bid to equal if not outdistance men at their own games. Academic parties of the era found women frantic to avoid other women lest they seem inferior by association. Mary considered it grotesque. She thoroughly enjoyed women, liked to go shopping or out to dinner with a female chum. She made friends at work and saw these women socially, independent of me. Her best friend was an elegant African American woman who worked wrapping packages at a deluxe clothing store because she, as a black woman, could not find work as a physical therapist for which she had trained, nor even work on the floor of the dress shop as a vendeuse. The two of them laughed and shopped (oh, all those heels and with those great legs!) and went to the movies together while I sat at my desk absorbing texts assigned to me.

Janyce reminded me of myself in Iowa City for being unwilling to accept the world's definition of her, a classic example of the Marked fighting the Unmarked's imposition of an identity. She was such high drama, so funny, so chic; she would have made a great drag queen. Still and all, she was a nice Cambridge girl, a dutiful daughter, a credit to her church group. Her wide circle of friends, white and black, included many in Roxbury, the principal neighborhood of African Americans at that time, which we would often visit in her company on Saturday nights. Those were the days before the southern migration and the dramatic decline and impoverishment of the area, a time when a white couple would not hesitate to walk the streets late at night returning to Dudley Square for the bus ride to Harvard Square. Many of Janyce's friends had, like herself, performed in amateur theater, so the Roxbury parties were very spirited. It was there I met her nominal boyfriend. Shortly after our first meeting I journeyed on my own one afternoon to his apartment and into his bed, an adventure assumed and executed without even the slightest verbal exchange except for a telephone call to establish the time and place for the assignation. It was all in the glance. It has always seemed to me that students of feminist theory who specialize in the male gaze ought to study the gay gaze. Its erotic power, how it compels, instructs, and demonstrates, without so much as a sound when perceived by another gay, is astounding, and perhaps tells much of what straight males instinctively seek to achieve in gazing at females. I will never forget my student at Lehman College in the eighties, a straight fellow, in fact, telling me that he knew I was gay because I "held the gaze too long" when looking into the eyes of another male.

As Mary and I established ourselves socially in Cambridge I hated the stiff formality of my assumed heterosexual personality. I was habituated to sensing masculine interest in me, whether desire, curiosity, nervous testing, indifference, or repugnance. Suddenly I had a persona denied or at least reduced. What is more, I was often frustrated for male sexual companionship. My fellow students seemed unlikely candidates for my attention, and I had never been much good at cruising. I met males haphazardly. There was the young man doing laundry in the basement of our apartment building who invited me into his rooms following some verbal minuet that had a subtext that excited him (he was not gay and thus immune to the power of the gaze), or the two sailors needing directions who stopped me one dark autumn evening as I was coming home with something for dinner. After pointing them on their way, I asked if they wanted a blow job, to which one said yes, the other no. We went into a nearby alleyway, the one undid his fly, the other stood watch. It was over in seconds, and I was cheerfully on my way with scarcely an interruption of the dinner schedule.

These lighthearted anecdotes do not reflect what became an increasingly urgent search for male partners. The Cambridge bank of the Charles River was a prominent pickup place that I avoided, partly because I lived so near and we often walked there as a couple, partly because I feared meeting Harvard acquaintances, for whom I was masquerading as a standard-issue young married man. When I was sufficiently liquored up to be fearless I went out on the streets at night into Boston, funnily enough more than once getting into bed with a guy who told me of doing it with professors I knew at Harvard. I discovered that prostitutes all knew that when the subway shut down you could usually find a taxi driver who would exchange a good blow job for a free trip home. I discovered the principal gay bar of Boston, built on the site of the infamous Cocoanut Grove nightclub, a place that over a decade before had erupted one night into fire, asphyxiating the hundreds inside who had been pressed and smashed against the exit doors that opened inward. I recoiled at the association, yet, glancing about the tawdry smoke-filled interior filled with men acting out in that campy, self-mocking way that I would describe in retrospect as a kind of defense against low self-esteem, I thought that only a place of such a hideous memory could serve as the site for the sexually charged get-togethers of homosexual men. That such an idea came to me indicates how the charade I was living was taking its toll upon my own self-worth. The men in the bar seemed demented, to me. Better the streets, I thought, although I ran the risk of physical violence or police cruelty, all of which I avoided except for a couple of close calls that sent me home to Mary wracked with tremors of fear and crying. She said nothing, took me in, and comforted me.

Mother died May 28, 1954. The news came in a telephone call while we were eating dinner, and I immediately began to weep despite the fact that we had two friends with us. I had not seen her since the summer of 1952, our only subsequent communication being through the letters she habitually wrote each of her children on Sunday afternoon and my considerably less conscientious replies. There was nothing to say, really; she did not like me married, did not like Mary, had not been at all sympathetic when the department had voted not to renew my scholarship after the first year, indifferent to my having to take a night job to get sufficient money to continue. She had been kind enough to agree to pay $50 a month toward the psychiatrist's fee I was incurring when I, trendy as usual, joined every other Harvard student in seeking counseling, although the money was sent on with an implied sigh of impatience at my weakness that I could read in the language of the letter that always accompanied the check. I flew back to Iowa City to join my siblings for the funeral, the first meeting since we all had gathered at dinner to send my eldest siblings off to college in 1940. We were to meet only one more time as a group of six, in 1973. Considering the essential indifference and isolation of the six siblings, on these occasions we demonstrated our extraordinary capacity for nonstop animated and witty conversation, which, of course, an observer might describe as a desperate effort to keep the interaction free of substance and psychic pertinence. Because my mother and I had a fractured relationship, never repaired after the revelation of my sexual orientation, her death filled me with the deepest regret: so much could have been said, two really warm and loving people might have united in their regard for one another, a mother could have been proud of a bright and vivacious son out to conquer the world. That I have had to live with the memory of our great divide pained me for many years until finally she faded into the mists of time.

A year and three months later, Mary died, on August 28, 1955. We had moved two days before to Attleboro, Massachusetts, just a short drive from the town of Norton, the site of Wheaton College, where I had been hired as an instructor. The day had started early for me, who was busily churning out lecture notes for classes that were to begin in two weeks. It was broken by the arrival of two guys from graduate school who came to lunch; Mary could not resist starting up our Cambridge social life way down in Attleboro. After they went off, we left the dishes where they were and retired for an afternoon of lovemaking and napping. While Mary continued to sleep, I went to my desk. After an hour Mary came to my study door to complain of feeling sick, returned thirty minutes later to ask me to call a doctor. This was serious. I was rigid with fear as I went to use our neighbor's phone, since ours was not yet installed. They gave me a doctor's name, I called, he came, and I ushered him into our bedroom, settling myself outside the door. While he was examining Mary, the cat, which I had shut in the kitchen, let out a yowl, and almost simultaneously I heard Mary groan. The doctor came to the door of the bedroom to say, "I'm afraid she's done for." I stared at her body, afraid to go near. She seemed to be sleeping, nothing more. But she was dead, gone, stolen away just like that.

I lived through the next two weeks glazed over, without a conscious sense of the experience, as one so often finds it described by the newly bereaved. State of shock, I guess is what it is. I went back to the neighbor, and in swift succession called my five siblings, whose responses were typical—expressions of concern, mingled with regret that previous obligations would keep them from coming to Iowa to be with me during the days preceding the funeral and interment in the Powers family plot in Ames. At least my brother agreed to come to the service itself. I also called our two luncheon guests, who guaranteed that they would hasten down to take me away back to Cambridge. And then there was the undertaker, nice enough to offer to take our cat off my hands, as he and his assistant loaded Mary's corpse into their hearse. The next morning I visited the old couple for whom we had house-sat that summer to break the news; they gave me $300 in cash, since this was the days before credit cards, so I could book a flight to Iowa. I went to Attleboro, declined to see Mary laid out in her wedding dress in the coffin, was given the autopsy results—"coronary insufficiency," whatever that meant—arranged for the cremation, flew to Iowa, waited for the ashes because in Massachusetts in those days there was a legal delay for cremation, a period of "thinking it over" (courtesy of the lobbying of the Roman Catholic Church, which wanted, I guess, a lot of bodies floating about in the afterlife but could not imagine a deity who might re-create bodies from ashes if that was so important to him), sat with Mary's parents, aunts, and cousins, and, thankfully, Bill Calder, who flew out to be with me.

Dulled and stupid, I was helped through this event by Mary's parents, who were aware that I was alone, still a very young person without family, in their home and mourning the death of my wife. (I did not notice I was young then; at eighty I cannot imagine how the poor kid went through it all.) As the funeral procession formed in the vestibule of the church where four years earlier we had been married, I stepped back, but they insisted that I precede them down the aisle. "You are the husband," Mary's mother whispered to me with a little encouraging smile, as the tears poured down her cheeks. I sobbed loudly as the organist played Mary's favorite hymn, which began, "Oh, God, our help in ages past, our hope in years to come," and which to this day makes me choke up, crying for the futility of such an invocation—hope, indeed! Eventually I drove off with my brother and his wife to Sioux City, Iowa, bidding Bill goodbye at the airport there a day later. I sat stupidly for three days, vacantly watching my little nieces and nephew gamboling on the lawn, then returned to Ames, spending another nightmare day with my parents-in-law, stupefied by their grief, who then drove me to the airport in Des Moines, the silence at our last lunch together broken only by their saying, these two old people, who had just lost their only child, "Go back, start dating, Charlie, forget about Mary, get another girl, you're young." I arrived in Boston, went to live for a bit with Bill's family, letting myself be tended to by them, then I moved myself back to an apartment in Cambridge, set up my desk, got my suit and tie ready, drove down to Norton, walked onto a platform, set my notes down on a lectern, looked out at sixty girls, and said, "Good Morning." It was September 1955 and my teaching career had begun.

THE HARVARD YEARS: A NOTE OF CLARIFICATION

I entered graduate school in September 1952 and was awarded the PhD degree in classical philology in February 1960 (the alternative midyear date for awarding degrees, done without ceremony, as a bookkeeping procedure). My career in classics was unplanned. Excellent faculty and a love of Greek literature kept me in classes where I could study the texts in the original language at the State University of Iowa; it was sheer joy, all of it. Although I had never given my future serious thought, my professors groomed me for graduate school and steered me to Harvard, from which I received a small scholarship. My performance there was spotty, bad enough at first to encourage the faculty not to renew the scholarship in the hopes that I would withdraw. Instead I stayed on and took a night watchman's job to pay the tuition. In the first semester of this new arrangement (fall 1953) I received A's in all four seminars in which I was enrolled; as a consequence the department chair found money to ease my way. The courses I took were uniformly uninformative, poorly taught, and a definite waste of time, with each self-obsessed "star" Harvard professor delivering a two-hour monologue either on something canned that required no immediate thought or on random unconnected notions after the manner of stream-of-consciousness writing—with one exception, the seminar in Lucretius offered by Peter Elder, who made it into a tea party in his rooms in Lowell House, where some exceedingly bright graduate students (some of them the real champs of the profession in the next two or three decades) sat about and read each other the papers they were working on, while Elder poured tea and made pointed, illuminating, valuable comments. Such was the stimulation that I later wrote my paper up for a journal. The other moment of real learning came when I was a teaching fellow in the spring of 1955, the pay for which was a measly $400 for three courses. One was an undergraduate senior seminar in Euripides' *Alcestis*, conducted for two of the brightest students imaginable, working with whom inspired me to research the subject well enough to create a second paper for a journal. The tough questions on the *Aeneid* that my Virgil seminar threw at me drove me to so close a study of the poem that I was mining my research for books and articles for years to come. As a graduate student, however, I was pretty much a flop; at the end of the term 1954–55 I had not made an impression on any faculty, nor found any of them sufficiently congenial for us to work together on a dissertation. For that matter, I had not even thought out a topic. William Calder took pity on me and steered me to Sterling Dow, who was always greedy for the glory of being Doktorvater. He was an epigraphist with whom I had nothing in common, but he dreamed up a subject, dull as it was, that I managed to research without any more trouble than fighting off terminal boredom, and which was reduced into a scholarly article a few years later that has, to my amazement, been cited more than anything else I have written. In 1955 I left Harvard to start teaching full-time at Wheaton College. That plus the death of my first wife set back dramatically any progress on the dissertation, which seriously undermined my relationship with Dow, which was conducted from this point on by letter. I finally sat down to the dissertation in June 1958 when I was by that time teaching at Yale, the father of one son, and expecting my second wife's second delivery in November. Needless to say, I had had serious distractions, but I managed to finish the dissertation one week before my second son was born. Dow and I had a contentious relationship that ended in his examination of me on Greek history in the spring of 1959 as part of a two-hour oral examination divided between a defense of the dissertation and examinations in four fields. I did not do well, which colored the rest of my responses to the other faculty on that occasion, and they voted to ask me to repeat in the subsequent semester, a polite way of saying, *You fail.* My lousy performance at this event was partly inspired by sheer nervousness and partly by too many martinis for lunch; it was not enough that I had failed, but in their post-exam discussion with me on the matter I sat there crying—I must have been really drunk. One of the great anecdotes of the classics profession, I am told. I am inherently vicious enough a raconteur to appreciate its worth. In the fall of 1959 I journeyed once again from New Haven to Cambridge and there found the entire faculty sitting for the examination, which, before it started, the chair assured me I would pass, clearly aligning himself with the majority force in the department who did not take to Dow and his animosities. Pass I did, but the tension left me shaken, and by the following spring I entered the psychiatric ward of Grace–New Haven Hospital for a two-week recuperative stay, suffering from severe depression. I have nothing but grim memories of Harvard University and its Classics Department, but I owe the institution the incomparable glory and status that comes from brandishing a Harvard PhD on my curriculum vitae or in conversation, plus, during the thirty years I spent in Cambridge later on, the chance to swim in the superb Blodgett Pool at the reduced fee offered alumni, and then the crown jewel of my Harvard experience, a yearly pass to the Widener Library, the use of which through the years makes up for any indignity or other horror that I might have sustained.

# FOUR

# FALLING IN LOVE
# WITH LOVE

*The new Penelope Pendleton Beye and her husband,*
*lost in the swoon of it all at the reception following their*
*wedding in Deerfield, New Hampshire, June 16, 1956*
*(Courtesy of the author)*

In the months after Mary's death, I, like almost everyone else in such a situation, went through the motions of living mechanically. Feelings of intense loneliness and an emotional vertigo brought on by dislocation were half the time blocked by the anxieties arising from my new job. No sooner had I settled into an apartment (although "settled" does not describe the frantic flailing that marked the move) than I found myself five days a week on the highway making the hour journey between Cambridge and Norton, scarcely noticing the road as my brain was furiously reviewing the material I was en route to offer or wearily parsing afterward to determine whether I had made sense.

I was appointed an instructor in classics at Wheaton for the academic year 1955–56. I was too shy even to ask about my salary in the interview, and no one, neither the retiring chair nor the dean, thought to bring it up. We were all WASPs; no one mentioned money, plus we were college professors, in those days really too high-minded to talk about salary. It was not uncommon for faculty in the more prestigious New England institutions to have what used to be called "old money." Well, I did not, so I was pleased to figure out from my first salary check that I was making about $3,000 a year. Bottom of the heap, no PhD yet, I was barely one step above a teaching fellow, the title Harvard used for graduate student slaveys such as myself, who the preceding year haltingly and ineptly taught three two-hour undergraduate seminars for what I love to call bupkis.

Once Wheaton would have been called a girls' college, until "girl" became considered almost as abusive as the infamous "n-word." At some level the students were being trained to become "ladies." I was startled to discover that the girls were not allowed to smoke outdoors going from class to class on campus, whereas the male faculty were—habituating the girls, I suppose, to the social fact that "decent" women—that is, "ladies"—did not smoke on a public street. One still heard talk of an education that would make the girls "well rounded," whatever that could mean, probably able to hold their own when the highlights of middle-class culture—Wagner's Ring, for instance, a trip to Paris, *The New Yorker*—might happen to come up for discussion. This presumably ensured that they were attractive women, and thus suitable helpmates for whatever man might bring them to the altar. Getting a man was a major undertaking. Christmas vacation in the senior year was a now-or-never moment from which fortunate girls returned sporting engagement rings, and wedding plans were the big talk of the final semester.

I was lucky to have a job. This was entirely due to Sterling Dow, who had agreed to be my dissertation adviser, although not a page of that document had yet been written. He was proud of the network of positions where he tried to control the staffing. Unlike some of his colleagues who had no notion of the bread-and-butter realities of the profession, Dow kept in touch with students past and present, shuffling them around in the job market as though it were a chessboard and at the same time shoring up his national reputation. Wheaton College, it must be said, was an entirely unimportant institution, as I myself was a very minor figure in Professor Dow's machinations. Still, despite my dismal graduate school record, and my never having even studied with him, Dow's overweening ego had a place even for me; I was his student, like it or not, so a job must be found.

As it was, I was going to replace another Dow student who

was going on to Yale, a fellow known to all as Ted Doyle, whom at the time I scarcely knew although he was destined to become one of my closest, most important friends. Edwin Joseph Doyle certainly was much more to Dow's liking, being an epigraphist, his mentor's own hard-nosed specialty, and a habitué of the American School of Classical Studies in Athens, Dow's home away from home. He had been slotted into Wheaton by Dow, however, because he was otherwise a dubious candidate for advancement. An Irish Catholic from Boston whom, as he himself often remarked, the classics faculty would immediately associate with every police officer and tavern owner in the city, not to mention the men of Harvard's Buildings and Grounds, he was also notoriously slow at finishing his graduate work; some called him lazy. Still, he was off to Yale for the academic year 1955–56 as yet without the degree because Frank Brown, the chair at Yale, told Dow he needed an epigraphist; Doyle was the right man at the right time, dissertation or no. I think it could be said that his war record, which included the landing at Salerno in 1943 and the fight up through the Italian peninsula into Germany, made up for a lot.

I was contracted to teach five courses a term, a schedule not uncommon in the forties and fifties, but a workload at which present-day academics would faint (and we are not even talking about preparation and grading). My main effort was a lecture course in classical civilization, Greece in the fall, Rome in the spring. For decades the department had traditionally emphasized history and archaeology, and far more students enrolled in classical civilization than in courses in Greek or Latin. On paper that may sound like a high-minded academic decision, but the reality was that ancient language courses were difficult (despite the fact that before Vatican II every Catholic boy of whatever intellect was forced to master one or both), and the girls shunned them. A lecture course, however, which emphasized art, literature, and archaeology, along with the history, would be easy enough for most anybody, and, if taught in a fashion that was amusing and colorful (read: lots of slides), would prove popular as well, and thus a breadwinner for the department. By the mid-fifties as the classics profession nationwide was beginning to look nervously at declining enrollments, the more realistic department chairs knew enough to move away from language instruction with schemes to ward off administrators pushing budget cuts. The Wheaton tradition of archaeology and history put them well ahead of the curve.

It was *essential*, therefore, that the successful candidate for the job be able to teach this course, and Dow, the historian, was the natural guarantor of this credential. As it was, I knew next to nothing about ancient history; I had not studied it much as an undergraduate and never as a graduate student. Since I had done no work with Dow (beyond hemming and hawing on the ridiculous subject of the putative dissertation that he had dreamed up for me), he had no experience of my complete ignorance of the subject. As he was intent upon keeping the Wheaton College position in his control, and with no other more likely candidate on the horizon, he prudently did not investigate, or perhaps he didn't care. Needless to say, I did next to no preparation over the summer months beyond checking some serious tomes out of Widener Library and occasionally inspecting their titles as they sat on my desk. Consequently, the first few months of my teaching career were extraordinary for the effort at preparation.

Every night I read the requisite pages of J. B. Bury's *A History of Greece to the Death of Alexander the Great*, turned them into an outline or script, took advantage of the many times I had acted in plays to memorize my spiel more or less, and did the same with H. J. Rose's *A Handbook of Greek Literature*. I'd like to say, continuing the actor/theater metaphor, that I went out there as just another hoofer and came back a star, or whatever it was that Warner Baxter said to Ruby Keeler. The fact of the matter is that I bombed; in the enrollment for the second term over half the students elected *not* to continue. It was a stunning rejection and well deserved. I was just reciting the "facts" of Greek civilization. My predecessor Ted had built that course up from nothing in three years to the popularity that I in three months had annihilated. I knew from hearing him that his anecdotes and gossip from the professional world of classics were both amusing and charming. He brought that raconteur's skill into the classroom and combined it with a seasoned teacher's disinclination to grade hard in a general education lecture course. I was too rigid, far too serious. As he said to me years later, when discussing the matter, I was a Protestant and he was a Catholic; there was no hint of absolution either for me or for my students in my classes. I am sure that my personal tragedy did not loosen me up either. Luckily my chair was sympathetic to the neophyte's dilemma, and the administration renewed my contract, so I had the chance to learn from my mistakes.

While I was involved in this disaster, my life in Cambridge took on pleasing complications. This came about through the machinations of another Harvard graduate student named Mark whom I had met a year earlier and with whom I had had a desultory sexual relationship all the previous summer. After Mary's death most people my age avoided me. Only ten years after the war, and they seemed to have forgotten that young people can die too, that men can lose spouses. I was lucky to have Bill's family out in Concord to visit. Even better, his younger brother Freddy came to live with me in Cambridge to avoid having to live in his Harvard dorm or to commute; it was ideal for me having someone never home but always a psychic presence. But Mark was forever urging me to marry again. "You were so happy married," he would remind me. He himself was planning to marry, so the subject was never far from his mind, although one might think that two men lying naked in bed together would not be onto that topic. He brought up his classmate in the school of architecture, a woman named Penny

Pendleton, who as a matter of fact had introduced him to Mary and me, since she lived in our old building. We had met her at a sherry party in the apartment of our neighbor Joan, no doubt making one of our over-the-top flamboyant entrances. At least Penny had been suitably dazzled, for I know that she wrote her mother after that night—I saw the letter years later—confessing that she had "met the man I want to marry, but he is already taken." Now I was free again, but I had no interest, not even in making it with a man.

But Mark was persistent. It became October, and he organized a potluck supper mostly with architecture students. This would be easy, since almost none of them knew me and my sad story. Penny, of course, was there; she flashed me a deeply sympathetic look as she entered but said nothing. After dinner I offered to drive her home. She asked me in for a drink, and somehow we were disrobing within half an hour. I cannot believe that we had expressed ourselves at the dinner table; how did we move so rapidly into the erotics? I do know that a few weeks before Mary died, we had all been at Joan's wedding, in fact we had all helped out, since it was a small affair that Joan herself arranged. In the car coming back I was sufficiently drunk to give Penny, who was sitting next to me, a kiss or two, but I cannot believe that this was any invitation then or later. True enough, Penny nursed a great crush on me. And I? Well, for someone who had found so much of his definition in sexual intercourse, perhaps I responded to the message of availability with a deep yearning for the security "doing it" would bring. This night I looked down at her as she lay in bed to announce—rather sternly, as I recall—that I had been having homosexual relationships since I was fourteen or fifteen, that I had always been attracted to men. It was important to me that this was clear. Penny did not seem to register any great emotion at this revelation, but then she was usually a mask. We did not make love, however, because I turned out to be impotent. She reacted as though this were a natural consequence of my emotional state, but I was horrified and shocked. The hyper-virility of teenage sex does not prepare one for the sexual miscues, inadequacies, and failures of the adult male. The next night I went over to Mark's and astonished us both by throwing myself on him, not stopping until I had satisfied myself into exhaustion. By rights that should have finished me off for a bit, but the very next night I returned to Penny's bed. Was I there for more than to demonstrate that everything was in working order?

Nevertheless, that evening established us as a couple. I had known Penny as a neighbor and friendly face at parties. Suddenly we were lovers. We were certainly perfectly matched for hours of intercourse, just as we were able to match each other martini for martini, a drink to which Penny introduced me. It is amazing to me in retrospect that I, who am in essence a male who lusts after other males, could not get enough of our coupling together, nights, afternoons, mornings, whenever we had a chance moment, wherever. The bedroom is the obvious place, but I remember on a weekend with friends our taking a canoe out on a lake and bringing it ashore on a small island, where we suddenly lay down on the grass and I pumped away into her, and at the end muffling our orgasmic groans and shouts. Sound carries so well across a lake, and we did not want our picnicking friends to think that murder was being committed. The intensity of our sexual relationship provoked me simplemindedly to tell, not ask, Penny that we should marry. And, she, ever the mask, always silent, did not disagree. But did she ever agree? Well, I guess at the altar she gave a positive response to the question posed by the minister.

What a strange courtship. I was so clearly manic, and I am sure Mary's death had put me over the top. In retrospect I wonder if Penny was clinically depressed; as a personality she could be so wan, so quiet. In the beginning it was restful, she seemed so easy to dominate after my experience of Mary's powerful presence. But behind the mask I uncovered a fierceness. She had a twin brother with whom she was in constant competition, and by extension with all males. He studied engineering; she would be an architect—engineering, so to speak, with style, flair, and imagination, and yet a profession that is to this day notoriously dominated by males. She was determined to break through the conventions of polite female behavior that her proper mother and a succession of boarding schools had tried to instill in her; it was from her lips that I heard for the second time in my life the word "fuck." She had lost her virginity young, as she was quick to tell me. For a college student of the fifties she was very promiscuous. She told our daughters, as I learned later, that she much resented the sexual freedom of males. Completely comfortable with one-night stands, she could have been a gay male. It seemed that she had worked her way through all the grad students in the architecture studios, but when I met them I noticed that they did not give her lingering looks, which made me believe that there had never been much of a relationship with any of them. But sleeping with everyone in your circle is a great way to exert a kind of control and establish a presence through the group. I always thought her sex drive was partly fueled by her insecurity about speaking. Sex was her means of establishing contact; the quiet person came alive. I responded with all the pent-up frustration that grief and sexual denial fueled in me. She could not have been more different from Mary. Slightly dark when tan, sallow otherwise, she was tall, lean, had the body of an adolescent boy, slim-hipped, with breasts that needed no support until motherhood and breast-feeding changed her shape. She was like Mary, I imagine, in that she thought she was the perfect match in sexual freedom with a man who had been sleeping with males since he was fourteen.

She was delighted that I had no parents with whom she would have to deal. The previous summer she had in fact met Mary's parents when they visited Mary and me in Cambridge, so that difficult hurdle had already been passed. In our inchoate fantasies of our impending wedding and honeymoon, I had in mind a visit to Iowa to show her off to friends, and that would necessarily involve the difficult visit to Ames. But in the immediate future I had to meet her parents, about whom she had told me very little. On almost any personal subject she believed in the motto "Don't ask, don't tell." As so many of the more affluent preppy Harvardians of the time, Penny affected the style of dressing shabby; she seemed always to be in her oldest clothes, drab skirts threadbare from years of wear, frayed tennis sneakers. Since she drove an old Buick, which she used, she said, for visiting her parents on "the farm" in New Hampshire, we two Iowans, who were familiar with a farming population that drove Buicks because they rode high and were less likely to be damaged in the ruts on farm roads, assumed that Penny was a poor scholarship student from a family scratching out a living on the hard New England soil. Thus, when I was prepared to be gracious and not condescend, I was surprised to be ushered into the presence of a magnificently dressed, handsome, commanding white-haired gentleman with a cane whom she introduced as her father, the Admiral. And there beside him with all the appropriate diamonds and strands of pearls was her elegant white-haired mother. So this was the dear old farm couple down from the country, where, as I learned later, they lived in a restored eighteenth-century farmhouse on several hundred acres that had been in Penny's mother's family for six generations.

Penny was my introduction into modernity and the imperatives of style. The one subject on which she was articulate was architecture; she did not simply talk, she lectured. Having taken Sigfried Giedion's course at the School of Design and almost memorized his *Space, Time & Architecture,* she was ready to comment on any architectural feature she came upon. It made for the most exhilarating strolls through cities. Walter Gropius was her teacher and god; I discovered the Bauhaus and everything it implied. The affectionate tour she gave me of Gropius's Graduate Center dorm and dining hall at Harvard and the Saarinen buildings at MIT completely shook up my aesthetic assumptions. I, who prided myself on the professional association of one of my uncles in Oak Park with Frank Lloyd Wright, discovered that I knew nothing about anything. I will never forget our first visits to New York together as she took me through the architecture galleries at MoMA, then out on the town to see the Manufacturers Hanover Trust Bank on Forty-third and Fifth Avenue, the Seagram Building, Lever House, and the other gems of the time. My allegiance to classical antiquity and its restatement in the Italian Renaissance had to be rethought in Penny's observations about the inherent classical aesthetics of modernism and minimalism. Talking art and architecture with Penny was an explosive expansion of my aesthetic sensibility that was another side to all the sex and the martinis. It was a delirium from which we never thought to wake up, but somehow through it all Penny finished the term and got her degree, and I read my students' exams and turned in the grades.

And then we were married, June 16, 1955, a scant nine and a half months after Mary's death. No one mentioned the fact, except Mary's parents, who sent what I read as genuine love and encouragement in their congratulations. Penny's parents were not at all enthusiastic, first that I was a widower—they were horrified that Penny chose to wear something relatively somber with a black belt to the rehearsal dinner in memory of Mary—and then I have to think that the Admiral, who had a lot of experience with males in close proximity, scented the perfume in the underwear, so to speak; the more manic I became, the more fruitcake was my performance, and the mounting stresses of the buildup to the wedding had me dancing in the air. The historic church in Deerfield, New Hampshire, followed by a reception under a large tent on the farm, would have satisfied my mother's every snobbish yearning. As we left the church, Penny caught her heel in the threshold, breaking it off, and so had to hobble on my arm to the car waiting to take us away. After the reception we drove to nearby Concord to change clothes, and in getting into the apartment where they were laid out, she tripped on a sharp object, cutting herself deeply enough to require emergency suturing and an anti-tetanus shot at the local ER. A week later in Minneapolis, after I fainted on the dance floor, they diagnosed me sick enough with mononucleosis that Penny was encouraged to do all the driving back to Massachusetts. Those are the scenes that an Ingmar Bergman would have foregrounded in his film of a doomed marriage. If not that, then a shot of our friend Joan's jaw dropping in shock when she cried out, "You're kidding!" after we proudly informed her that we were getting married.

But did I love her? Looking back, at eighty, I would say that this was the deepest, most complicated relationship of my life. Years after our divorce, whenever we met I was always agitated and troubled; there was something deeply moving there. Love? Guilt? Frustration? Yearning? Annoyance? At the outset we were more engaged with each other than I have ever been with anyone before or since. We were drunk on the sex, drunk on the martinis, of a mind that you cannot have ecstasy without two people like us, just as there is no martini without gin and vermouth. It is odd that Penny, who was reared on upper-middle-class notions of married life, who had bought a trousseau (at her mother's insistence), who had bridesmaids, who wrote thank-you notes on specially prepared stationery, who had struggled to finish her degree work before the wedding so that she could go out to get an architectural job after we married, was utterly indifferent to the wedding, went through the paces because of her mother, whom she despised for her attitude; but what is worse, she recognized that I, supposedly the man from the bohemian life who was going to rescue her from her mediocrity, was just as hung up on the wedding as anyone. In fact, while Penny had slaved to finish her coursework, she had delegated me to negotiate with her mother on the wedding details. It was odd, and so gay, and I am sure Admiral Pendleton in the background marked it all the time, that the prospective mother-in-law and son-in-law sat together by the hour in the Cambridge apartment I still shared with Freddy talking of which champagne, what kinds of hors d'oeuvres, flowers, caterers, what car to use driving away from the church, on and on and on. It was a Martha Stewart moment *avant la lettre*.

I began my second year of teaching as a married man again. Penny and I took over the apartment where I had been living with Freddy, and she proceeded to give a more minimalist line to the interiors. There was a racket of sawing and hammering, but not much she could do in the rented ground floor of an old Victorian. More important, she got a job, and then discovered she was pregnant when she missed her period two months in a row. We were frightened; this was unexpected—more than that, not even imagined. In 1956 nobody we knew was having babies in Cambridge, Massachusetts. It must be said: not at all wanted. And yet Penny's pregnancy gave me a glow of pride, such a sense of accomplishment that it was hard to remember that my part in all this was simply a split-second orgasm. Did this demonstrate that underneath it all I did not think myself a man? But that now, if I were to stand in the great shower of life among all those naked fellows with the water coursing down their torsos and dripping off their extended penises, I would finally be one of them, because I would have fathered a child?

A month later she was in Mount Auburn Hospital following a miscarriage. "Some bum sperm met up with the egg," explained the burly doctor, looking down at me as he leaned on the corridor wall after he had performed a D&C. I suddenly felt inadequate, forlorn. Thank you, Doctor! I suppose that is one way to describe a miscarriage. Our lives subsided into the comfortable routine where once again we worked, we drank, and we made love. And by November Penny missed her period again. In the seven years from 1956 to 1962 she became pregnant six times and brought to term four babies. It turns out that we did not know anything about birth control. The diaphragm was the device for birth control before the invention of the pill. This was the woman's department, as I thought of it. Mary used it, as she did everything else, absentmindedly, intermittently, but she never became pregnant. She was diabetic, and doctors have told me that diabetics have a hard time conceiving. Mary and I started out our sexual career with me using a condom. It was all part of the crazy fun of doing it with a woman. Penny, who was a much more organized person, had a diaphragm to put on when we first went to bed. But our use of it was a calamity. My eureka moment came years later when I took my daughters to a gynecologist for their first prescription for some kind of birth control device. As I sat in the waiting room leafing through her reading material, I encountered a brochure titled "The Use of the Diaphragm." I read that if you are going to indulge in marathon sex—not that the writer of the brochure phrased it quite like that—the diaphragm must be removed between orgasms and treated with more of the spermicide that one spreads on the rim. Or something like that. I can't really remember. Penny had never bothered learning about the fine art of the diaphragm. She had just been lucky. Well, in our orgies of wine and roses, her luck had run out. What is appalling is that we never figured it out, never asked a doctor, never did anything but meekly submit to our fate.

I knew nothing about the diaphragm, nor the orifice in which it was inserted. "Cunnilingus" is a word I had never heard until well into my thirties, I believe. It is odd that a man whose sexual experience from the beginning was so focused upon his mouth did not think to employ it when he began to have sex with a woman. It is commonplace that every high school girl nowadays goes down on her boyfriend, but neither of my two wives ever wanted to do the same with me. That was the proper 1950s with two somewhat improper females. When I saw *The Vagina Monologues* in my early seventies, I was interested in the women quoted who knew nothing of their vaginas, who had never thought to take a look with a mirror at their vaginas. My wives never talked about their vaginas. I never went near that orifice except with my penis, which otherwise bobbed around as a focus of our attention whenever I was nude. Even stranger is that when Penny and I were in the last stages of marital breakup, long since retired to separate bedrooms, engulfed in rage and resentment, we sometimes fell down into my bed as a drunken spill-over from angry quarreling in a standing position, where we would have angry sex dominated by my ferocious cunnilingus.

Penny and I moved into a house outside of New Haven in the summer of 1957, and she bore our first son a month later; I struggled to finish my dissertation way, way late and finished in a rush of despair and exhaustion in November 1958, one week before our second son was born. We moved to Palo Alto in 1960, one month before our older daughter was born on October 10. In November 1961, at the birth of our second daughter, we were so drunk when we presented ourselves to the emergency room that we were both wheeled to the delivery room for the labor. The attending obstetrician, a devout Roman Catholic, told us in all seriousness a month later that it was in our best interests to foreclose the chance of any further pregnancies.

It is difficult to describe the combination of despair, entrapment, loneliness, and betrayal that these unwanted pregnancies produced, especially in a woman who so desperately wanted to make her mark in a man's world, and found herself alone at home being a mother. It is more difficult because at the very same time we both deeply loved all four of our children, took great pride in them, and wanted to give them the affectionate care that neither one of us felt we had received. They were darling, darling little children, and grew up into utterly enchanting adults, not to mention witty, caring human beings who love each other as much as their own families. I can say that in so many moments of my life when I happened to catch sight of one or another of them I was filled with a rush of love, a love in kind and intensity that no other person has ever inspired in me. It is also true that as time went by this paternal passion was sometimes tempered by pangs of the terrible guilt I have felt at the resentment they habitually inspired in me as I and Penny struggled to "do the right thing" by them. My adult children and I skirt the subject of their growing up unless we are remembering funny anecdotes of their early years. They will be better off, I imagine, once I am dead as their mother is, and they will not have to deal with memories actualized in a living presence.

Young people nowadays will say to me, "Four children! And so close together! How did you do it?" Well, we drank a lot, for one thing, and then we gave up a lot for them. We were grim, or grimmer than we need have been; eventually the two of us stopped talking to each other when we were alone—what could have been said would not have contributed joy, so silence was the more honorable option. One night not too long ago my husband, Richard, and I set out to watch Leonardo DiCaprio and Kate Winslet in *Revolutionary Road*, and even before the film had reached its halfway point I told him to turn it off. I was almost physically ill with the revulsion that my memory induced. Ah, Penny, it was all so wonderful at the beginning, and then it wasn't. I suppose if we could have kept up the intense sexuality that brought us together, if we had not become tired, me too tired to perform, if we had not become bored with each other, become two slightly tight drabs who managed the house . . . if, if, if. . . . In February 1966 we were with Ted Doyle at the San Francisco airport to see him off on his eight-month sabbatical leave (from which he was not destined to return alive). By this time he had been my colleague at Yale, and later at Stanford, and become father, brother, father confessor, uncle, to ourselves and the children. Now he looked us in the eye, kissed us both, and said so gently and sadly, "Be nice to each other." His very last words to us.

Domestic life was a list of chores and obligations never quite satisfied. All the time I would remember the sexual life of my teens as though it had happened to another person, seen through a scrim, except when I focused precisely for a masturbatory moment. Our move to Woodbridge, Connecticut, put me on a country lane miles from the university and New Haven, miles away from men on the street. Yale itself was my first experience of an all-male institution since Andover. It was like a high-class locker room, with all its jostling and joking, farting and belching, a place I had never inhabited, although it engaged my erotic imagination. I was initially put off by the dramatic change from my previous teaching position; I was inherently more comfortable talking to the girls.

For the most part the men were amiable, good-looking, well-to-do WASPs. They ran the gamut from specimens resembling the Winklevoss twins to stumblers like G. W. Bush. Clearly Admissions had one criterion: blond gentile. A great number were there because it was the thing to do. I remember talking with a mother who came to consult about her son's academic failures, a woman who in gesture and looks bore an eerie resemblance to Carole Lombard, who complained to me with a languid and glamorous sigh, "Well, can't he buy his way through Yale like his father did?" This question shocked me, but was answered, so to speak, by another student who was in danger of failing, who came to me weeks before the final to say that his father wanted me to tutor him so he could pass and was prepared to offer me something like a thousand dollars for the effort. That was a stupendous sum in those days and in my naïveté I could only try to explain to the youngster that I could not conceivably do a tutoring job in so short a time that would warrant the fee, not recognizing until years later that it was a bribe he was offering me.

The boys were sexually attractive, of course, but I was not reacting, until one young fellow so shocked and angered me that I did the unpardonable—had sex with him. Slightly older, he enrolled in Beginning Greek as a requirement for the Episcopal ministry. He was such a stereotypical Episcopalian I could barely repress a laugh: tall, good-looking, preppy, the jaw jutting out ambitiously under slim lips set in a line, the silver-blue eyes with their earnest gaze, the marbles-in-the-mouth Upper East Side way of talking, masculine gentility at its very best. Shortly into the semester he was floundering badly; no extra effort on my part seemed to rouse him to work harder. One evening he invited me around to his club for a drink, where he explained that worry over his diabetic girlfriend had put him off track. The thought of my late wife, whose diabetes surely shortened her life, brought on a whiskey-fueled sympathy. I said I would give him a pass and expect him to make good in the second semester.

But then his effort registered even less, he grew more nonchalant, the girlfriend had disappeared from the scene. I went from puzzled to angry. He must have learned that the "diabetes" angle would get to me. By the end of the term I had stopped being friendly whenever I encountered him. But he was no dummy; his solution was to bring me back to his club "to talk over the situation." Why did I go? That is the question. How complicit was I in what ensued? I like to think it was because I always hope for the best with students even when their failure is obvious. This time he had another tack, in retrospect I would say something dimly erotic. We sat in a small darkened side room, me in a chair, he perched on a kind of counter, squatting, as soldiers often do, a pose that brought his crotch, very visible and foregrounded by the spread of his thighs, into my direct line of vision. He was ratcheting up the operatics, confessing a kind of desperation, that his "hopes" would soon be "nothing more than laughable dreams" when he failed my course. Since antiquity young handsome males have played their looks to their advantage with their elders, in some cultures with more awareness than others. The fakery of his language, his pose, his careless obviousness—everything said contempt.

As I think back on it, he was doing Marlene Dietrich to my Emil Jannings. He was so sure of himself, sure that he could provoke precisely the response he wanted from me, that is, another sentimental surrender to his need for a passing grade. Suddenly I had to strike back, and probably because I was drunk and horny I impulsively said harshly and coldly to the widespread thighs before me, "I'll pass you in the course if I can give you a blow job." He sucked in his breath as though he had been hit, looked me in the eye warily, a boxer ready to ward off any blow that was about to descend upon him. I am sure that this was not what he was bargaining for. There was a long silence, during which time I had a pang of fear: Had I gone too far? Then he said:

"Okay, come over to my room. I live off campus."

He gave me the address. I told him I would be there midmorning next day, and fled away. The next fifteen or so hours were an agony. It was the first great moral crisis of my teaching career (leave aside the dynamics of my marriage); the guilt was overwhelming, paralyzing me. Still, in the sober cold light of next morning's day as I started to drive into New Haven, only the lust and contempt remained. But when he opened the door to me, freshly showered, immaculate, standing tall, smiling politely, the very model of a young cleric, I quailed at what I had said to him. As we stood facing each other in the living room, I suddenly burst out, "I can't do this, I shouldn't be here." But I was rooted to the spot; I couldn't bring myself to leave. "Oh, god, what should I do?" He smiled and suddenly cut short my anguished waffling.

"Look! You work it out, okay? I am going to take my midmorning pee." He was slowly unzipping his khakis as he spoke, turning abruptly toward the bathroom. Without shutting the door, he began to urinate, I could hear him at it. His obviousness enraged me all over again.

"Okay, we're going to do it," I shouted out angrily. He emerged and gestured with his head to the bedroom door. What began as an act of humiliation and revenge changed its character when I got next to this gorgeous body lying naked on the bed. The experience filled me with a profound sense of well-being and joy. Indeed, I was shocked at how truly wonderful I suddenly felt. Years later when I was teaching at Boston University, a student from one of those exclusive suburbs on Long Island or from Connecticut told me that she had taken my course because a family friend had once been my student at Yale and said I was a "brilliant" teacher. And it was he. Had he ever learned Greek, I wondered, at least enough to read the New Testament? Wasn't that required of all the Divinity School candidates? Or did the passing grade from me give him certification? "Do you remember him at all?" she inquired. "He's such a great guy. I babysit for them all the time."

Yale in those days was an old boys' club into which I was pleased to see that I could fit. The very manner in which I was hired has always amused and gratified me. At the December 1956 Philadelphia meeting of the American Philological Association, Professor Dow had invited me to join his group for dinner at the famous, and expensive, Bookbinders Restaurant in the city, an event charged with hidden significance, since Dow was much too cheap to frequent such places ordinarily. In addition to three or four of his students, Dow had invited Frank Brown, who, as I have mentioned, was the chair of the Yale Classics Department. Fifty years ago when the old-boy network controlled the job process there was no neutral mechanism for those offering jobs and those seeking them. Opportunities were not posted on a public list; young people entering the field had no means for making themselves known other than what their mentors could do for them. Precious little, as you can imagine, for women or Jews or those from obscure institutions. The young men seated at the table in Bookbinders were in a very enviable position, yet as usual I was too naïve to understand this. When I slipped into a seat at the table I did not understand that Dow was setting up a certain one of these students to make himself extremely presentable to Professor Brown, since, as was known to some though not to me, there was an opening at Yale. As it happened, I innocently took a seat next to Brown at the circular table, I am sure to Dow's consternation, for, as I figured out subsequently, Dow had invited me and some of the others only as filler material so that his candidate intended for Brown's attention would not be too obvious. It was the same ploy one uses when planning to get a man and woman interested in one another.

Anyone would imagine that I sat next to Brown because I was ambitious, but in fact I was pretty ignorant of academic politics in those days. He did not wear the customary identifying name tag attached to his lapel, which only convention nerds wore in the evening. When I began by asking Brown who he was and where he taught, I sensed a frisson among the other young men, all of whom knew exactly. But it charmed Brown, clearly enough, as did our subsequent argument over the virtues of city and country life; the persiflage we aimed at each other was sharp and peppery, all style and very little substance. The following week I was surprised to receive a note from Brown inviting me to present myself as a candidate for the opening at Yale. Thunderstruck, and very pleasantly surprised, I consulted with Dow, who predictably encouraged me to stay put at Wheaton. My parents-in-law, however, strongly urged me to consider New Haven. The Admiral had finished his career as naval commandant at Yale, and they had made a great circle of friends in the four years they had been there. I went down, made some kind of agreeable impression (I loved it that the classics faculty was startled to discover that so modest a fellow was staying at the posh, posh New Haven Lawn Club, not knowing that my parents-in-law had reserved rooms for me), was offered the job, and so was hired. And I entered the group of eleven young male junior faculty as Brown's favorite. That automatically disqualified me for attention from the reigning expert on matters literary, the eminent Bernard Knox, who could not stand Brown, as I was told in later years. I have always felt that, more to the point, Knox could not tolerate even the slightest whiff of the pouf, he was so much of the mind-set of the men who fought as he had with the Republican Army in Spain. His classical antiquity, his writing on epic and tragedy, demonstrate a rugged, romantically male view of things—irony was not his thing.

Ted Doyle, who had joined the faculty a year before me, became my closest friend and ally. He was an acute student of the politics and personalities of the department as well as of the major university figures; he was my refresher course in academic maneuvering, which, of course, I first learned from overhearing my mother, the paradigm busybody, gossipy "faculty widow," but without her bitterness and with his own marvelous deep, deep cynicism. The boys called him Uncle Teddy Boo, and he was indeed the quintessential uncle, coming out for dinner, bouncing the boys on his knee, gently mediating in moments of household Sturm und Drang. Curiously enough, he gave me a key to his apartment in New Haven with the remark that I might want to take a nap someday. I did in fact once take someone there for a sexual matinee, which, as I realized only years later, was probably his purpose for the loan of the key. He left Yale because he had not finished his dissertation by the specified deadline, and took himself and his new PhD to Stanford, where he convinced me to follow in 1960.

In my third and last year at Yale I agreed to an informal tutorial in Homer at the request of an exceedingly bright undergraduate.

When a colleague in the Russian Department asked if he could join us, offering his rooms as a meeting place along with a bottle of sherry, we became a seminar of sorts. A half century later I vividly remember the hours of our meetings, as does the young student, who rose to be one of the truly eminent classicists of the late twentieth century. Those tutorials with him were inspiration enough that I was able to write *The "Iliad," the "Odyssey," and the Epic Tradition* for Doubleday in 1965 from the notes I began then and refined over the next few years. It was like the paper on Euripides' *Alcestis* that came out of my preparations for bright students in a senior seminar at Harvard: my best writing and thinking are always in dialogue with students. I cannot imagine what it means when a colleague says, "I am a scholar, not a teacher."

In my last term at Yale I cracked up. One night I laid myself down onto the country lane before our house and wouldn't get up until Penny called a psychologist friend, who came to take me for a voluntary admission to the psychiatric wing of Grace–New Haven Hospital for two weeks' stay as a patient with the privilege of leaving in the daytime to teach my courses. The immediate provocation was my drunken groping of a student departing the dinner party we had just given graduating majors in classics. He politely and tactfully rejected my advances as I walked him to his car, but it was the contempt I registered that provoked my despair. Sixty years later I can see the scene, hear the gentle, muted disgust in his "Don't."

Grace–New Haven was not a diagnostic ward, necessarily, but a holding pit, if one can call it that, for people who had lost it for the moment and needed a controlled place where they could figure out what they were going to do next. It was like a vacation, being with nice middle-class people my age, housewives who had taken too many tranquilizers and driven into the guardrail, junior executives who had stood on the platform all day somehow unable to board any of the trains heading to Manhattan, faculty who started thinking of suicide as something more than a literary symbol or motif. It was like a vacation, I say, because the people there did not have to maintain the pretense of the happy home and family in suburbia any longer. For me personally it suggested what a toll being the paterfamilias was taking. It was decided that Penny and the children would go to her parents' at the farm and I would stay and consult a psychiatrist over the summer months. The three months were relatively worthless; his attempt at a Freudian guided tour of my childhood in that abbreviated time went nowhere. He might have considered various calamities—that my mother died in 1954, my first wife died in 1955, that I moved house three times in the previous three years, I had remarried in 1956, become a father twice since, finished a dissertation, failed my orals in humiliation, accepted my PhD as an ironic and meaningless triumph. He fastened on my groping that kid, and could not get beyond it. For him it was all about homosexuality, whereas I saw that moment of rejection as one thing too many, the last straw, as it were. He encouraged me to abstain, and the depression would go away. Abstention was not difficult, since almost no prospects crossed my path, which made the groping all the more laughably grotesque.

At the end of the summer I was so immersed in our move that there was room for only the very occasional erotic thought in my calculations. I drove a station wagon–load of stuff to Palo Alto, giving a ride to three of Freddy's younger brother's friends to share the expenses, a grueling ride lightened only by the diversion of spending one night in a crummy motel with three boys in their underpants, one of whom with the cutest ass imaginable sharing the bed with me. Another night, when we stayed in that boy's parents' home, we refreshed ourselves after the long day's drive in the cellar shower, where I had the pleasure of watching the boys splashing about in their nakedness, talking together, as well as sensing my disinclination for aesthetic reasons to introduce my tubby self into the mix, seeing them as a male version of the traditional ancient Greek Three Graces. Once arrived, I had houses to inspect, then the very pregnant Penny and the two boys to greet at the airport, and needed to consult with the housekeeper we had engaged for four months to help with the transition, do the real estate deal, notify movers, arrange the furniture, arrange for schooling, find an obstetrician, note the due date of early October, get an office set up, look over the teaching material. It was not a life for casual sexual engagement with males, even if in this so aggressively heterosexual suburban community of what gays call "breeders" one might spot a man with invitation in his eyes on the streets where no one ever, ever walked. We were in California.

I never would have gone to Stanford if it had not been for Ted Doyle. Ted left such an empty space in Connecticut. He and I had struggled to grow the enrollments in Greek at Yale, and the results were finally having an effect on the entire undergraduate classics program. Suddenly he wasn't there to share, to give advice, to pull the oar. Out in Woodbridge Uncle Teddy Boo had been such a fixture of family meals and family walks in the woods that suddenly the gap was palpable. We were on the phone all the time. He wanted to hear the gossip of the Yale department, I was enchanted by his stories of sunny California, the glamour of it all, as well as his humorous takes on the business of settling in at a university that was definitely no "Ivy." He was as amusing on the vulgar rich of California as he had been on the repressed stuffy Brahmins of New England. As time went by he began encouraging me to think of moving there myself, telling me that he was sure that he could arrange an appointment with Brooks Otis, the recently appointed chair of the Stanford Classics Department.

Penny thought it was a great idea; it would be warm like the Hawaii in which she had spent her youth. Frank Brown thought it was a silly idea, insisting that, while there was no chance for junior faculty to advance at Yale, he would personally put me in line for a superior appointment elsewhere, and that he did not at all think Stanford was worth it. (He rolled his eyes at the mention of Otis—I should have paid closer attention.) Stanford in those days had recently been for the country club set, the jeunesse dorée of California. (I could never understand in *Double Indemnity* how Phyllis Dietrichson's gross husband was an alumnus.) But major changes were taking place: the trustees were determined to transform Stanford into the "Harvard of the West." A new dean of the College of Liberal Arts, the aristocratic Philip Rhinelander (yes, *those* Rhinelanders), was charged with making a set of academically glamorous hires. That meant raiding the Ivies, and to get the maximum bang for the buck, he went after very junior people. I was the perfect candidate, although how I personally came to be hired was bizarre. It was through Ted's manipulation of Stanford's new chair, Brooks Otis. Otis, a serious Christian, the son of a clergyman and scion of several grand old Boston families, was Rhinelander's friend and Harvard classmate. His previous academic life had been spent in a small liberal arts college. With no experience in building up a department in a major university of vast pretensions, he relied on Ted, who was infinitely political and deeply, cynically subversive, ready to play the Boston Irish servant to the Boston Brahmin grandee. (Ted could never resist saying that Brooks, who came from an impecunious branch of the Otis Elevator family, "was born on the wrong side of the shaft.") At a certain point in the cold of the winter Ted called to say that Otis had been promised another appointment by the dean. Otis did not want to go to the national meetings to do the hiring, Ted claimed, and was quite ready to consider me for the position. It was to be an interview by telephone.

It was another instance of the impulsive, capricious streak in my decision making. To move my family across the continent on the strength of a brief telephone call with a man whose WASP background would guarantee that he would be as repressed as I in the course of it, and to trust in the blandishments of Ted, who I knew perfectly well was the master of blarney, in retrospect seems crazy. The telephone interview went off well enough, as obviously it would when the communicants were on their best behavior. My one stipulation was that Otis provide me with an adequate office, since I had a large library. To this he agreed. That slight morsel was the only matter of substance in our negotiation.

Otis and I disliked each other the instant we met. Since I know people who admire him, I have to believe it was chemistry on my part. Very shortly I understood how I repelled him. It was me waving my hands, and my loud laugh. He was always asking people if I was Jewish; he must have seen me as the masculine equivalent of Bella Abzug. Very shortly I hated him for betraying me. When I walked into his office to introduce myself, his first words were to announce the unexpected death of a senior colleague, which would necessitate my taking on his graduate seminar in comparative grammar. I understood that few would be prepared on such short notice to offer so complicated a subject on the graduate level. Still, his request for me to start out in a new teaching situation with an overload of that magnitude seemed particularly ungenerous. Worse, the large office he had promised turned out to be a smallish room that I was to share with some nonentity named William. When I remonstrated, he replied with what I came to understand as his standard evasion: "We must do the Christian thing by William." A couple weeks brooding among my books in a makeshift office at home amid the screams and cries of three little ones brought me to the breaking point. Fueled by martinis, flooded with rage, I went to its source. There at his home in the presence of his wife, I flat-out lied, saying Penny could no longer endure me having an office at home and was packing to go back East with the children. The silence was broken by Mrs. Otis saying in a steely voice, "Brooks, get him an office tomorrow." Within days

I was ensconced in a grand space that Dean Rhinelander found for me in his decanal suite. Oh, how Otis must have hated me! I always felt his determination to rid himself of me began in that moment.

I did not get along with the other two senior faculty members much better. The psychiatrist in New Haven had observed more than once that since I did not do sports as a child I lacked an understanding of competition and cooperation; on the one hand, I was not aggressive enough, on the other, I could not get along easily. Maybe it was because I was armed with this new self-knowledge that I pushed to get that bigger office. Other efforts were not so successful. Another senior colleague, a Brit, of the type who thought all us "natives" were simpletons, would offer me his uncomprehending stare whenever I advanced some literary critical notion, a "take" on some text or other. I remember giving him an offprint of my second article, after the fashion of junior colleagues attempting to secure their position, and his remarking that my thesis was obvious and scarcely worth the effort. My other senior colleague was a large elderly lady whose smile in retrospect I now see was exactly like that menacing little-girl smile on the face of Janice Soprano, sister to Tony in *The Sopranos*, revealing reservoirs of malice, resentment, and rage that made the on-looker tremble. She could reduce the Englishman to rubble. At one departmental meeting when he was using that bleating voice and those elocutionary hesitations that mark the English upper classes, she slapped her fat fist down on the conference table and shouted out, "Stop stammering and spitting, get it out!" which reduced him to tears. She was, I hasten to say, impartial in her brutalities. When I first ventured to speak at a departmental meeting she shouted at me, "Shut up, you mutt, you're new here." So much for team spirit.

In forty-two years of college teaching I have had four periods in which fate has given me students of such caliber that the classroom hours were sheer joy. My years at Stanford were the first of these. Students who presented themselves for instruction in ancient Greek or Latin for lectures in the ancient literatures and cultures were not only intelligent enough to master the subject easily, they wrote well, they asked seriously good questions, they treasured their instructor; as he, them. I think of some of the alumni of those classes: the poet Sharon Olds, the theologian Elaine Pagels, the actress Kathleen Chalfant, the ancient historian Michael Gagarin, the documentary filmmaker Henry Chalfant, are just a few whom my failing memory has retained. Students like these inspired me to make every classroom hour worthy of their intelligence, and after a few years I was able to begin work on *Ancient Greek Literature and Society*, my second book for Doubleday. The "Society" in the title reflected what I had learned from Yale University, where the archaeological historical approach to antiquity anchored the literature, art, and ideas in a context, something that was keenly missing from Harvard's Germanic emphasis on zeitgeist.

After the gray and gritty landscape of New England, Palo Alto and the Stanford campus seemed to us to resemble a resort; everyone was blond and athletic, their clothing casual and scanty, the constant sunshine glittered on the giant green fronds of palm trees as they swayed in the breezes. I was amused that Stanford had a prohibition against boys wearing shorts to class in those days. It was probably an extension of the age-old masculine insistence that in displays of power a male will be fully clothed, while a woman will bare her legs; one thinks of the Wall Street law firms that even today require women to wear dresses. I initially thought the prohibition of shorts was to cover over the intensely erotic thighs of the boys—well, erotic to me, who can find nothing more alluring than the gentle cover of golden hairs on the perfectly muscled golden brown leg of a soccer player, although it is doubtful that the front office was thinking this way. Still, one thinks of the Yale Admissions Office, which from the invention of photography up to the beginning of the seventies photographed every entering freshman in the nude for the files. Think how Yale could grow their endowment if they put those photos on the auction block at Sotheby's! The physical presence of the Stanford boys affected me as no other group of students had. Partly it was the growing self-conscious sensuality of American youngsters, especially in California, culminating in the Monterey Pop Festival of June 1967, which ushered in a celebratory atmosphere among the youth of the American bourgeoisie that had a run of about a decade. The boys just advertised their sensual, physical selves more, whether aware or not.

Two anecdotes will establish the delight that I felt. Stanford recreational swimming was segregated by gender, which was more or less universal fifty years ago. Males swam nude, ostensibly because the original swimsuits were made of wool, which shed lint into the filter system and was thus to be avoided, and Stanford continued the custom. I swam at noon almost every day, then climbed onto the permanent spectator bleachers to lie down and nap or eat my lunch. Over time a number of my students got in the habit of joining me on the bleachers, where we had some pretty high-class bull sessions. They were not only bright young men, they were very earnest. So it was a kind of Socratic moment for me, lounging about talking into the face and crotch at the same time of any number of lovely naked lads. One fellow used to arrive, flop down in front of my body stretched out on a bleacher, straddle the bleacher, and present his delicious penis and testicles on the level of my head about two feet away, open his sandwich bag, and munch away. We once discussed it years later, and decided that it was an unconscious response on his part to an instinctive feeling that I was attracted to him, and subconsciously he wanted to gain the support and favor of the alpha male.

The most amusing experience of this sort was in a small

upper-level Latin course with four students and myself sitting around in my office translating a text. The group consisted of one young woman, two fellows evidently a couple (although no one acknowledged it as such), myself, and then, well, this Adonis, a thoroughly unlikely, utterly square, utterly hunky young blond with great skill in the Latin language, hence his presence as a freshman in so advanced a course. He was a shy prep school boy from Connecticut, spoke when spoken to, smiled in a dazzling way, but his great claim to attraction was his introduction into our world of what soon swept the youth of the nation: he wore skintight Levi's without underwear. When he was in the throes of the work of translating aloud in class, he would slide down on the sofa until the barest tip of his butt was still supporting him on the frame, thus allowing in the long line of his outstretched body the glorious mound of his good-sized genitals to take pride of place, and if we were lucky the outline of the penis and the testicles was clearly evident. Three sets of eyes—I don't know about the girl—left the Latin text in the book to fasten on delights infinitely greater. It was when our eyes met that we acknowledged our sexual orientation, something I had never done in or out of class at Yale. Homosexuality was beginning to exist in the consciousness of at least the better educated, more sophisticated children of the bourgeoisie. In the same way, the staid proper Boston Brahmin–like stance of San Francisco Jews was being given a shake-up by East Coast Jewish students at Stanford like the young woman from New York who campaigned for student office with the slogan, "Tippecanoe and Super Jew! Vote for Jewdy!"

In the summer of 1962 I went to Europe for the first time, specifically for a month in Greece and a month in Italy, and it was, of course, a major turning point in my life, for the firsthand experience of the remains of antiquity; for the willingness to leave Penny alone with four children, the youngest an eight-month-old baby; for the extraordinary pleasure of traveling with a young male with whom I had a most satisfactory emotional and sexual relationship during the trip; and, perhaps not least, for the psychic disfigurement of the attendant guilt with which I was filled when I beheld my wife and family on my return. Fifty years on I can still feel a tinge of guilt remembering that episode, but also I know that it had to be that way, I had to be free, if only for a brief time.

If I were writing a novel about the experience, I would start the events with a description of the circumstances of the death of my first wife's mother, who had moved with her husband to the Livermore Valley in 1960 to be near their niece at the same time we had gone to Stanford. I had conscientiously kept up with them, Penny and I had visited them in Iowa, and when they moved their furniture to California they brought along and gave to me the great round mahogany Victorian dining table that they remembered I had loved. All the summer of 1961 she lay dying hideously of stomach cancer in the hospital in Livermore and I drove over as many nights as I could manage to sit and talk with her. It was awful, and I was truly grateful when she died, but if nothing else I understood *pietas*. I brought her husband, now befuddled with grief and age, back to Palo Alto and undertook to go with him on the train along with the coffin back to Ames. It was one gross moment after another until in the very early morning on the train three hours out of Des Moines a porter leaned across me to say something to my father-in-law, and I felt his very hard erection pressing into my upper arm. He moved on and I jumped up and met him as he paused briefly at the entrance to the smoking lounge and men's toilets at the end of the car. Within seconds he had determined the area was deserted and hustled us into one of the little rooms, pulled down the toilet seat, pushed me down, unzipped his fly, and brought himself out, and I took him into my hands and into my mouth. He came with a muffled moan and a grand explosion. The sheer physicality of this, the energy of our desires—my first experience since the psychiatrist had advised abstention, and to this day memorable as a powerful reaffirmation of my identity— could not have been more erotic, utterly satisfying, reassuring, psychologically validating, putting me at complete peace with myself even before I had myself off after he had scurried out the door. It sparked a peaceful, joyful glow that stayed with me through the next two days, from overseeing the unloading of the coffin in Des Moines until we arrived at the grave site, where my mood of serenity and fulfillment elicited from me out of nowhere the whispered words, "*Requiem aeternam dona eis, Domine, et lux perpetua luceat eis. Requiescant in pace.*" I had done what I must for my mother-in-law and my late wife; now I could leave the old man with his unmarried sister-in-law and take a jet back to the coast.

Our fourth child was born the following November. Penny and I were never able to shed the guilt we felt at her birth, particularly when the infant was born with a condition that prevented her left eye from opening for three months. It seemed a mark of rebuke directed at our reluctant parenthood. We doubled our efforts to be exemplary parents and housekeepers, saved from descending into a truly destructive cycle of grimness by the natural effervescence with which my manic personality is endowed, not to mention the endless resort to good manners and the repression of true feeling that was a legacy of the homes from which we sprang. In order to supplement my meager salary I took a job at a local junior college teaching evening classes. Days were filled. Time set aside for class preparation, office hours, and grading seemed to soak up every empty space on my academic calendar not already blocked out for teaching. I looked nervously at the list of research projects I had set out for myself, knowing that I was not producing as much as a young man should. The moment I walked in the door at home I had three little ones clambering for my attention, eager to show me the results of whatever project they had achieved that day, and now there was a fourth who needed a bottle or there was a diaper to be changed. Penny greeted me with the kind of listless gesture of surrender that said, *They're all yours for a while, buddy.* At least we had a student helper who put the children to bed and assisted with bedside reading, which gave us two beleaguered adults a quiet moment to have a drink before I had to hit the trail for the night teaching. I set off with a perfunctory kiss and Penny's warning, "Watch the road," a reminder of the time that I confessed to having fallen half-asleep at the wheel on the way home from the junior college.

The junior faculty at Stanford, who were all of them just as tired as we were, sought remedy in weekend drinking parties, sometimes with stand-up buffets to temper the effect of all the alcohol. One night we were among twenty or twenty-five standing in the living room of a house just around the corner from us, and then it was eight and no food had appeared, guests took note, sought out the hostess, and it turned out that she had just cracked mentally. In any case, she was sitting at a table in a little room off the kitchen playing solitaire and humming. The other women scurried to turn out the food that was there onto plates, and we all ate in a kind of drunken stupor, or was it a hushed something or other? It was so 1960s Palo Alto–Stanford young marrieds. One night at a cocktail party—and I remember this scene so vividly—I sat in a chair drunkenly staring at the equally intoxicated wife of an English Department colleague who was crawling on all fours under a large table nearby, at which point I blurted out to Ted, who sat next to me, "Penny bores me, Ted." He took his big fat Irish finger, put it to my lips, and said sweetly and softly, "Don't say that, don't think that." In retrospect it would all have been so much better if I had had a guy on the side. But where to find one? I was too tired even to care.

As winter turned into spring Ted invited me for drinks at a bar with some guy who worked in the library. He was a slim fellow about my age, who proceeded to get as tipsy as myself, as always

seemed to happen in a bar with Ted. When I excused myself to go
to the men's room my new friend went with me. We stood side by
side pissing away, and as we were finishing I reached over to take
his penis in my hand and watched it grow stiff, while he stood there
silent and acquiescent. Without a word we repacked our pants and
joined Ted, who meanwhile had paid the bill and was heading out
to his car. My friend agreed to drive me back to the faculty parking lot for my car. Once there, we began to kiss each other passionately, only interrupted by his moaning whisper, "I didn't know
this was going to happen." I was so desperate for a man I felt I
would explode and fell upon him as though it were a rape. I was
out of my mind. Once we had finished, we pulled our clothes together, said a muffled farewell, and each drove off to his respective
family.

On the way home I stopped for something Penny wanted in the
nearby supermarket. I was still sufficiently drunk that I dropped
everything to the floor at least once, and as I knelt to pick things
up, I looked at the long aisle, the food products running along
the shelves on each side of me, the unforgiving uniform lighting
taking definition out of everything in my view, recognizing then
a sensation of California that I would read a few years hence in the
descriptions of the place by Joan Didion. Unaccountably I heard
myself shout out in my brain as though I were Scarlett O'Hara:
*As God is my witness, I am going to go to Europe.*

Well, someone up there heard me, because on the fifth of
August I was on a plane for Athens. Days after my moment in the
parking lot five students from my Beginning Greek class asked if
I would tutor them through June and July so that they could advance through second year and start the third year in the fall. They
were all bright as hell, motivated, each willing to pay me the ten
dollars an hour that I asked. At $250 a week for eight weeks, this
would give me $2,000, an enormous sum of money in those days.
Then another student— indeed, I remembered him well as one of

those boys from the Latin class who had gazed ardently at the youth in the tight, tight jeans—asked if I would consider tutoring him in August. When he mentioned that traveling with his father in Europe would prevent his studying with the other five, all I heard was the word "Europe." Yes, I would tutor him, but we would have our lessons while traveling a month in Greece and a month in Italy. Like every other rich young kid, he had been to those places a million times, but he was happy with the idea of sitting about studying while I viewed the sights, and then having a lesson.

But what about my obligations at home? Our oldest child would celebrate his fifth birthday while I was gone. I encouraged Penny to take the children home to her parents in New Hampshire, but she refused. As a Navy child she had plenty of examples of women left with children while the husband was overseas—her own father during the war, for instance. She insisted that she would be fine. The guilt I feel to this day is mitigated by knowing that, as she confessed later to my daughters, since it was only the lack of money that kept her from walking out, she probably was entirely happy to have a life to herself for two months, to be a parent to her children without Mr. Overbearing Manic around the house.

Imagine being thirty-two years old, taking the first extended vacation since you were fifteen. Imagine having studied intensively the culture and history of ancient Greece and Rome since you were nineteen, having lectured on these subjects for the past seven years, and now you are visiting every major site of these peoples, looking at objects and architecture about which you have an immediate and intuitive understanding. Imagine that the young man with whom you are traveling turns out to be more intelligent than you had imagined, serious about studying the original Greek text of Homer's *Iliad* and Herodotus's *Histories*. Imagine spending the cool hours of the morning and the late afternoon visiting sites and museums while spending the midday lying about listening to the young man translate his prepared material and sight-read still further. I have rarely known a student to make such progress in the two months available; such was the agreeable impression made upon me that I can remember these forty-odd years later the passages of Greek that occasioned the most discussion. To this day I will come across marginalia in my *Iliad* text where I have indicated that the idea came from him.

When we first got our hotel room in Athens and were about to take our siesta, each in his underwear across the room from each other in his own bed, almost the first thing out of his mouth was a stammered—what was it? I have to call it a prepared speech— in which he politely rejected anything sexual in the two months ahead. I stifled my disappointment; after all, he was paying the bills, and I was his teacher. Imagine my delight when fifteen minutes later I watched him striding across the room with a tent pole pushing out his shorts. My God, he was so handsome, well built, and bursting with sexual energy. It was almost but not quite a love affair. Certainly it was the most extended, complex, complete physical relationship with another man that I had ever had up to that point. If he was a novice or insecure about many aspects of lovemaking, I was simply lacking in experience, certainly recent experience, so what we were doing each day had a delicious tentative quality, a shared surprise at the pleasure and ecstasy of it all. It was not love because we did not want love with each other; he knew he was not ready for that, and I knew that I was already in enough of a danger zone with my emotions. In every other way it was bliss, not the least being the wicked pleasure every morning of watching the man at the hotel desk react to my young friend's settling our bill rather than the older fellow he took to be the sugar daddy.

Needless to say, my return to Palo Alto was a shock. The French and Italians have a word for the psychological state; it is called "the reentry," since it is their custom for the entire country to shut down, so to speak, while everyone takes an extended vacation. For

me there was the sheer fright of giving up the young man, returning to all the domestic problems in my relationship with Penny.
There was the added guilt that reading Simone de Beauvoir's *The
Second Sex* while overseas brought to me. Being a woman in a
patriarchal culture was bad, being the wife of such a demanding
person was worse; how could she not be victimized? It made me
sick to the stomach and sexually impotent. How could I deal with
the guilt of my failure at sex? Did my two impossibly wonderful
months with the young man call me home to gayness for once and
for always? The months in Greece and Italy made me determined
to find a way to spend a year in the Mediterranean lands with my
whole family. That would be my redemption. Miraculously enough,
it happened. Our departmental secretary showed me a brief
mailing that she had tacked onto the office bulletin board. The
Archaeological Institute of America announced the Olivia James
Traveling Fellowship set up for travel in Greek lands for poets,
artists, writers, scholars, anyone with a love of the ancient world.

This was the gift of a woman named Olivia James, who originally donated the money to the Smithsonian for the noble purpose
I mentioned. The trustees of that institution, not thinking they
had the competence to choose, handed it off to the Archaeological
Institute. Of course, the archaeology establishment managed to
convert it to their own purposes. The first holder of the fellowship was a man closely connected with the archaeological establishment, a resident at the American School of Classical Studies
in Athens, who got it from the AIA without competition so he
could complete his architectural drawings of the Parthenon. So
much for travel in Greek lands for poets, musicians, and that ilk!
I was the second holder of the fellowship, and certainly its least
likely, not being an archaeologist, historian, epigraphist, or prac-
titioner of any of the hard-nosed disciplines the AIA loves. Who
knows how my improbable appointment came about? My old
boss at Wheaton speculated that since I had asked Sterling Dow,

my dissertation director, who also happened to be a major figure in epigraphical circles, and Frank Brown, my old boss at Yale, a leading archaeologist, to write recommendations, I was shoo-in. Who could compete with those names?

My trip in the previous summer prejudiced me in favor of Rome as a place to settle my family while I was traveling around Greek lands. I had not counted on the rivalry between the American Academy in Rome and the American School in Athens; it is like the Red Sox and the Yankees, only more so, with trustees drawn from the Social Register. The clique around the American School insisted that I should live in Athens. But I had an argument when the American School establishment made their displeasure known. After all, in addition to the Greek mainland the Greeks had also settled the peninsula of Italy south of Rome and Sicily, as well as the area of Turkey. Were we to live in Istanbul?

Rome it was. We sailed for Genoa on Cunard's *Mauretania*, a nine-day crossing. With the help of a friend I found an improbably grand apartment: ten large rooms with very high ceilings, furnished in pieces of real or fake eighteenth-century provenance, Persian carpets on the floor, a large children's nursery, a maid's room, pantry, kitchen, two terraces giving out to a view of gardens and fountains in the grounds on the floor below. If ever you see Bertolucci's *Il Conformista*, watch for the scene where the protagonist goes to see his heroin-addicted mother in her grand Fascist villa. The camera pans along a street notorious during the Fascist era and one of the palaces on the street was where we lived on the second floor. A genuine marchesa was subletting the place while her husband pursued his diplomatic career. We hired a live-in cook from friends who were returning to the United States; engaged a capable, no-nonsense English girl who came out from London as au pair; and took on the gatekeeper's sister, who did the cleaning when she wasn't washing our mountains of dirty clothes in the bathroom tub. We had the travel grant, my parents-in-law gave us some money, I took some money from a small inheritance, and somehow it all worked in a thoroughly enchanted way. I traveled through Greece, Turkey, Sicily, and southern Italy, just as I promised. Sometimes I traveled with a Greek American student of mine who could talk to the people of Greece, sometimes Penny joined me, as when I went through Turkey, sometimes I went alone, as when I traveled through Sicily. We traveled together on small trips to see the art and architecture of Italy, then on a longer one later to France and England. My years of yearning and dreams were realized.

It took an enormous toll on our marriage. Traveling by ship with four very small children, establishing a family in a large apartment with live-in help—these are not idyllic adventures for everyone, especially when it requires some fluency in the Italian language. It was only much later I learned, in couples therapy when she finally felt free to speak her mind, how much Penny, who had been forcibly resettled every two years as a Navy child, truly disliked traveling. She hated our year in Rome because she had little talent for foreign languages, so managing our cook and cleaning help was a double nightmare of administration and translation. All the free time that having the help bestowed upon her was gone in her frustration at not being able to practice architecture with it; she did not want to walk the streets of Rome looking at pretty buildings and sit for espresso in piazzas and watch the people. Watching her husband move farther away in his manic enthusiasm for living abroad was already too much for her. At the beginning in the fall when I went off to Greece and Turkey I summoned her to join me and my traveling companion (completely platonic) in Izmir. She arrived, thinking, I imagine, that now was our chance to become the young lovers we had been at the start. At her arrival she handed on to me the heavy baggage of my guilt for my failure at lovemaking in recent years, my depression at seeing her sad, and yet gamely trying to pretend she was having a good time. All the joy of the experience of discovery and adventure that had filled me utterly in the previous weeks evaporated at seeing her grimly try to enjoy the party.

While we were living in Rome, Professor Otis wrote to inform me that he would not support me for tenure when the time came. I was in the first year of my second three-year contract at Stanford while on this leave. So I had two years to work out my immediate future. I immediately wrote to a friend at Boston University, the very same friend who had found us the wonderful Roman apartment, asking her to keep a lookout for anything coming up in the Boston area. After our migrations to unfamiliar locales, where we had had the usual agitation of integration, my instinct was to return to a place we knew. So far I had gotten jobs through personal intervention (Dow at Wheaton), luck combined with charm (Yale), and friendly persuasion (my friend Ted working on Otis). My friend wrote back to tell me that coincidentally she was leaving Boston University in two years' time to move with her husband to Princeton (this time it was lucky coincidence). When we returned to California after the months of letters, I made a flight to Boston to talk with the administration at Boston University, and they invited me to join the faculty in September 1966 with the prospect of becoming the department head in the academic year 1967–68.

Did I discuss this move with Penny? Not really, but she agreed in the sense that she never said no. Perhaps, as an unwilling wanderer most of her life, she thought of Boston as home. She had attended Abbott Academy, a prep school north of the city, for three years, after which she had gone to college and graduate school on the north side of the Charles River. Our year together in Rome, 1963–64, changed me forever; I fell in love with Rome hard. For those who do, they say when they are away from the city that they are "Romesick." The year in Rome changed Penny as well. Because there was so much help with us in Rome, she as well as myself was free from the quotidian distraction of child care and housework, free to take long solitary walks through that incredibly beautiful city and think. I doubt that for Penny, frustrated in so many ways, those thoughts were pleasant, but the experience of being free of domestic chores made her more than ever determined to get outside the home. How could Boston not beckon to her, the city where she had first begun to have a career?

Once we were back in Palo Alto a depression set in for both of us; it was hard to live together again in a small house when we had lost so much to connect us. It was hard to come back to the reality of suburban California after a year in so glamorous a city as Rome, especially from so splendid an apartment. After driving our family across the country in a little under a week, we bedded down in our house, home sweet home, only to have my four-year-old daughter declare at breakfast, "I don't like this motel. When are we leaving?"

We encountered a remarkable change in the student body, particularly the new graduate students in classics, which forecasted a general shift in the culture of American youth. In the fall term of the academic year 1964–65, as I approached the spot where my Homer seminar was scheduled, I saw the students unaccountably standing outside the building as though waiting, and moreover they all seemed to be smoking the same cigarette, which they were passing around among themselves. Once we had reassembled and I began, I quickly sensed an undertone of hilarity, which in the course of the two hours occasionally broke into giggles and even laughter at what I had to think was only minimally humorous. They were stoned, of course, but I had no understanding of this. At least not then, but it rapidly became an obvious feature of more events than I would like. I began to recognize a new kind of insouciance, a marvelous disconnect, sometimes adding a wonderful long-distance focus on the material at hand, sometimes just descending into a vague pit where any understanding was threatening to be demolished. Ironically enough, it resembled what I now encounter all the time in my dotage as my friends and I carry on conversations in which we often forget the thread in the middle of speaking. The only things missing are the giggles and the munchies. In connection with the Homer seminar I began to organize my lecture notes on Homer, which resulted in writing a specimen chapter through the winter months. In January 1965 I sent it off to Doubleday, and—miracle of miracles—got a contract with them, so I had to sit down and turn out a manuscript. The writing usually took place back at my office in late inebriated evenings when I had done my duty by the kiddies, and could escape the silence that filled the space between Penny and me once we were alone. It was so like backstage at the theater once the curtain comes down. The resolutely manufactured good cheer had ended; there was no ill will, really, just nothing more to say.

The increasingly obvious emptiness of our relationship naturally troubled me. I was tormented by a sense of failure that I assigned pure and simple to my being gay, without a thought to the commonplace truth that marriage over a time often produces profound ennui in the partners. I was not intimate enough with enough people in Palo Alto to get a sense of this. I learned much later from my older sister that she and Penny had had long discussions about the marriage when she was spending a couple of months with us, and that she had urged Penny to take a lover. Easier said than done in the kind of antiseptic suburban world in which we lived.

By August my manuscript was finished, and I sent it off to a former student and close friend in New York. Shortly thereafter I flew to New York to discuss it with him. While I was away Penny got into some kind of relationship—hard to determine their emotional seriousness—with a young man who did work for us at the time, a nineteen-year-old student at a college in San Francisco. Poor fellow, he must have been damaged goods. I remember watching the film *Days of Wine and Roses* with him, a very sad story of a young couple and their destructive alcoholism, and his saying with a sigh at the end that that was the story of his parents all over again. One night he and I went to walk the dog, and in the dark of the Stanford grounds as we sat watching the dog run off the leash, I made a serious pass at him, which I guess at first he was too startled to resist, but then recovered himself and made me stop. In the thunder and lightning of the aftermath of their affair I remember one or the other of them telling me that the next morning he had come to Penny with the story of my attack, and she had taken him straightaway to bed. This was a matter of the moment because he was scheduled to move away at the end of the summer.

It was months later, when he moved back for a longer stretch, that I sensed the two of them becoming more and more moody and weird, and then one morning as I was getting the children ready for school I happened to notice them playing footsie under the dining room table as I was at the stove. My reaction was a disgrace. At first controlled, of course, I singled out the boy for a lunch date to force him to confess to me. My confrontation with Penny was muted by the fact that her recently widowed mother had just flown in from Honolulu, leis around her neck and all, making the evening meal something Neil Simon could have rendered hilarious. Still, I managed to act out after the old lady had gone to bed. There was even yelling and screaming, difficult to cover over in an open-flow modern house. How I could have behaved so haunts me to this day, I, the veteran of such flagrant adultery, I, the sensitive barometer of the waning affections between us two. It was the triumph of male chauvinistic piggery, the atavistic belief in wife as property, the pompous control mechanisms of a professor with his student, and of course deep and dangerous and, oh, so sad, the desperate flailings of a man called fag and fairy too many times. And, oh, I shudder to think it, but there must have been the insane jealousy, insane anger at coming up the loser, insane because I somehow had imagined that

she and I were equals in the running for this young man's affections. Pathetic delusions, gross misjudgments, distortions of view,
all of these elements were in the mix of a suburban nightmare in
our beautiful glass box in Palo Alto. In the face of my howling,
real or repressed depending upon those present, the people in
my household were all so nice to me. I remember sitting about at
a grand Easter dinner, Penny, the sad, sad young man who had
begun boarding with friends of ours, the friends themselves, their
children, our children, chocolate bunnies, Easter eggs, the whole
of us putting on good cheer. How long, O, Lord, how long? The
most ridiculous moment must have been when I was alone with
the two and manically, merrily urging them to take the summer
off and go to Europe together to have a proper time together,
while I stayed with the children. They stared at me as though
I were a mad dog who might break loose from the leash at any
moment.

Weeks before this our entire lives had been darkened by the
tragic suicide of a graduate student who had joined the department in the fall of the previous year—in fact, one of those merry
lads puffing away on the marijuana cigarette. I had become his
dissertation adviser, friend, and great admirer as I watched in fascination his public unveiling of his homosexuality at a time when
this was still a very delicate maneuver, particularly for someone
who advertised himself as interested in a teaching career. He was
perhaps twenty-six, tall, blond, very Irish, with a tough-guy mouth.
He had a kind of mean, aggressive way of presenting himself. He
had just resigned from the Navy, where he had served on the
staff of the admiral of the Sixth Fleet, carried himself like a military officer, and was so much of a no-nonsense guy when I first
met him that I quailed. The first thing to go was the crew cut as
he let his hair down—in more ways than one. In the next eight
months he turned himself into a wise-ass, loudmouthed, entirely
funny, campy, gay alternate version of that original persona. It was

fabulous, since he kept the person he was intact but absolutely different. His intelligence promised me that I was in for a treat as we worked on his dissertation. Our discussions often took place at the end of the afternoon, and just as often I would invite him home to dinner. Penny adored him, the children adored him, he was so much fun, every time a new and delightful experience.

One Monday he came to dinner, and as sometimes would happen Penny and I drank enough to get tipsy. Our student live-in was out for the evening, so our guest took it upon himself to read to the children and put them to bed. Naturally I felt terribly embarrassed the next day and insisted that he come to dinner again to redeem the previous evening. He laughed at the idea, but came along in any case after we had spent another hour in my office going over his proposal. He was so bright, but so determined to push the limits that getting something acceptable put together was a chore. The evening was delightful, he was in his element, Penny and I were on our best behavior. Then came Wednesday, and as I learned later he drove to San Gregorio Beach on the ocean considerably to the west of Palo Alto, arranged himself on a blanket, took fifty Nebutal pills, and died. From the letters he'd sent out and the arrangements he had made it was clear that he had planned this as early as Monday, so that those two days with him had been when he was already intent on leaving life. That was almost a half century ago, and yet as I write this, my heart skips a beat; somehow my emotion is just as strong as when we were told on the following Thursday.

When his father and brother came out to retrieve his possessions, Penny and I asked them to dinner. It was a strange evening. The father was a widower, by his remarks I would say a relatively devout Catholic, the brother was a crew-cut, blond, eminently nononsense butch version of the dead young man, indeed, much as when he first came to Stanford. Penny and I had recently been to a mass that Ted had arranged for the repose of his soul at the student Catholic chapel. It was a normal five o'clock mass attended by anyone in the area, which Ted had arranged to be designated as a special requiem. Penny and I went to this in deepest grief, and, filled with our memories of funerals in Catholic Italy, dressed completely in black, she replete with a black picture hat and veil, both of us with dark glasses; the other congregants, everyday people on their way home from work, looked at this apparition and stood back to let us enter.

The father said the burial in Cleveland had been in consecrated ground, despite his suicide. The father and brother were not prepared to recognize the fact of the suicide in Cleveland, although on another level they acknowledged that their son and brother had killed himself, and on still another level, if the language used was ambiguous enough, they could say that he was also tormented by the fact that he was gay. It seemed to me so important that those two acknowledge the suicide and the gayness; otherwise what would have been the point to the suicide? It seemed to me to be urgent that this be acknowledged, that this was so. No suicide in the closet, that's what I was thinking, I guess. They were both nice guys; we sat around in our house after dinner and got incredibly drunk—my, they could drink a lot! But then, as my mother would have said, they were Irish. It was just the four of us talking about him, and death, and suicide, and sexuality, and the desperation of it all, and we more or less abandoned for the night any notion of the peace of God which passeth all understanding and all that.

The year before had been hard. Admiral Pendleton died just before Christmas 1964, shortly thereafter the teenage son of Professor Otis died when his car went off the road, then the wife of my British colleague was killed in a head-on collision with him at the wheel. Penny came back from her father's funeral to attend two more, the first three of her life. No wonder she was ready for an affair with a sexy, loving, insatiable nineteen-year-old—just what my sister Holly had been urging for over a year. "When you are trying to raise four children and keep your family intact, adultery works way better than divorce," was what she advised. Now, in the summer of 1966, we were going back to where it all began for us two.

# FIVE

# "BE NICE TO EACH OTHER"

*October 14, 1972. We are setting off for a neighbor's bar mitzvah thinking ourselves to be very European after our year in Rome, myself especially imagining I could pass for Fellini, but at the temple the mother of the bar mitzvah boy will exclaim, "The one goyish family we invite, and they arrive looking like they just walked out of some shtetl!"* (Jon Wagner)

$B$y 1967 we were living in Brookline, Massachusetts, a suburban part of greater Boston, in a large Edwardian house (sometimes I like to say mansion), with our children sleeping in four bedrooms on the second floor and we in a suite on the third. At my urging Penny had gone back to work, at first nervously and tentatively part-time. This was an enormous challenge to her, ten years dormant, away from new ideas and techniques while living in the barren, empty lands of suburbia. I had been adamant that she network through her former classmates still in the Boston area, despite their obvious head start on her in the profession. ("Do not be nervous, do not be embarrassed.") She found some studio work, then got into a much more serious full-time job when I guaranteed to do the housework, shopping, all that sort of thing, with the abundant assistance of a cleaning woman who came in the afternoons and acted as chaperone on days when I could not make it home. In the days before she did so radical a revisionist rethinking of our life together, Penny used to say quite fervently, "I have to thank you for pushing me; I never would have had the nerve to do it myself."

From our house in Brookline I could walk to work, and the children, we thought, would prosper intellectually because, according to the superintendent of schools, the school in the neighborhood into which we had moved had a student body that was over ninety-five percent Jewish. I was now the chairman of the

department, but I kept a very large office on the third floor of
our house and directed most of my operations from there, relying
on my efficient secretary to hold the fort at the university. (I had
discovered that, if you keep your office door closed and appear at
only very specific moments, you can function perfectly well from
the home, sort of like the performance of the Wizard of Oz behind the screen.) We had a large front hall flanked by a dining
room and a living room, small parlors, a butler's pantry, and a huge
kitchen, enough space that I indulged my love of parties by inviting people to dinner as a kind of reflex, strangers, old friends, my
children's friends, always a weird mix, over which I presided,
shouting and laughing in my usual manic fashion. It was nothing
to me to have a sit-down dinner for twenty people twice a week.
Nor, for that matter, to cook up a batch of pastries for the kids
when they came home from school. Once for my birthday a group
of the children's friends gave me a book entitled *How to Be a Jewish Mother* with the inscription, *To Mr. Beye who is more of a
Jewish mother than our mothers.* The house was a teenage ren-
dezvous after school, and we made a recreation room for the children in a part of the basement. I was hard at work on the third
floor, pretty much insulated from the sound but not from the
occasional fumes of marijuana floating up through the hot-air
venting system, when I would pound downstairs shouting and
screaming, and they, the simpletons who never made the connection, would wonder how I knew. Sometimes when we had dinner
parties on the weekend the children entertained down below after their group had eaten with us. We turned a blind eye to their
drinking and doping, I must admit, as we were busy upstairs having
our own party. I can well remember a strange intersection when
a lad from belowstairs came up to use the toilet by the kitchen and
I collided with him as he emerged to head back downstairs. We
caught each other to keep from falling—both somewhat tight, I
imagine—and without thinking I took him more firmly in my arms

and gave him a long wet kiss from which he did not withdraw. We separated and never said a word.

Penny was often *"en charette,"* as they say in the business (meaning "in the cart"—in nineteenth-century Paris, a cart carried student architectural drawings on their way to be judged, and the students would sometimes jump on to make last-minute alterations; hence, meaning working up to the deadline, pulling an all-nighter). She did not always come home from her office for these parties, since she was not the least bit inclined to small talk, or for that matter much big talk either. I remember once discussing Penny with a woman who had known her from childhood, who replied to my "Still waters run deep" with, "Well, sometimes they run shallow too." My older boy, when he announced that he would not attend college and I began the typical lament, insisted that the constant dinner party conversation he had heard and participated in for the previous four years had been as all-inclusive and deep as any undergraduate experience in a liberal arts college. Nonsense, of course, but you get the idea of what those dinner parties might have been like. My deepest satisfaction probably came intuitively from knowing that like my father before me, I was a professor, an author, department chair, a father, a man who presided over a splendid table, and who lived in a large house.

The great difference, however, was that I felt forlorn, ignorant of how to get myself any gay sexual experience. It was an embarrassment, but I did not know how to find myself in the gay community. I was a middle-class married man with four children and an imposing title—professor and chairman. Odd that I was somehow so enveloped in that cultural persona that I was afraid that if you took the wrapping off there would be no one there. The Stonewall riots took place in June 1969. At the time I knew nothing of them, immersed as I was in family life and career-building, and scarcely looking at the papers. The news came slowly, when it was no longer news, and I took note of the tough bitches who fought back against the hated police—hated, feared by me. How I envied and admired and was intimidated by them as well, these gay warriors, wimp that I was. Where was I? Who was I? Did I end up being this Brookline burgher because I could never face the police? Mother? I did not want to go down that road. How did I get here from where I once was as a teenager in Iowa? I felt sad, lonely, and desperate for masculine company.

There were gay students at Boston University, men like no one I had encountered before. I was frightened because some were so forward, so obvious, so determined to enfold me in their sexual embrace. One day, while I was walking on the sidewalk toward my office, a student in a parked convertible looked over at me and, when our eyes locked and the gaze held, jumped over the side of the car and followed me into the building where I had darted because I was scared. I went into the nearest men's room and he followed, and we met in a stall. Another day at the university a student came to my office on a visit. He was a bright, witty, talky kid who was always eccentrically dressed in suits, with a colorful handkerchief in his breast pocket. The motive for his attentions was never clear, since he was not enrolled in any of my classes. He had recently brought me back, from a weekend trip to Paris, a luscious tie from something new in Paris called Le Drugstore, for no reason at all except that it amused him. On this visit he outdid me as usual in manic talking, but once we were seated and the door to the office was closed, he laid his hand on my thigh. Startled, I stared at the hand, not saying a word, and watched as it moved to unzip my fly, and within minutes he had knelt down to take me in his mouth. I stared down at his bobbing head, losing myself to the pleasure he was giving me, thunderstruck to be so out of control, he the student, me the professor, and then surrendered. It had been so long. On another occasion a young fellow threw open the door of my office after a particularly rousing lecture when I was still coming off my high, and shouted laughingly, "Bravo, bravo." Before I could manage to invite him in or dismiss him, he was standing beside me, pushing the door shut with his foot, and then hugging me with a few muffled bravos still muttered in my ear. The embrace turned into a very long and wet kiss from him, and somehow or another in minutes we were naked on the floor. Then he positioned himself so that I could enter him and all the time I could hear my secretary in the outer office carrying on her work. It was too surreal for me. I played at being hip but I really wasn't ready for the sixties, and here we were almost upon the seventies! The one constant I noticed then, and it remains with me as a memory now, was that all these young men were the instigators, they approached as friends, wanted nothing, did not haunt me, never introduced the dynamics of our professional relationship—teacher/student—if there was one. But, oh, I did not know to what lengths I could go with these young men, what to do.

Then it was that I discovered hustlers. In the late sixties and early seventies, in addition to the commonplace phenomenon of young working-class males selling themselves near the intercity bus depot, there was that very Bostonian custom of young graduate students for hire on a couple of streets near the public garden. (A *Boston Globe* article on the subject had the figure of 70 percent of these people for hire claiming to be students at one of Boston's many institutions of higher education; their customers, they claimed, were largely married men from the suburbs.) This all came to an end years before the AIDS epidemic when the complaints of the well-heeled tenants of the adjacent apartment buildings finally moved the police to do enough sweeps to clear the area permanently. It could be hilariously annoying. Friends of mine were told by an elderly professor dinner guest that as he stood on the curb to hail a cab a couple of young men complained that he was trying to take over the space where they customarily stood each evening.

My discovery of this came about because I took up ceramics.

The catalyst was an old artist friend who taught the use of the potter's wheel at the Boston Center for Adult Education, which was lodged in an enormous old mansion on Commonwealth Avenue right around the corner from the center of this sex trade. So I more or less took up hustlers together with the ceramics, and along the way threw and fired an impressive array of pots, pitchers, and plates while having the experience of so many interesting, interesting young men burned into my memory. Since my office was a very short drive away I could indulge myself with something better than sex on the hoof, which, while it cost me more, also gave me a chance to lie back on my wonderful Victorian lounge chair to talk with these fellows as I had done with the boys of my youth. The delight of these encounters was that we had nothing to gain from each other that was not immediately obvious, and, more important, we had no roles to play. I remember so many great bodies, shining eyes, eager smiles, so many conversations. I think of a young African American from Atlanta who was taking a summer biology course before entering Harvard Medical School, who discussed with me the experience, so new to him, of the professed liberalism and veiled racism of the Bostonians who crossed his path. There was another fellow working on his doctorate in psychology with one of my Boston University colleagues, with whom I sat for more than an hour arguing the relative merits of teaching versus research. And then there was the very funny young working-class boy from Providence, Rhode Island, no student at all, only sixteen, who at first thought I was a detective and was going to arrest him. He talked fast and furiously about his life, how he and his buddies came to Boston once a month and made, as he said, "good money," how his older brother used to come to Boston to hustle as well, but he had gotten married, and how he still urged his older brother to come along and earn a little extra money, but the brother would not. He came with me to my office, where we stripped and he proceeded to lower himself onto my erection, and it was all I could do to get him to stop talking, talking, talking. Then there was the young man I picked up on Commonwealth Avenue who was hitching, not hustling, who embarrassed me by his weary disgust with my proposition, so I quickly changed the subject, learned that it was his nineteenth birthday, that the next day he was sailing out on his first cruise as a Coast Guard recruit all the way to Puerto Rico. I enthusiastically supplied him with all the information I could muster from memories of my visit over twenty years earlier. We even pulled over so I could get paper and a pen from the glove compartment to write it all down. When we reached the neighborhood where I was to drop him off he surprisingly asked:

"You still want to suck me off?"

"What made you change your mind?"

"You ain't like all those queers."

Who knew what that meant? I brought the car over into the secluded shadows, where he pulled down his pants.

Boston University in 1966 was definitely a step down for someone who had taught at Harvard, Yale, and Stanford. The institution nursed a profound sense of inferiority when it measured itself against the two giants across the Charles, not to mention Boston College, Brandeis, and Wellesley. It was founded by Methodist businessmen, a fact that itself was a blot in the eyes of snobs who evaluated things in Boston in terms of "old money," membership in the Congregational or Episcopal Church, and a prep-school education where muscled boys went out for crew before becoming doctors or lawyers. Proud immigrant parents sent their first-generation American children off to Boston University with their lunch sandwiches in their satchels along with books and papers. As one administrator said to me, "We are educating people into the midlevel bureaucracies." That was all changing when I arrived. Dormitories were being built, Jewish youngsters from the New York area who had trouble getting past the quotas at so many schools were applying for entrance because Boston University was not filling its freshman class each year. Jewish faculty who faced a similar discrimination as academics were eager to be hired, and there were places for them. Ironically, a decade or so earlier a petition to the trustees by the leaders of the Boston Jewish community to give support to a significant Jewish presence in the university in return for considerable endowment funds had been rejected. One began to hear the humorous appellation "Boston Jewniversity." For someone who had once counted the possible Jewish names on a class list in the desperate hope that an interesting group of students would be in the class this was happy news, although the student I usually faced was more often a budding Brenda Patimkin than a Susan Sontag.

The great surprise was the contingent of offbeat youngsters who had somehow or another dropped out after their freshman year somewhere else, more often than not from one of the institutional elites. They had migrated to Boston because it was becoming the place to be if one was young. Surprisingly they more and more turned up in the Classics Department as majors. We were different, kooky maybe, certainly hip. Whatever it was, the best were as good as any I had taught at Stanford, and looser, more prone to thinking outside the box. They had something to say that provoked me in every seminar I taught. Anyone who reads the preface of my *Epic and Romance in the "Argonautica" of Apollonius* will note the names of the students from my Apollonius seminar at Boston University who were so damn bright, but what is more, who kept prodding me to put in print what my professional conditioning made me too timid to do on my own. This was the second, after Stanford, of the great teaching experiences in my forty-two-year career.

When I was being interviewed about coming to Boston University, the dean of the College of Liberal Arts talked about my becoming chairman "to make things new in classics." "He means getting rid of deadwood like me," said the retiring chair, who was sitting in on the meeting. This was the middle of the sixties, and I thought I was hot stuff, in my denims, my open shirt, the hair that came to my shoulders. I was as puerile as they come, reveling in a teenage sensibility that I never had when I was a teenager. I remember once out dancing with Penny at some rock-and-roll joint, shirt open to my waist, wriggling my ass in my tight, tight pants, and hearing someone in the crowd say, "My God, that's a professor from BU." Groovy!

Still, I had the goods, or so they thought; Doubleday had just published *The "Iliad," the "Odyssey," and the Epic Tradition* as an Anchor Books original, which was quite a prestigious label in those days; the reviews had been good both in the popular press and, surprise, surprise, in such academic journals as the English *Classical Review*, not to mention being put on the reading list at both Oxford and Cambridge. My Classical Civilization survey course was so oversubscribed beyond the two-hundred-seat limit that the dean in desperation asked me if, please, would I give it a second time on the same day. I calculated that an insignificant department like Classics should do what it could when it could so as to have the chits to call in later on. In a very short time the department faculty grew from three to nine and we were ensconced in our very own brownstone on Bay State Road with offices, seminar rooms, and a library. Budget problems were never ours. As the assistant dean who handled the money explained to me, "Oh, Lord, Charlie, compared to the other departments this little pissant operation hardly shows up on the books. Spend what you like." The number of majors grew dramatically, and more important we were attracting seriously intelligent students who made class such a joy. As the hit song from 1968 began, "Those were the days, my friend, we thought they'd never end . . ."

In 1971 the trustees of Boston University appointed John Silber president. He had been the dean of the College of Arts and Sciences at the University of Texas at Austin, where he had lost a power struggle with the powerful Frank Erwin of the Board of Regents, who found him autocratic, arbitrary, and insubordinate. Dr. Silber may have lost that round, but he was determined to win the next battle. The BU faculty and staff were no match for him and the crew he brought with him. It was like the Communist take-over of Eastern Europe, perhaps in more ways than one. I remember a meeting with all the departmental chairmen and the Presidential Search Committee when they were discussing the Silber candidacy. The alarm went off for me when one of them described in his sweet, feeble old gentleman's way a telephone conversation he had had with his professional counterpart at Texas who prefaced the interview with, "Is this line tapped? Is this being recorded?" I registered the fear and paranoia in Austin, which all too soon became the tone at Boston University. Silber had a very specific idea of what he wanted to do, an identity for the university and a rationale for the college of liberal arts. His critics would say that he was brutal and ruthless in putting these in place. Anyone who has spent a life in academia knows that change comes at glacial speed; the structure of a university generally gives much more power to the faculty than, say, the employees in a corporation are given, so that administrations as a rule can only get what they want through enormous amounts of cooperation. Most would argue that this is a virtue, since the university is thought to be a *repository* of the collective wisdom. A leader who wants immediate change must have special talents. This one certainly blew me out of the water, and severely limited my role in the university. My reaction to him is there to read in Nora Ephron's 1977 *Esquire* article "Academic Gore," for which I was interviewed extensively by her.

Among the figures in the entourage who accompanied him to the university was the very brilliant and electric William Arrowsmith, whose writings I much admired, and with whom I had always had what passed for friendly relations. His interests ranged over all ancient literature, his translation of the Latin *Satyricon* of

Petronius being as accomplished as his several translations of Greek tragic drama. Another was the very prickly prima donna Donald Carne-Ross, who began his classical career back in the fifties as the producer of the *Third Programme* on the BBC, which broadcast a rich variety of classical literature, and who is best remembered now for encouraging Christopher Logue to make a translation of the *Iliad*, although he knew no Greek. Carne-Ross and Arrowsmith were passionate believers in the contemporary cultural relevance of antiquity, unmediated by criticism, academic or otherwise, or scholarship. That was an easier position for Carne-Ross to pull off, of course, who had no special degree in the field and thus was innocent of its scholarship. For instance, he read the poems of Pindar as a serious exposition of ideas of godhead relevant to us in the here and now. We could not have been more different. My take on Pindar is that he is the author of certain texts that date to the fifth century B.C.E., written in a hard-to-understand dialect and style, needing a lot of parsing, that these texts reflect certain political and social realities of their time, and that they are most of all important as evidence for the attitudes that may have then been contemporary. As for Pindar's so-called religious ideas, they seem to me so much decoration for complicated choral odes, danced and sung, that depend upon the obvious for an audience to comprehend. In any case, I subscribe utterly to Louis MacNeice's dictum in the poem *Autumn Journal*: "It was all so unimaginably different, and all so long ago." Pindar's poems are of their time, and I can only hope to get a vague estimation of them through my imperfect learning and understanding of that period, as well as the inevitable subjectivity that informs anyone's opinion on anything.

Arrowsmith and Carne-Ross—both notorious, not unlike their leader, for their quick tempers and exaggerated notions of their worth—swelled in anger whenever I suggested this point of view, as did Dr. Silber, who was intent on renewing American culture with a heavy dose of ancient learning. My caution that we knew antiquity so imperfectly that it was at best a very imperfect guide to life made him consider me a nihilist. Those gentlemen would have been only too happy if I had left the university. I had tenure, however, and while it was in their power to fire all the junior faculty I had assembled (which indeed they did), they were stuck with me. In the time-honored tradition of the academy, they proceeded to make my life as miserable as possible, so that I would be driven to seek employment elsewhere. This meant (1) ignoring me, for which I have always been grateful, since I thus had so much more time for my own work; (2) denying me pay rises, which I sued annually to be given and in each instance won; and (3) encouraging students not to take my courses, an iffy maneuver not usually successful, but to which I was impervious, having been an academic star too long to care.

I was lucky to get out of town for the first year of the Silber reign. It all started with a memo from the dean of the College of Liberal Arts in 1971 asking heads of departments to nominate an outstanding member of their faculty for an early sabbatical leave, that is, after six instead of seven years of service. Immediately I thought of myself and counted up on my fingers. I would be eligible for sabbatical no sooner than 1973–74. Was it not reasonable of me to consider my first years there as exemplary, my performance certainly outstanding? But would the dean think that I was too frightfully overbearing to nominate *myself* for this reward? No, not at all, was his genial response. (God love him!) I immediately applied for and received a sizable grant from the National Endowment for the Humanities, which supplemented the half-salary sabbatical I would be getting. I then shot off a letter of inquiry to our former landlady in Rome, the elegant marchesa, who replied that she was so taken with our previous tenancy that she would evict her current tenants, redecorate, and make the place even more splendid than before. The wonderful fact was that I had managed to save up some other money (what my older son always likes to call "serious coin") from taking on part-time visiting professorships at Brandeis, Brown, and Wellesley; I had to figure tuitions for four children in private schools. So we were scheduled to spend the academic year 1972–73 again in Rome.

This would be an expensive year, but it was extraordinary. On the whole, Penny and I were doing quite well financially in the modest way of academics. She was beginning to make a decent salary at her work, I had been given a hefty raise the previous year, which doubled the pay of the previous few years, and we each had a bit of money, mine from an inheritance and hers from an ongoing trust fund. It so happened that I had been spending my first years at Boston University building up the department's moribund reputation by going about the country lecturing at universities, where I would generally be given a slight honorarium along with my travel expenses; I was doing it a lot and managed to bank quite a bit from those gigs.

When I first mentioned the possibility of the sabbatical and my hopes for taking the family for a second year in Rome, Penny immediately declined to come along, pointing out that she was just in the early stages of a major design project for a school building. I thought it only reasonable, even if it was mostly attractive as being a decorous form of separation that covered the fact that we had definitely drifted apart. Still I am ashamed to admit that at the moment of her announcement I experienced a flash of anger and resentment that "the wife" would disobey her lord and master. Mother's maxims on the gendered roles in marriage seem to have sunk deep into my psyche. It makes me think of my mother-in-law, whose response to the news of our impending divorce a few years later was a puzzled, "But he was always a good provider."

This was not an easy time for Penny. She had given herself over completely to establishing herself as an architect in the Boston area. But before that she plunged into the qualifying examinations for board certification; they are many, they require study and memorization, and it is normal to fail parts of them more than once. Once she had worked herself past this enormous hurdle, she immediately was given more serious work. As I said before, this is very definitely still a man's profession, and women who enter it have to perform twice as well in order to be judged the male's equivalent. Initially she did minor detail work on several buildings near major highways in the Boston area, so that we could amuse ourselves as a family by driving along and pointing out, "That's one of Mom's buildings," even if she had only worked on realigning all the restrooms when the new code for the handicapped required special measurements for wheelchair access.

A year earlier in January 1970, Penny had endured extreme physical and mental anguish when she barely survived an automobile accident. She was in the process of driving a dinner guest back to his motel when she skidded on the ice and the car went into a tree. She was not wearing a seat belt and the steering wheel on impact did severe damage to several of her internal organs. Luckily her passenger survived with only minor injuries. During the week when the doctors could not guarantee her survival, and I with the help of our student live-in kept the children calm with the illusion that their mother's accident was minor, I worried over the morality of this lie, if she did indeed die without their seeing her. (They told us at noon that Daddy had broken his leg in an accident, they came to pick us up from school at three with the news that he was dead.) The hospital sent her home at the start of what turned out to be an enormous blizzard, which eventually killed the power, so we sat by candlelight in the kitchen with the oven door to the gas-fueled stove opened, a cozy family scene in some respects, everyone so thankful that she was alive and we were all safe. The event, like the death of her father in 1964, seemed to change Penny in a significant way: she began to treasure and assign value to the days of her life, or so I imagined from gauging a new sharpness and urgency in her remarks. Her life was ready for major change; she was back in a city where she was positioned to live life to the full, which had certainly not been possible during the decade of suburban living. She recuperated very slowly, but it was uneventful. As soon as she could in April she was back to work as busy as ever.

In the late summer of that same year, she suffered the sudden loss of her twin brother to an unexpected heart attack at age thirty-nine. Her brother's death came with a peculiar circumstance. On the day he died we were on our way to Maine to visit our younger son, who was enrolled in an athletic camp there. We had spent the night at the farm alone, because Penny's mother was on the Cape at the moment. Curiously Penny took it into her head to call her brother, something she almost never did, and in fact after giving the idea a second thought she changed her mind. In the morning as we were about to leave, Penny complained of chest pains, and since they continued I wanted to stop at a clinic on our way north, which she refused to do. At noon the pains stopped. By four we were back at the farm, where her mother greeted us with, "Penny, Brian's dead." He had come in to work that morning complaining of chest pains, and his secretary had finally convinced him to go down to the company infirmary, where they quickly summoned an ambulance to take him to the hospital, and he was dead on arrival *at noon*. He had been alone at home the night before because his wife and children were with her parents. I begged Penny to go to her doctor for an EKG. The tests showed no problem, but we were interested to hear the doctor say that there were data for the supernatural experiences of twins, which he himself could not imagine trying to account for. Penny, who had trouble expressing herself on mundanities, was never able to go into murkier matters unless she was quite liquored up, so I cannot imagine what she was feeling.

Since I wanted to feel free to travel during the upcoming year abroad, I offered a recently graduated student couple who wanted a year abroad a chance to stay with us, junior chaperones for the children, now ages ten, eleven, thirteen, and fourteen. I did not plan on hiring a cook, since I felt supremely confident at turning out the meals as I was now doing for us at home in Brookline. I loved shopping; the washing and the cleaning were shared by me and the student couple. It was rather slapdash, but we all managed to laugh a lot, and with a little exertion everything seemed to go along just fine. It was only years later that my sons confessed to sneaking out nights to go to a nearby jazz club; as far as I knew they were asleep in their rooms after doing their homework. The children went to the Overseas School of Rome as the boys had on our previous visit, while the student couple found jobs to occupy their days and get into the Roman scene; and I occasionally paid a visit to the library at the American Academy so as to justify the fact that I was a professor on official leave.

I was working on the manuscript of *Ancient Greek Literature and Society* for Doubleday, so I had plenty to read and to study at my desk in the marchesa's apartment. I started my day out on the terrace off the kitchen drinking coffee, where I saluted the maids I could see on other terrazzi beating carpets and shaking dust mops. Naturally I was an object of furious curiosity in the neighborhood. Italian males cannot boil water, let alone tend to the household tasks. Here I was, *il professore*, a grand American academic, doing the kitchen work. It was a perversion of endless fascination for everyone on Via Bartolomeo Eustachio. I went out with my string bag to shop in the small stores and markets, where I would plan meals for the day. Much of the rest of the day I wandered the city of Rome serendipitously, encountering architectural and sculptural detail of extraordinary variety in every little street and alley. On weekends the family went to the miles of uninterrupted sandy beach at Sabaudia or from time to time in colder weather on trips to some site I thought might be interesting. My children claim to this day that our roaming throughout Italy during that year was fun, memorable, and educational. It has provided us with a strong bond of mutual interests that we can hold on to as a point of reference as they become middle-aged and preoccupied with the lives they themselves have created.

The hours of two to four p.m. were *riposo* in those days in Rome before the European Union and its stock markets made the Mediterraneans change their style of life; the children were at school, and I returned to the empty, quiet apartment. There was a young man who frequently came for lunch and stayed to nap. He was a twenty-one-year-old mechanic whom I had met two years previously through friends on whose custom-built sports car he had worked. This unlikely relationship—he was Sicilian-born, and had no education beyond the age of twelve—was not just about sex. He was straight but very intelligent and very witty. We had met in 1970 at lunch at my friends' apartment where we spoke in Italian because he was there, and I was startled by his admiration for my own wit, which he, incredibly enough, could grasp through the language barrier. He was patient and tolerant enough to make out my meaning through the barrage of my constant linguistic errors, and I realized that he too had a great sense of humor, and wanted some witty exchange to bounce back and forth. It was odd the way we clicked that day; here we were, these kindred spirits despite the enormous gap in age, class, and nationality. It was certainly helped by his great good looks, dark, Sicilian, and Arabic, and his attraction to the glamour so often attached to Americans in decades past. When he learned that I was staying on in Rome for a few days and was changing hotels, he offered to help me move my luggage. That, of course, precipitated a visit to my new hotel room and, as these things so often happen, I made a discreet pass at him, which he probably had anticipated. In any case, we began a relationship, very much that of the typical Mediterranean straight male who will offer his penis to be pleasured in whatever way the other fellow chooses, although this young man was good enough then to lie back so that I could pleasure myself with my body against his. This continued during my sabbatical year on endless weekday afternoons when he would arrive smelling of the strong soap he had just used to wash the grease of the mechanic's shop from his hands, and I would serve him some salad and pasta, the both of us jabbering away in some kind of intelligibility before moving on to my bed. I never felt the need for another male that entire year.

How could I have spent time with him, I know people must ask. So ignorant that he questioned why President Kennedy had let himself in for assassination by visiting this foreign country, Texas; that he could ask, one day when we were in Piazza Navona, and I proposed our visiting Sant'Agnese to see the architecture of Borromini, if it was because this Borromini was an American. No, I liked the male smell of him, the rough, aggressive sureness of his movements, his intelligence, acuity, the kindness, the tenderness. His great passion was his late-model car, constantly polished, perfectly tuned, in which he delighted in taking me for rides outside of Rome. A favorite haunt was the end of the runway at Fiumicino, where we could stand and face jets thundering down and then lifting off over one's head. But most of the time he simply worked hard at the BMW garage off the Piazza del Popolo and turned most of his earnings over to his family with whom he lived. Sometimes he returned in the evening to play cards with my children, who found him to be great company. He could have been an older brother. We were a very odd twosome, I know, but I truly enjoyed his company. One of our great pleasures that year was sitting at the back of the theater showing Pasolini's *Decameron*, where all the characters speak in Neapolitan dialect, and his whispering a translation into Italian for me. It took us several viewings for me to get it right.

Years later my younger daughter complained bitterly that my bringing her and her siblings to Europe upset the fabric of their social life in the United States, but I stick with my older daughter's remark about Rome being the "vacation from life." Penny hated going abroad for that reason, insisting that coming back to "real life" was too painful. She came for two weeks at Christmas, a glamorous time in Rome, where shops know how to dream up glitz, in the Piazza Navona especially, where the peasant shepherds came from the hills in their sheepskin outfits to play on their pipes while roaming about. I stayed back in the flat, ostensibly to write, so that Penny might have maximum time with the children alone. It vexed me when my mechanic friend met her and she invited him to join them all in the evening to go out to see the Christmas spectacles. He so obviously found her attractive, and she for whatever reason put on her charm. It was classic domestic farce with a special slant. If I had had more of a sense of humor about our marital predicament I could have relaxed and had a much better time.

During the year abroad Penny had moved into an apartment so we could rent the large house to an academic family in Boston on sabbatical. As I learned after the fact, she had done so in order to live with a young man in his late twenties who had left his wife and baby child for this adventure. In January of my Roman year I flew to the States to deliver a triad of lectures in New York, and made a date with Penny, while her mother was in Florida, to spend a weekend on the farm, where we could do our income tax form, which we filed jointly. Afterward she drove me to the airport for my flight back to Rome and on the way tearfully told me the story of the young lover, and confessed her heartbreak and depression because he had decided to return to his wife for the baby's sake. All laudable, all understandable, but all very sad, nonetheless. I comforted her as best I could with many a hug and squeeze, and then waved goodbye.

Upon my return she seemed not to be able to face moving back. We formally separated, although at first she was afraid and cried out to me, "Don't let me do this." I lived with the children in the house until the following summer, when she moved in while I took a vacation in England. In London while staying with friends of our family I watched the interplay between the mother and her twelve-year-old daughter. In the previous winter when I was living alone with the children in Brookline, my older girl had descended for breakfast one day to announce that she had begun menstruation. I was horrified that she had not had her mother on hand for this significant moment of change in a woman's life, although she had stilled my vaporings by putting her hand on my arm and murmuring, "Cool it, Dad." With the memory of that while watching the mother and daughter, I thought over our situation. Our house was enormous, Penny and I had long since stopped sleeping in the same bed. We had the top floor, she in one room, me in the extra-large room accommodating both my desk and my bed, and a kind of sitting room in between. We had never thrown dishes at each other, snarled, or screamed. Why couldn't we continue to live in the same house? True enough, she was involved with a man, and that might prove awkward. She would have to see him elsewhere, of course. I telephoned her and proposed a meeting for the two of us. We met and decided to fly to Québec City to discuss our life together. Again the man who would film the story of our marriage would have a brilliant piece of imagery. As we stood before the Delta check-in desk at Logan Airport, rather grimly fixated on walking across the minefields of the compact we were working on, there came into view a giant aircraft moving up and across the glass facade of the terminal to obscure the view of the runway lying behind. As we learned later, the plane we were to board had crashed on landing and the authorities had positioned that giant aircraft to block our view of the crash. Instantly, the large departures board read "Cancelled" next to our flight, and the ticket counter became a hive of activity as crew, staff, and clergy worked the crowd of relatives waiting for news. We gave up the idea of a flight and went back into Boston, looking across the divider at the empty lanes leading to Logan, kept empty for the ambulances, which now did not need to come; there were no survivors.

The plane crash was certainly the image for our reunion. The first knotty problem was Penny's lover, who was very much determined to remain on the scene. He was a man in his forties with whom Penny had had dealings as a client of her firm, who promptly complained of marital boredom and moved into her bed while nominally remaining husband-in-residence for his wife. He took to coming over, and as he was a pleasant enough, if dull fellow, I would invite him to dinner. A major problem was his wife, who evidently went berserk when he stayed out all night. She was enough aware of the situation that she knew Penny's name, and, I guess, that she lived at home again. More than once, just when I was busy turning out breakfast treats for my children, I would get these frantic calls from her wanting to know where the guilty twosome was, and I would have to say I did not know and did not care, for which response I was treated to a shrill tirade on the perversity of a male who did not want to track his spouse. Oy!, as we used to say in Brookline. He was good with his hands, and I well remember him one evening resewing all the big leather buttons on my leather greatcoat, no small feat of manual dexterity. One evening as he sat waiting for Penny to return from work he hesitantly explored with me the possibility of his moving in with us, living together with Penny in her bedroom, and otherwise appearing as a roomer in the household. It would all be quite discreet, he claimed, because we had our suite of rooms on the floor above the children. I told him that I would find it impossibly frustrating because I found him sexually attractive, and such an arrangement would only work if he were to sleep with me as well from time to time. This man was as conventional as you could get, so I was surprised that he would even listen to such a suggestion, but he did, and he pondered, and then he said that he would have to try it out. Of course, I had quite forgotten my wife's competitive streak. When he told her what we had discussed, she went into a frenzy of rage, so that was the end of that scheme and almost the end of the poor guy's relationship with her.

Penny in the fifteen or sixteen years of our marriage had always been repressed, demonstrative and overtly angry only when she had had enough to drink. Suddenly now that she was back in the house she grew openly sarcastic, frequently nasty. What bothered me was that she would lash out at me in front of the children. We had almost never before displayed animosity in front of them. This was a worrisome and ugly turn that I did not know how to stop or control. It is sad too that the memory of us as a couple the children retain is this ugly one based on these last two years, which is really only a small fraction of our married life. Someone might say that the fundamental truth of the emotion of that final period was so compelling that everything else was naturally blotted out, yet I have to remember that when directly after my return from Rome we told the children that we planned to separate they were astounded, unable to imagine that we were even in disagreement, let alone marital shambles. Years later I decided that what made this mild-mannered, repressed, and basically decent woman behave that way was a fierce determination not to be, as she would see it, bullied by my over-the-top personality, cheerfulness, feigned or real, and relentless verbosity. She had had enough of that, no more Charlie center stage all the time. I have always thought it is a telling insight into her competitiveness that after her terrible accident she pursued a relationship with the man who had been with her in the wreck. He was a high school friend of mine, one of those many athletes with whom I'd both had sex and double-dated, who by chance had a business appointment in the Boston area, which was what brought him to our house for dinner and a chance to meet again as middle-aged men. Naturally, nothing was said, but I would imagine Penny intuited readily enough his and my relationship. He told me years later that Penny was determined to have a relationship with him—God knows he was a gorgeous wreck of his younger self—and more than once flew to the city where he lived to meet. He was clearly puzzled that he should be so attractive to her, but I am sure that the lure was that he had been with me so many times as a teenager.

The continuing furor of our lives led me to suggest finally that we go to a marriage counselor. If asking Penny to move back home had been a mistake, this was certainly a very positive idea. Penny and I went to a therapist every Monday for two hours over the next two years. He had said at the beginning that while he hoped to be impartial, he was disposed to keeping a marriage together rather than see its dissolution. I thought him remarkably fair, Penny thought he was biased toward the male. I loved it that there was a third party to hear our replies to each other's questions, and who was able to note more or less objectively when we were openly contradicting previous assertions, or even in the same session suddenly adopting opposite views. I was frightened to discover how angry Penny was, because I never felt that deep anger before, awed that her anger had been there and I was oblivious, guilty about how she felt I had undermined her, had betrayed her in the deepest emotional way. I thought I had been true to her in whatever way I could. I was always there, I was devoted to the family, to the household; my heart was in my home. She could never forgive me my sexual proclivities. I did not consider that negotiable. It was a given of me from the day we met. She blamed it for my loss of sexual interest in her, even though she was surrounded by middle-aged men who confided to her the same situation in their homes. She was in fact having an affair with a man her age who both could not leave his wife and could not stand her anymore. In the last six months of the second year of counseling she began to repeat herself frequently with the statement that I had "ruined" her life, and that I "must therefore pay." At last I said, "For the sake of argument, all right, I have ruined your life. Now it is ruined, it cannot be unruined, so what am I to do?" "You must pay," was all she could say, again and again. The awful truth was that she loved me, loved me in a way that I did not, could not, never had loved her, that she loved me at the beginning, and that her love went on even when she found the strength to feel contempt for me. When her mother said to me after we were divorced, "You took your laughter away," she was talking of something else whether she understood or not.

In the end I think Penny and I both paid with that dreadful inky black all-enveloping cloud of failure that covered us whenever we had to think of our shared past. The therapy eventually ran its course, when the doctor said to us, "I always vote for marriage and against divorce. But, I am sad to say, I don't think this marriage can be saved." The sense of failure was crushing, but somehow it was as though a priest had given us absolution, even perhaps his benediction. *Go forth, my son and daughter, and find lives for yourselves.* I went down to a little seaside town south of Boston and bought an old ramshackle house where I could get away from whatever the house in Brookline held for us. It was 1975. I was forty-five, Penny was forty-four, our children were eighteen, seventeen, fifteen, and fourteen. As we were packing up the house for our separate moves, she held up a mah-jongg set her mother had brought back from China and said with a shy and wistful little smile, "I suppose when we're old we'll end up playing mah-jongg together." Whenever we met in later years, when finally we were civil and sensitive to one another, there was always that feeling of peering out across the wreckage of the crashed aircraft to see dimly that, yes, there was another survivor sitting there, dazed but still alive.

The end of our marriage proved to be good for Penny. When she was fifty she met a handsome virile man of thirty-two who was so smitten with her that he could not leave her side, despite her insistence that he keep some distance, since once snared she would never again be entrapped in marriage. She was eventually the first woman to become an associate of a major Boston architectural firm; at her memorial service a young woman from that place described most fondly her mentoring of the junior females employed there. It was then I learned from another speaker of her strenuous efforts to promote female faculty at the aggressively and notoriously sexist Harvard University.

# SIX

# AND THEN I WAS GAY

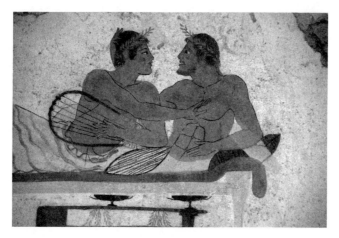

*Detail of the fresco from the so-called Tomb of the Diver, Paes-
tum, Italy, circa 470 B.C.E. A common motif of ancient Greek art
was the symposium scene in which an older (bearded) male
reclines next to a youth (beardless) on the banquet couch and
engages him in flirtatious erotic banter. The Greeks of the classical period much valued the amatory relationship between
men and boys in their late teens, which they considered to be a
cornerstone of a cohesive society and the basis of a strong military posture. (Rita Willaert)*

Within a year Penny and I had divorced and sold the house. She moved with the girls to an apartment in Brookline and they continued to go to Brookline High School. The older boy, who had rejected college and gone to work in a restaurant, moved to Canada, where the children had once gone to a summer camp, and in a short time married the daughter of the owners, resuming a teenage crush on a serious basis. In a few years he had landed-immigrant status and had become a father. His brother followed in his footsteps in abandoning education and going into the restaurant business, but in his case the marvelous instinct for cooking led him through a chain of experience eventually into the kitchen of the Ritz-Carlton as a first step to a career as a chef. The girls went off with me to Athens for the school year 1978–79. I was delighted to have this one year with them when I could create a semblance of a family again. I liked there to be people around, having grown up in a house with ten or more wandering about. Apparently I had begun to experience the empty nest syndrome, unless that is nothing more than a journalist's invention.

After cooking meals and running a household for several years, I was alone, and I noticed it. With my share of the sale of the Brookline house, I contributed, as the court demanded, to a fund for my children's education, and kept out enough to make a down payment on a two-family house in Cambridge. Penny and I had such a different attitude toward real estate. She was the heir to an ancestral farm of many hundreds of acres, but had spent her childhood living in rented rooms as her father moved the family from one Navy base to another. The war years sent her and her family into an exaggerated spin of dwellings, until finally she found root in a boarding school, and then in her dormitory room at Radcliffe, and finally in the apartment building where Mary and I lived on the top floor. When I met her she had never cooked a meal in her life. Domestic life, housekeeping, these were not skills she learned at home. When we divorced she lived in rented rooms for the rest of her life. I, on the other hand, who had grown up in a large and comfortable house, living at the same address until I was sixteen, yearned for that permanence again. I thought it would be the great house in Brookline, and well remember the day I left it forever with the real estate agent, who held my hand as I sat in her car sobbing.

My return to Cambridge was inevitable. I was single. I was hungry for emotion and sex. I wanted males. I wanted the sophistication of Cambridge. But I also remembered a life there with Mary and with Penny, and my memory told me we were young and jolly. I wanted that back again. The two-family house I bought was traditional for the neighborhood, with one apartment upstairs and one below. My neighbors in the other two-family houses were all elderly Irish Catholic working people, who nodded but were not overly friendly. I did not present myself as gay, and when young men lived with me, local storekeepers would sometimes refer to them quite innocently as nephews. At other times the front bedroom in my new house was inhabited by various children at different stages of their growing up into adulthood, my second son before he joined a group of friends to rent out a giant apartment, my younger daughter when she needed a place to stay on vacation when she went off to college.

I kept a low profile, and on one occasion was ingenious in protecting my image. An old acquaintance from graduate school days, more recently in my life when I was a visiting professor at Vassar, had suffered a stroke that left him slightly demented from the medication he was taking. I made the great mistake of telling him to drop by if ever he came to Cambridge, and weeks later he arrived to stay for a week, not at all what I'd had in mind. He was an enormously fat, chain-smoking alcoholic of incredible genius and with the hideous ill temper that often accompanies such gifts. He had recently decided that he was gay, and was making a great drama of coming out. This consisted largely in discovering gay Irish drinking songs, which, since he himself claimed Irish blood, was to be part of his new character. I did not allow smoking in my house, so he sat on my upstairs porch drinking and smoking most of the day while tossing the butts down to the sidewalk below. As he smoked and drank he bellowed out a tune off-key, the main refrain of which was repeated again and again: "I'm a-goin' to suck your cock, my boy." I kept hoping he was not audible from the street but discovered one day as I was sweeping up the butts that you could hear him loud and clear, and as I was making this discovery along came one of my formidable, stout old lady neighbors, who was looking up sternly in disbelief at the source of the sound on my balcony. I had the presence of mind to say quickly, "My friend, Father O'Neill, I had to remove him from his parish, poor old fellow," shaking my head and lowering my eyes in sadness, to which my good neighbor replied passionately as she squeezed my arm, "Oh, Lord, Mr. Beye, you are a saint."

I discovered a new substitute for parenting when I volunteered at the Cambridge City Hospital as an aide in the noninfectious surgical recovery ward Friday through Monday, six a.m. to noon. Once I had satisfied myself that I was not taking a job away from someone who might be paid to do what I did, I was happy to go there, make myself useful, feel wanted, touch other human beings, feed them, bathe them, get my first experience of senility and decrepitude. It was a strange experience, drawing on the memories of early fatherhood twenty-odd years before, when I was washing, powdering, and diapering old ladies. With the demented and the silent you had somehow to intuit. I never got used to insisting upon food for the old lady with the flailing arms pushing the tray away. I still think she should have been allowed to starve herself, but people who knew better said she was not really sending a message. As my younger son said, "Dad, you're the ward aide, not the doctor." The experience has made me resolve to do myself in when the time comes that I am failing.

Most patients were severely decayed, except I was surprised at the number of young men in that ward who had been struck by cars while out jogging. Washing one of them was an interesting experience in male-male interaction. He was a relatively young Hispanic getting ready for a visit from his family. His arms and hands were useless to him, strapped as they were on an inflexible frame, so he had not been able to wash up at all. "I stink, I stink," he kept saying as I was getting the tub of water and clothes and soap ready for his sponge bath, "wash me good." He stood before me while I knelt with the washing materials and proceeded to scrub him. Of course, the smell was most profound around his genitals and anus. I had no problem cleaning him behind, and took a deep breath and proceeded to take his penis in my hand, pull back the foreskin, and carefully soap and wash him thoroughly there as well. I took my time, was careful, we kept a volume of conversation, and interestingly enough he did not allow himself to become even the least bit engorged in the process. It occurred to me that gay males who have such experience of the naked male body should undertake work of this kind, since they might be more neutral than other caregivers.

As I started work in the Cambridge City Hospital I was winding down another volunteer career of ten or twelve years' duration: teaching in the medium-security Norfolk State Prison. Boston University offered a degree in liberal arts there, of which I was the classics faculty. The program was limited to long-term inmates, since at the rate they could take courses it was going to be a while before they got their degree. One might wonder why an inmate student would enroll in a classical civilization or a classical literature course. First, because they had to take what was offered. Second, because taking a course was free, and it took a little time off an inmate's sentence if he completed the semester. Third, it is very boring serving time in prison and something is better than nothing. Fourth, there were intelligent, intellectually curious men in Norfolk who had never had a chance for something like college courses. I found it sometimes frightening, often exhilarating, occasionally stupid and boring, and every so often quite sexy. I discovered that, contrary to my incredibly naïve liberal bias, many men are in prison because they are dangerous, violence-prone, and sometimes clearly psychopathic. Like the other teachers in the program, I declined the protection of a guard to which I was entitled, and never felt fear, even as I walked across the open courtyard big as a football field in which all the men were milling at the time of day I arrived for class. But one day was different when I walked into an empty room by mistake, only to see a man standing before me who advanced slowly and lethally like a leopard, speaking gibberish, and I was, as they say, scared shitless, until he, for whatever reason, stopped his forward movement and fell silent, and I walked out the door. Equally repulsive were the simpleminded and ignorant, who could talk for hours if they got going, and stopping them was difficult. But some guys could cut through my verbiage with quick intelligent questions or comments, often harsh, unyielding, and there were no compromises due to politeness. I had initially started volunteering at Norfolk because I was sick to death of the average Boston University student who appeared in my general education course. These guys were a real inspiration.

The class read a lot of Homeric epic and the tragic dramas. Their take on these pieces was different primarily because almost all of them had killed someone, not a few in the Vietnam War, but others in domestic quarrels or botched robberies. We also had a couple of career killers, who were hardened to their work like anyone in a business, although murdering someone for whatever motive changes a person. The texts we read resonated in ways I had never known before. The men who came back from Vietnam to find their wives had been cheating on them, and beat them up badly, or cut them up, or sometimes killed them, read about Clytemnestra, who was sleeping with Aigisthus while Agamemnon was at Troy. Kill the bitch, was their take. Nothing about how she was exacting some kind of symbolic revenge for Agamemnon's killing of Iphigenia. I had a student who had killed his wife and two baby daughters in a drug-induced madness and now was a gentle, utterly destroyed fellow living with that knowledge and memory. *Medea* meant something different to him than to other men. (I couldn't bring myself to introduce Euripides' play about Herakles and the madness sent him by Hera when he kills his children in a rampage.) Most of the men responded instantly to the weariness Achilles voices in the *Iliad* over the killing, the fundamental emptiness of life. It was not a middle-class conceit with them, something learned in literature classes, and I sometimes felt so inadequate.

When I started teaching at Boston University, the students were what my mother used to call "diamonds in the rough," that is, exceptional young men and women who were willing to take the risk, make the effort, try out something unknown to their parents called a college education. But over time the demographic became suburban kids of medium or meager talents. What is more nauseating than not overly bright youngsters whose entire lives have been lived between a fake colonial cottage, a 7-Eleven, and a shopping mall? Any prisoner would be more interesting and rewarding than that, I reasoned, and I was not wrong. I also said that the experience could sometimes be sexy, but not really. The men were not good-looking as they are in the films. Prison inmates are generally speaking losers, and losers are not as a rule good-looking, otherwise they would have conned themselves into a better life. The better-looking guys in my class were all the bottoms for the tough guys who protected them. After a while you could spot couples who would never appear so on the outside, because of course they wouldn't be; physical relationships in a prison are imposed out of desperation. Of course, I maintained a professional aloofness that I assumed was a formidable armor against any identification, and was amused to meet one of the men on the outside when he had been paroled who said casually over coffee, "You know, we thought you'd want some cock off us in there, and there was plenty available for you." So much for professional dignity!

The divorce decree stipulated that I contribute most of my money to a fund for my children's education, a demand of Penny's despite my angry protestations that if they wished they could go to Boston University for free. Like most people in the education business, I have a much less sentimental view of the expensive institutions of higher learning, but Penny won that round. Still, I had enough to maintain the two-family house in Cambridge, an expense pretty much covered by the tenants who rented the downstairs. And I had my broken-down house near the seashore, which may have been shabby, but with two bathrooms, four bedrooms, and the other obvious spaces was big enough for wonderful parties as well as stay-over guests. Between these two dwellings, and, I would say, because of them, I experienced at age forty-five the first serious male romantic relationships I had ever had, other than that one Mediterranean trip with my student fourteen years earlier. One of them lasted a summer, one three years, one two years, and one turned into an on-and-off involvement for a decade. Three of the men were essentially heterosexual, although each in his own way tried out the various physical possibilities of male-male sexual partnership. The fourth was thoroughly gay, and wanted everyone to know it, once he himself had accepted his orientation. Where anyone might find fault with my love life was that at my age I was in love with men in their early twenties, the age of my sons, more or less. Others might think it limited, that so much of our pleasure derived from my fellating my partners and enjoying frottage thereafter on their naked bodies. But this is more often than not an instinctive homosexual behavior. For those who cannot grasp this, think of Léonide Massine, who was resolutely heterosexual and went on to marry, but started as the lover for many years of Sergei Diaghilev, the great ballet impresario. When he was once asked how it was that he could have sex with Diaghilev, he shrugged and said it was Diaghilev's mouth and his penis, and that he had the warmest regard for the great man.

The first of these four was a young married English fellow, who worked as a taxi driver, spent his time writing poems and novels, took a night course with me, and taught me more about the Sumerian Gilgamesh poems than I had ever known, much to my shame, since I billed myself as an expert in ancient epic poetry. But, as he often points out, he learned what he knew about Homer's poems in that course, and went on to use that knowledge professionally many, many years later. He lived with his wife and baby son as dorm parents in one of the local colleges. In springtime at the end of term we attended the same poetry reading. I was giving him a ride home afterward and on the way I must have fallen into one of my more sour moods, because as we pulled up in front of the dorm, he turned to me to say, "You must be happy. I don't like to see you like this." And with that he leaned across to kiss me on the mouth, slowly, gently, a kiss charged with emotion, or so I received it. He left the car with me in it, completely stunned. The next day I saw him across the way on campus, and when I saw how he averted his gaze when he saw me, I hastened to his side to say reassuringly, "Thank you for the kiss. It bucked me up, and you needn't be the least bit embarrassed." It was as neutral as I could manage, and he did indeed smile at me, as though all were to be completely forgotten, or understood as an aberration.

He was off to England for the summer, so I quite put him out of my mind. Therefore I was startled to get his call in September announcing excitedly that he and his wife had just landed at Kennedy. All that emotion, and for what? Three days later he was in my office to tell me of their travels, but there was more. Soon the door was locked and we were lying on the couch. Was I the aggressor, was it mutual? Did he bring himself forward to me? I can't remember now. Within days we were taking an afternoon drive to the house at the shore, both of us nervous at what could be before us, he especially, since other than the fleeting moment in my office, this was new for him. He was a married man, a romantic lad with a long history of beautiful girlfriends taken and left, a lapsed Catholic with all the baggage that entails. Orphaned of his mother at nine, he was not only bereft but young, he had been my student, he admired my writing, he insisted that we stop at a liquor store so he could get a nip of brandy, for his "cold." He built a fire in the bedroom that had a window looking out to the sea, we stripped and got under the covers, shivering in the cold and musty air of a shut-up summer house, waiting for the room to warm up. I was ready to fall in love; he needed some kind of daddy figure in bed or out. As he told me later during his summer in London, he had had to watch his father take on a new wife, and at the same time hear himself dismissed as "good for nothing." If I could say that he appeared at the right moment, he often said the same about me. He was as highly sexed as I, a handsome English lad, emotionally needy, married because of a pregnancy and unhappy with it, confused, at some kind of dead end for which this completely new experience seemed to offer a way out. Illusions all, but they fueled a powerfully romantic afternoon for the both of us then and other afternoons, until it was finally too cold, even with the fireplace as a blazing inferno.

Sex in Cambridge meant dodging my children's visits, and, curiously enough at this stage of my life, coming out of the shell of a married life, I somehow felt that anyone who saw me and this young man together on the street or walking into my house could tell, just sense the emotions coursing back and forth between us. There was the famous day when I was on the telephone in my office and he walked in, and as I saw him I became dizzy—it was right out of one of the "bodice-ripper" romance narratives—and moments later a colleague of mine entered and almost immediately backed out. Later she excused herself for "barging in." I protested that there was nothing wrong in that, to which she replied, "Oh, my God, the atmosphere in there. You could cut it with a knife. I was so embarrassed." She talked as though we were naked on the sofa before her very eyes. She knew nothing about us, and still she had had this sensation.

We could not get enough of each other. He took to inviting me to dinner if only to have more time together, and I stupidly went along with it, just as besotted as he. His wife was a budding academic with whom I could talk seriously, dandling the child on my knee, watching my love out of the corner of my eye preparing dinner, letting my eye pass down over his wonderfully rounded rear end in his tight English corduroy pants. I brought these sinister evening visits to an end after what seemed a blatant hint contained in a dream his wife described. She dreamed that she, her husband, and I were sitting about, just as we were when she recounted it, staring at the fake Persian carpet on the floor. In the dream, she recalled, her husband and I lunged forward from our seats, began to wrestle on the carpet, rolling around and around, panting and groaning, until one of us flung out his leg and hit a tall Chinese vase (a fantasy prop in the dream) standing at the edge of the carpet. It toppled over and shattered into pieces everywhere. She finished this recital with, "And then I dreamt that I asked you to leave because you two were damaging everything." I have always marveled at the perception of this woman. Was she conscious of what she was intending? Our relationship continued, of course, in other venues. But then it came to its first halt at the end of the winter term when I invited my lover to come with me all expenses paid for a week's trip to California where I would be giving lectures. After a day thinking it over, he said no; there was a startling anguish in his voice as he explained that he could not face waking up every morning naked in bed with me for what it might mean about his sexuality. His misery made me guilty, which took the zest out of what we were doing. We became listless, started to "talk things over," the grim prelude to the end. But we stayed celibate friends as we had been to begin with. The romance, for better or worse, started up again much later.

Ending the romance was the professional thing to do, I knew; it was ethical, diplomatic, and sensible, but I hated being without him. What I did next was sheer lunacy; I must have been truly deranged at the time. It turned out well, as a matter of fact, but I cannot remember the moment without wondering at myself. The new semester began, and with it new lectures, new students. Three days into the term another young man joined the class of thirty studying something Greek in English translation. He was a slightly older chap, lines were beginning to appear on his face, unusually tall, slim, good looking, with blond hair that hung to his shoulders, presenting a smiling friendly countenance to the world at large. At the end of the hour he approached my desk to ask if it was too late to enroll. It was not, so we went along to my office to get the necessary bureaucracy rolling. As we stood next to each other, he peering over my shoulder to tell me the answers to the questions on the form, the smell of him, tired, faintly unwashed, that powerful man smell, began to overcome me. I turned slightly and asked:

"Have you ever slept with a man?"

Without missing a beat, and keeping his eyes on the form we were filling out, he replied evenly, "Well, yes, once in high school, with one of my teachers."

"Then, will you come to dinner this evening?"

Thus began my second love affair. The young man was in his

last year and a half of college, the product of divorce, alcoholism, the loss of family fortunes, only too ironically aware of old money, American aristocracy, and failure. To support himself he worked on the railroad as a switchman, living randomly here and there, waiting for September when he was to move into a kind of communal home in Cambridge.

For the next two months we were together a great many nights, he broke up with his nominal girlfriend and decided to move with me to the shore for the summer. The sheer pleasure of secure housing I am sure was a major factor in his decision. Gregarious fellow that he was, he introduced me to households of people all around my Cambridge home, young people I never would have known, who have remained friends to this day, all of them, weirdly enough, now somewhere in their fifties and sixties, anguishing over their children's progress in life. Sexually he was less inhibited than other essentially straight males about the physical possibilities of our lovemaking, a decided plus, but at the same time his relatively low libido (or maybe job-induced fatigue) left me desiring much more from him. Still, he was witty, friendly, attentive, although at first, just as we had made the decision to spend the summer at the shore, he backed out the night we were to move down, and I spent wretched hours on a single bed mattress with him, in the room of the apartment he occupied with friends, first arguing, then crying, then sleeping awkwardly and intermittently. When he had awakened, drunk his coffee, and looked out the window for a bit, he turned to me to announce he had thought it through again and was ready to go to live with me in the house at the shore. I can still remember later that morning his brother saying in a meditative way, "Free room and board? Some guy who will give him head every morning? You don't get that offer every day."

His schedule was a killer; the railroad dispatchers called him at any time, day or night, and he fitted his study hours and classroom appearances to that. My role was immediately parental, or

so I conceived it, preparing his lunch bucket no matter what hour
while he showered, putting a meal on the table when he came home
exhausted and dirty. Our days were mostly consumed by our respective tasks, with him taking random naps to catch up on sleep,
and we walked on the beach. Mostly we talked and talked; he was
a font of ideas on every subject. There were evenings when we both
sat reading; he had brought his library of books with him, which
I thought was so endearing. Still, we had those mornings when I
brought him his coffee and he opened his eyes, yawned, stretched
that long, long body, arching his back so that his erection bobbing
provocatively before us became the unspoken next item on the
agenda.

He had a week's vacation coming to him and we drove to Vir-
ginia, where he had relatives and I had an old friend in Richmond.
Nothing illustrates the difference in our generations than his last-
minute preparation for driving nonstop as far south from Boston
as we could in one day: he smoked a joint, explaining that otherwise he could not have tolerated the boredom of handling the steering wheel hour after hour. It made me wonder about his moving
those huge freight trains around. The visit was just as I could have
wished. We stayed in the old family plantation, now cut up into
apartments and bereft of the fields that once swept all the way to
the river, but presided over by the same kind of southern gentry
you get in the films; yes, the word "gracious" comes to mind. Their
graciousness, I must say, nearly lost a beat when they began to
understand in the course of our stay that the dear old professor
was having his way with their charming nephew. One evening the
uncle, who was my age, sat up with me drinking and talking, and
when suddenly he told me that he imagined his nephew was quite
a "hot young thing," I didn't know what he expected in reply. The
visit to my friend in Richmond was more relaxing because more
honest. He could not have imagined my traveling with such a handsome young guy for any other than totally carnal reasons.

In September, as planned, my young friend packed up his books and decamped to the commune, where he immediately lost himself in the group life for which he had been planning ever since I met him. Although he was only blocks away from me in Cambridge, he stopped our relationship. Not a word was said, nothing harsh, no scenes, and whenever we met as he was jogging or we collided at the supermarket, he smiled in a distant sort of way. I was sad to see him go, but of course I had to make it into my own drama, and thus insisted to myself how I understood that his shattered childhood had taught him how to move on without a murmur or backward glance, moving from one parent to another, being disowned through death, disappearance, and drunkenness. In another decade we would occasionally meet in New York, where he had begun his career and eventually married, and even more recently I was delighted to lunch with him again in London, where he now lives, and to discover that on the verge of sixty he is as disarmingly sweet and charming and funny as he ever was. More than anything else I learned from him the possibility of an inherent goodness of heart.

And then I managed a third year abroad. It had long been arranged that I was to be appointed the visiting professor at the American School of Classical Studies at Athens for the academic year 1978–79. It could not have come at a better time, since I had had the misfortune to pass three kidney stones in the preceding year, and because they stuck in the ureter and this was in the days before ultrasound, the doctors had to anesthetize me and go inside. A year off was very much needed. Despite all the nasty things I habitually say about the administration at Boston University, I must note here that they granted me another sabbatical a year in advance of the normal seventh year. Parenthetically I will add an astounding detail connected with both the institution and the kidney stones. As I was lying at home recovering yet again from a stone, I heard the front door open and someone ascending the stairs to my room. I had left a note on the door indicating visitors were to do just that. There appeared in the doorway a young man, part of the Texas entourage who came with Dr. Silber, who was scarcely even known to me, since of course I was the "evil" one and was to be shunned. As it was, however, he explained that he knew the departmental secretary's husband, from whom he had heard of my troubles. With that he approached the bed, pulled down my pajama bottoms, and gave me one of the best blow jobs I had ever had, then just as mysteriously hoped for my good health to return, and left.

At the time of the trip to Athens my sons were grown up and on their own, so only my two daughters and I were to go, along with a school friend of theirs. They had been living with their mother following our divorce, but the court decree gave me permission to take them abroad. The younger went to school for her senior year at an American-style international institution in a posh suburb of Athens with the children of the diplomatic corps and the rest of the *jeunesse dorée d'Athènes*. The older went for her freshman year at an American-style, English-language liberal arts college in Athens. It catered to everyone in Athens who anticipated getting an education in the States and wanted to learn the ropes ahead of time, not to mention the children of Greek Americans whose parents wanted them to have a year in the old country without their missing out on their progress in the American system.

Their school chum was with us for a month-long tour of England, Germany, and Italy, but dropped out in August, thank heaven, before we sailed from Brindisi for Patras. I write "thank heaven" because the emotions of teenage girls are as volatile as their capacity for friendship, and during that month I was always the one who had to pair with whoever was the outcast girl as the relationships shifted day by day. Because we were originally to be four people, the director of the American School allotted us the splendid large marble palace—it almost was—on the school grounds connected to the equally imposing Gennadius Library by a long portico of Ionic columns. Each of my years abroad were lived in a style I never knew at home, making Europe a repository of unrealistic fantasies and memories that I have trouble squaring with demonstrations in the streets and all the other paraphernalia of the modern discontents seen on the television. As in Rome, so here in Athens I brought my own peculiar style to the grand house in which we were to live. It was a shock to the Greeks when I announced that I intended to do the cooking as well as various other domestic tasks. The school sent cleaning women over once a week, but, for instance, I did the laundry, and many is the time that I was hanging the wash out on the line when the school gardeners arrived for work in the morning and dubiously saluted me as I smiled and nodded, my mouth filled with clothespins. Luckily none of these men had to witness me indoors standing at the sink and stove.

The year in Athens was another intellectually challenging time for me; it constitutes the third of the four glorious moments of my career. The American School is a resident academic program for American graduate students who take a year off from their normal program to study in Athens. Principally archaeologists, epigraphists, and numismatists, they represent the so-called hard disciplines, what Dow used to call "solid stuff." Still there are always a few literati tossed into the mix, and occasionally the visiting professor represents the literary side of things, as I did. The school sends the students out on fabulous tours of the archaeological sites, where everyone aboard the bus must contribute a short paper on some special feature of one selected place. I shall be forever grateful for my participation as a visitor, since the concentrated and intellectually challenging review of the aesthetics and sociology of the architecture I received was mostly new to me. To be learning as a novice deeply and intensely when one is in fact almost fifty is as satisfying as it gets. It was also highly entertaining to be able to study close to hand the differences between the American Academy in Rome and the American School in Athens.

My only obligation during the year was to offer a seminar during the winter season. Given the no-nonsense quality of the students and the staff, I was a little hesitant to do something with Apollonius Rhodius's *Argonautica* because it was such an offbeat text; as I had gotten to know the students and their projects, an author like Apollonius seemed more and more alien to their training and current research. But I was determined to write a book on the *Argonautica*, so that was my current research interest and that was what they were going to get, like it or not. I could not have misread the students more completely. My seminar was subscribed to the limit, the students were keen to try out something new, they were quite enthusiastic; certainly I got enormously intelligent feedback from them, which helped me no end on the book. They were the very best of the then-current crop of students in U.S. graduate programs in classics; as such they were always prepared, always ready with background reading material, always alert. Plus they were for the most part a witty group, which seems necessary for a good read of the *Argonautica*.

Living with my teenage daughters in our grand palace pretty much put sex out of reach, although hardly the thought of it. Walking about Athens were hordes of nice-looking young soldiers who I knew from previous visits were often ready to sell themselves to supplement their paltry wages. I well remembered one evening in Athens a few years earlier when a cheerful fellow accosted me in Syntagma Square to propose that he would get for me one of the handsome young soldiers, *evzones*, as they are called, who paraded before the Parliament Building and Palace in a kind of kilt. He named a price, insisted that the soldier in question would provide space for us to spend the night, and added the special tourist treat that on the next day he would arrange to have my picture taken with the young man when he was back on duty. I didn't think such

treats would be mine on this trip. However, on the first school bus
trip one of the students who boarded introduced himself to me
and the older academic with whom I was sitting with every hint that
he was gay. He almost said as much, stopping only when he saw,
registered on our faces, the rebuff we were mounting psychologically. This was 1978, a decade after Stonewall and all the fallout in
aggressive gay action that followed it, but still my seat mate and I,
who both knew the other was gay, would never have mentioned it,
especially since I was a father living with my daughters there at
the school. How perverse it all was, seen in the perspective of history, only a month or so before Harvey Milk was assassinated in
San Francisco. Sometime in the winter I ran across this same young
man in the library when we had a chance to speak privately. He
suggested that he could visit me and I agreed. A day or two later,
when I had the house to myself, he came over and stayed for sex. I
was beyond horny at this point, to the extent that my penis and
orgasm mechanisms were pretty much out of whack. ("Use it or
lose it" is not just a cute joke.) He was entirely sympathetic when
he said, "You see, you should have come on to me on the bus that
first day. This is what we could have been doing all fall." It took several days to bring me back from the dead, so to speak, all of which
was simply a kindness on his part. He had originally suggested the
visit simply out of curiosity, and now was willing to continue visits
only when his free moments and inclinations coincided.

My older daughter began dating a fellow student from her college. He was a young Greek Cypriot who came from Khartoum,
where his family had been merchants for three generations. On the
first date she met him somewhere out in the street, but for the second she agreed that he would come to the front door. It was so
amusing, right out of those Hollywood films of the thirties and
forties. I opened the door to the young man, we introduced ourselves, I brought him into the living room, where he sat nervously
on the very edge of his chair, waiting for my daughter to descend

from her bedroom. Our conversation was the usual nonsense between father and suitor, except that I found his Mediterranean good looks most appealing and so was certainly not prepared to barricade the palace, as the traditional jealous father is supposed to do. A month later she asked if she could move in with him in the apartment his father maintained in Athens for his business trips. I hesitated only a bit, enthusiastic, I guess, because of my own fantasies of nights with this young man. Still, I thought that when one is young and sex is so good and the protagonists are both good-looking, kindly, and amusing people, why not? Who knows what is to come? But I took him aside to tell him that he must remember that we were Americans, I would not tolerate my daughter being his servant, as I assumed Greek women generally were. He laughed and reminded me that in Khartoum he had been going an American school and hanging out with Americans since he was in kindergarten, so he had a pretty good idea of the amount of cleaning and washing and cooking he would be doing. As it was, he had already come to our palace for dinner several times and watched me, the *megálos kathigitís*, the "great professor" (my joke title among friends), cook up and serve.

When winter set in, the tours ended, and it was time for me to teach my seminar on Apollonius's *Argonautica*. There is no reason to drag my reader through the thicket of exposition and interpretation, but the professor in me wants to say a few words about the poem in order to make a point about my changing attitude toward classical antiquity that began at this point and continued through the next decade. It is, I think, tied to my expanding awareness of what it means to be a gay person. So here follows my little lecture.

There is a variety of styles in ancient Greek literature, of which most moderns will have heard of tragedy, comedy, and epic. The Greeks had a strong sense of tradition and expected each style or genre, as we say, to conform to the convention. *Argonautica* is an epic poem, and the reader could expect a story of a valiant male leader and battles. Epic also traditionally portrays male bonding; think of Achilles and Patroklos, or, going back earlier, Gilgamesh and Enkidu in the Sumerian epic tale. The subordinate figure in each pairing corresponds to the sidekick of our own buddy stories, for instance Batman and Robin, except that in these ancient stories the bond is sundered by the death of the sidekick. Apollonius begins his story with a brief description of the traditional hero Herakles, who is also on board the good ship *Argo* with his boy toy Hylas, whom the poet says Herakles snatched from his father's farm. Gruff, tough Herakles is the good ol' boy hero, the pederast hero, an expression of the conservative Greek notion of valor. In the initial scenes of the poem Apollonius sets up beautiful teenage Jason as a counterpart, describing him having sex with Queen Hypsipyle and impregnating her. Enter the new aggressively heterosexual love hero into epic poetry.

Because the story of Jason and his band of Argonauts doing magical battle for the Golden Fleece with the help of the Princess Medea and her subsequent abduction would be known to the reader, the expectation would be that the story would follow the fairy tale pattern of the prince who performs a magic act with the help of an adoring princess and wins the prize—sometimes a treasure, sometimes the maiden herself. Apollonius has radically made Jason a timid and unsure man instead of the bold, decisive hero of tradition; he uses fawning and seduction to get what he wants from Medea, who more than once provides the direction. Half the poem describes the duo traveling after getting the fleece. As the shape of a traveling buddy narrative develops, the ancient reader, who naturally valorized males, would expect to slot Medea into the sidekick role. Well, you can see where this is going. As the poem progresses Jason takes backseat to Medea, the roles are reversed, and the poem delivers a witty shock. I only bring the matter up because I think that my interpretation reflects my own growing awareness of my gay self as opposed to the consciousness with which I wrote my earlier critical works. I began my career writing about the *Iliad* and the *Odyssey*, which feature two self-obsessed, aggressive, brutal, testosterone-charged males. That is the heroic tradition. I would not repudiate what I wrote, but I grew to feel somewhat remote from the ideal of the hero in the form of Achilles or Odysseus, just as in real life I found myself more and more estranged from the Arnold Schwarzenegger type of male, if I may use an example so extreme as to verge on caricature. What interested me in the *Argonautica* was that the narrator had managed to describe Jason, who formally is meant to resemble these earlier figures, in ways that poke fun at him and thus undercut his essential "heroism." The other intriguing maneuver is the introduction and enlargement of the character of Medea. This reversal is a shock to the epic system, irreverent, and funny. Needless to say, the major Apollonian scholars will have none of it. (As one put it, "We must not laugh at Jason," to which I say, *Why not? The narrator makes him laughable.*) I am not sure why they oppose this interpretation, although perhaps it is because the reversal I have suggested puts the hegemonic heterosexual epic hero at risk, to use the wonderful blather of postmodern criticism, vulnerable in a significant way to a woman. When you think about it from the historical perspective, there was the *Argonautica*—let's put it in the last few decades of the third century B.C.E. at a time when we are seeing a new emphasis upon the female, as in the emergence of female nude statuary, the new importance of the love goddess Aphrodite—in Egypt, seat of the Ptolemies, a dynasty known for its strong female royals. And, as we know, along comes Cleopatra VII, who certainly ran circles around Julius Caesar and Mark Antony at the end of the first century B.C.E. I know, I know, all the professionals are rolling their eyes, but since no one knows anything one way or the other, I prefer to go with this. It's all in my *Epic and Romance in the "Argonautica" of Apollonius*, published in 1982 by the Southern Illinois University Press.

That year in Athens a variety of friends and relatives took advantage of our great house on the hill to pay a visit, most important of all my former mother-in-law, Mary Pendleton. She was a sweetheart who gave me the money to buy a Volkswagen Golf while we were in Greece (with the proviso that I bring it back and hand it on to Penny upon my return). I had written a couple of times suggesting the idea of a visit, and one day she called from New Hampshire to say that she was on her way. Indomitable, eighty years old, she arrived on her own, and she has from that moment on been an inspiration in my own aging. Within days of her arrival she was prepared to walk across Athens and up to the Acropolis, dressed to the nines in an elegant blue tweed suit with a fur collar, and in her high-top Keds, which my son had once given her as a joke when she was out picking blueberries, but which she knew were perfect for walking across the uneven marble. As she moved briskly past the Parthenon to the other end of the summit, she seemed driven by a special urgency, and I marveled at how the experience of Greece was overwhelming her, when suddenly she cried out, pointing off into the distance. "There it is! There it is!"

"What, Mary?"

"The Hilton, where I stayed last time I was in Athens."

My daughters and I returned from our year in Athens; they were off to college, I to resume my miserable teaching job. I met the young man who was to become the third Mr. Right in the first years of my bachelorhood. He had been a student several years earlier, someone whose brilliance was as thrilling as his evident eccentricities. He was a first-rate artist, gifted at oil painting particularly; his acting talent was obvious from the many roles he had taken in theater, and was coupled with a masterful manner of theater criticism. But then, his writing in general was always first-rate. All his papers were memorable, but I will never forget the last, if only for the way he brought it to me. He was late with the paper, something I have always been harsh about, yet because of his great gifts, I had been lenient, telling him to bring it by midday following the assigned date. I opened my office door to his knock, and found him holding a cafeteria tray, which he handed me without a word and left. On the tray was a plate surrounded by three milkshakes, one strawberry, one vanilla, one blueberry, obviously a patriotic theme celebrating the coming bicentennial. (It was 1976.) On the plate was a hamburger bun, and inside, folded into the dimensions of an average hamburger patty, was the paper. It was, of course, another extraordinary piece of work.

After the close of the school year, when he learned that I had bought a house in a seashore town near his childhood home, he made a date to meet me at my house on the morning of the Fourth of July. In one of those chronological complexities that novelists tend to avoid, I had spent the night of the third in Cambridge, following the angry quarrel with the young man who had suddenly decided not to move with me to the shore, a night of sleeping fitfully on a mattress, as I have described. If that was not enough, I was due back in Cambridge in the early evening of the Fourth for a grand dinner party celebrating the bicentennial while watching the Boston Esplanade fireworks from a balcony across the Charles. It was the Fourth of July, traffic was light, and I set out to drive to the shore, after assuring myself that indeed my young man would be moving in after spending his day driving train engines around at the station. Tired as I was, I was interested to meet again this strange youngster, to uncover some new facet of the rather peculiar personality who had given me his term paper in a hamburger bun. The meeting, as I might have imagined, had its weirdnesses. He was physically a handsome lad, but he had tics—the most obvious was forever stroking his beard and mustache. There was a certain hesitation in his manner of speaking, although the choice of words showed his vast reading. He could be sullen, as though he were being forced to reveal more than he wished or ought. I had a feeling that he was gay, and that he wanted to reveal this to me. It was a common enough theme of timid young men wanting my confidence. I did not advertise my own sexual preference, naturally; I was a professor, this was 1976, I was only recently divorced, and I was the father of four children. But as the popular culture began to embrace gayness, more people noticed it in themselves at an ever earlier age.

Our meeting was almost as peculiar as the presentation of the paper, although far sadder. He got to the point very soon, although rapidly stroking his facial hair and stammering more than usual. Since his youth, he told me, his father had warned him especially against homosexuality. I thought that this was indeed odd; it is not to my mind a subject that needs bringing up with children, who not only know next to nothing about sexual desire and its manifestation, but at best certainly can only imagine the heterosexual paradigm. The result of this indoctrination, he continued, was that he had a morbid fear of homosexuality, and, what is more, a profound physical aversion at the very idea of homoerotic activity. He circled and approached his destination: for several years he was convinced that he was gay, but he could not even imagine what he would do about it. I told him that if he thought this, then his only chance for any happiness or at least psychological fulfillment was to find a male lover. With many a stammer, he conceded that he had in fact reached this conclusion himself; still, his basic aversion was so powerful that he was unable to act. He looked over at me, then asked if I myself was not capable of sex with males. Not that he was implying that I was homosexual, he quickly added, no, what it was he wished to know was whether I could act out something physical with another male. It was so strange a conversation, the two of us in the bright July sun at the seaside. Finally I could not tolerate the tension and indirection. I told him that I wanted to get naked with him in bed; with an enormous sigh of relief he silently followed me upstairs and into my bedroom. There ensued a painful half hour of fumbling and groping. Clearly enough he was excited, ready to reach out and hold me, willing to accept my physical gestures designed to arouse and satisfy him. He was lavish with his kissing, but he maintained himself rigid as a scientist might who was in a lab coat ready with his pen to note down data. At last I was the only one to reach an orgasm, after which we moved apart, got up, washed ourselves, and he took his leave after first shaking my hand and thanking me with complete seriousness.

So there upon my return from Athens was the future third Mr. Right in my local deli. At his announcement that he had recently moved to Cambridge, I invited him to dinner. He arrived washed, combed, and dressed as though he had made a definite effort to showcase how attractive he was, so I wondered what he had in mind besides food and conversation. Of course, we made it to bed later in the evening. This was the first of many nights together, frustrating, sad episodes in which he tried to satisfy his painful erection but was seriously inhibited. We kept at it, however, I selfishly pleasuring myself mightily the entire time, until finally, maybe the whole of a month later, he did achieve an orgasm. One hears all the time of women being so inhibited, but I did not imagine that the more or less automatic reaction of a male to stimulation could be so blocked. I have since learned that an orgasm requires the cooperation of the brain and the penis. Here was a young man whose father had initially made him demented, brainwashing him with those strange injunctions. That first night of success his spasms were so grand that at first I was afraid for him, then almost cried myself as I watched him sobbing with joy and relief.

We remained a couple for two years, until the late summer of 1981. Then it was that he told me he was not sure he could find a body so old as mine sexually exciting enough to continue. Poor fellow, his early deficits left him always monitoring his performance. I applauded his honesty, however, in this and everything else. He was an important teacher for me, all of twenty-five years younger. I learned so much about theater, Antonin Artaud's great declaration, "No more masterpieces," for instance, which he lived by; about art, about the importance of Odilon Redon, about Giacometti, about Beckett, about Monteverdi and his predecessors. For this overeducated classicist trained to know nothing else, he was a continuation of what my first wife, Mary, had done for me, not to mention the architectural education I got from Penny. We went to New York theater, we saw everything; we went to the museums, not the obvious MoMA or the Met, but the small museums that I had never heard of. His conversation was constantly intelligent, if sometimes tiresome in the way young people can be who are determined to tear down everything before building anew. I can honestly say that he enlarged my intellectual horizons profoundly. At the time, I was writing my Apollonius book, where in the preface I thank my Boston University seminar students, but on every page there is the uncredited influence of this remarkable young lover of mine who made me rethink what literature was all about, what antiquity was, and how I related to it.

He and I continued to live in the same neighborhood, although he almost always spent the night at my place. We did not broadcast our relationship in the neighborhood. I have mentioned that he was my "nephew" to the storekeepers, whether it was a euphemism or a case of their naïveté. About six months into our affair he decided to tell his parents that he was gay and use our continued sexual relationship as the proof. As I described earlier, he said, "I do not want them to go to their grave not knowing the truth of me, for then our relationship will have been incomplete." Well, of course, I thought of my mother and our awful one and only conversation on the subject, but at least from the time I was sixteen until her death she knew the true, whole me. At first his parents were enraged, and told him—just as I expected they would—that I was an evil monster who had perverted him. Needless to say, they never spoke to me, instead surrendering to such high drama as standing to the side and ignoring their son when they encountered the both of us in the lobby of a concert hall.

It was my first experience of a young person starting to identify himself as a gay male after he had discovered that same-sex relationships were natural and instinctive for him. He was eager to go to gay bars, the only one in Cambridge being a rather dreary spot next to MIT. I went there once, but what is there to say after, "I'm gay, I'm gay, I'm gay"?

Friends gave me a black-tie dinner for my fiftieth birthday. It was fun, from the hors d'oeuvres and champagne through to the baked Alaska at the end and beyond, when the guests gave brief testimonial performances and I gave a giant twenty-minute drunken response. Among the guests were old friends, three of my four children, and the three young men I have just described. As I reflected later about the evening, I was struck by the disquieting fact that my three children were the only guests present who did not know that those men were my lovers past and present. My young man's recent determination to tell the truth to his parents made my silence all the more painful. In one of life's great coincidences my older son had recently written to say that he was angry at my silence and evasion about the marriage in the years when it was fracturing. His letter seemed to demand a new truth. And so it was, when I knew that the children were spending Christmas with their mother on the ancestral farm, I wrote to him there asking him to share the contents of the letter with his siblings. I wrote that "I have been a practicing homosexual since I was fifteen," named a number of so-called family friends over the years with whom I had been intimate, revealed what role these three young men played in my life, sealed the envelope, sent it off, and waited for a reply. None came.

At roughly the same time, when I girded myself to tell some dear friends in New York—they were a couple I had known through Penny from her undergraduate days at Radcliffe-Harvard—about this wonderful young man and of course at the same time revealed my sexuality, they were congratulatory, enthusiastic, and kind. Encouraged by this, I began telling people piecemeal; but it was difficult for me and for friends of long standing to look at me, the twice-married father of four, and now grandfather of one, and see a gay male living with a young man in Cambridge. One woman, a very old friend, whom I encountered at a symphony performance, gave me an embrace because she had not seen me for a long time, then turned to notice the young man at my side and could only manage, "Well, yes, hmmm . . ." before turning away into the crowd. It is extraordinary how many people had trouble with this change in my public identity for years, until at last I invited them to a church to witness my wedding.

My children, however, came around easily enough. There was no answering letter from my son, but after the holidays, when my younger daughter was staying with me before going back to college, we went out to dinner, at which point she looked me in the eye and asked, "Well, do you want to know the reactions to the letter?" They were (1) Penny's: "He has cheapened our marriage by telling you"; (2) oldest son: "I don't want to know"; (3) second son: "No way! He taught me how to have sex with a woman! But, oh, my God! All those young guys hanging out for the night in his house? I never thought!"; (4) older daughter: "I want to kick myself for bad-mouthing all those gay guys in front of Dad, the ones I worked with last year. It was just because what I was wanting were some cuties to date me"; (5) and my younger daughter said nothing. My older daughter, moreover, then set out to learn about homosexuality, joining the gay support group on her campus and making friends in the gay community. With all the children there was always awkwardness, more, I think, because my lovers could easily have been their siblings, perhaps also from the fact that, as those things go, I had a stronger attachment to them than to my own flesh and blood, at least in some ways and for certain moments in time. I wonder if my children have been hurt by that more than they will admit. Still, I was blessed with their love as they all worked to understand their father in a new way.

Now everything was in the open at home, but not at work. There were many faculty in those days, the beginnings of the eighties, who were comfortable identifying themselves as gay. It was so ironic that I, who had once been so open, now was hesitant, at least in office situations where people knew me as a divorced professor with four children. People I had to deal with at the university were not enough well-known to me to bother explaining the permutations of my emotional life. It was just the beginning of a great shift in thinking: people could be married, or formerly married, and they could be gay. This was preceded by the devastation of the AIDS epidemic, which brought gay people widespread attention that they had not had before, and perhaps as much sympathy as opprobrium. For instance, when I went to my fortieth high school reunion in 1988 as a divorced man, seven years after the first case of AIDS had been identified in 1981, several classmates made an effort to tell me of young men in their neighborhood who were sick and dying of AIDS. I figured it was their way of acknowledging that the teenage boy whom they remembered as the queer, the fairy, the cocksucker was now endowed with a certain dignity known as "gay man."

My young lover, in addition to having doubts about continuing to find this fifty-year-old man acceptable as a sexual partner, was also chafing at the fact that I was the only male with whom he had had sex. As he began to move about in gay circles he discovered the widespread promiscuity that was and perhaps still is the norm of the gay experience. He and I wrestled with the interesting question of whether gay males act out a promiscuity that is inherent in their sexual predilection or whether heterosexual males would be far more promiscuous than they are if they were not bound to a wife and children. When we talked about gay baths, I told him that I was not psychologically up to having a partner whose other outlet was serial sex in evenings at the baths, although what was more powerful was my inability to hear of a companion telling of his exploits. My belief is that sexual intercourse is either a love-filled experience designed to bind two people closer together or it is more in the nature of a bowel movement, designed for much-needed physical relief. As the latter, it need not be commented upon or even mentioned, for that matter. At the time I had been reading about what they were calling the "gay disease" that was spreading in San Francisco, which made me cautious from a new perspective. I had only twice in my life gone into baths. Obviously it was a different experience from making out with one's high school acquaintances in the backseats of cars, and more like picking up hustlers from street corners and bringing them to one's office. From the two times I was in a bath I would say that the difference is the anonymity, the fact that one can move from one to another naked body and indulge as one chooses without any personal involvement.

Oddly enough, the first time I went into a bath was in the seventies, in Boston, and remarkably after a Classics Department reception at Harvard to which I was invited as an alumnus. There I met a former student who was himself a classics professor at one of the nearby institutions. We both got drunk and left the party together, when, to my great surprise, he suggested we go to the baths in downtown Boston. I knew him only as a thirty-five-year-old conventional married male, so this was really a shock of adjustment. We rolled around naked with a bunch of guys there, then took showers, put on our clothes, and went home without commenting on this novel experience together. A few months later when I was having coffee with him I was startled to hear him tell me that he had been back to the baths. In the rigid theater of my mind I could not cast him as a gay male, especially since he did not in any way change his manner or voice from the conventional fellow I had known forever. Where was the mask? The facade? I have often thought of that. He and I were old friends, intellectuals sharing the same knowledge, both married with children, and, as the evening at the baths showed, both at ease with same-sex experiences. Why didn't I build on that evening? Why didn't we become lovers? Wouldn't that have resolved problems of married life in Brookline?

My introduction to a sexual life had been with boys I knew well; I knew their families, where they lived, often their history, and it was from that context we could talk together before and after our encounters. That was my model for interaction with men who prostituted sex; some of the most interesting conversations I have had in Europe have been with young men postcoitally sitting and smoking a few cigarettes and describing their lives to me in answer to my questions. I could recount meeting all sorts of interesting young fellows here in the States. I don't think you get that kind of chatting in the baths. But the issue of the moment was that I was too old for my young friend, soon to become my ex-lover. He needed a greater validation of his sexual habits and of his body and person as performing elements in a sexual drama. So our breakup was all for the best for him. Good luck and God bless. We remained friends.

The fourth of the young men with whom I had serious romantic relationships was a student I noticed on the day of the inauguration of Ronald Reagan. It was also the first day of second term and he was sitting in my class. He used to make jokes about the coincidence of the first day of class and the inauguration, which is why I remember it. I remember picking him out of a class of twenty-five or thirty because he was ruggedly handsome and ugly at the same time, not to mention the unusually surly and unhappy look he could assume. Even when he showed his attractive side it was remarkable how glum he looked. I became more curious, even alarmed, and at last contrived to stroll with him from the class in the direction of the library, where we were both heading. We stopped at a bench on the way and chatted. I managed to get around to his unhappiness. He came from Colorado, had followed a girlfriend to Boston University, no sooner enrolled than she had left him to start up with another fellow. He stayed on. It was his second semester, he "guessed" he liked his classes; it seemed clear he was not an enthusiastic student, although his conversation marked him as intelligent. It was his first experience of the East Coast, which he did not like. He particularly did not like all the Jewish girls at Boston University; they weren't like girls back home. I could just imagine what the girls were like in his suburb. It was mostly Catholic, he said. He was an indifferent Catholic becoming more definitely lapsed. He was particularly repelled by the gay boys in his dorm and at the gym, where he played a lot of pickup basketball; they were always trying to hit on him, he thought, when he was showering. All of this was said in an angry voice, which was his most common mode, I could see. He used to work for a gay man at a newspaper in Denver, and once he and the guy had gotten it clear that they were not going to get it on, they were easy with each other, but these gay boys in his dorm, in the showers, he claimed, would not take no for an answer. He found it disgusting.

His Marlboro Man western swagger, gruffness, and angry tone, combined with the inevitable boyishness of being twenty, I found particularly charming. I contrived to talk with him whenever I could. As the weather turned warm I planned to install some used lumber as a fence at my property in Cambridge and asked if he would like to earn money helping me. He abruptly volunteered to work for free. Our work together on this project was, I am sure, what most fathers and sons experience, although my sons and I had never gotten ourselves into this. He and I fought over every detail. I am by nature a controlling figure; in this instance I was twice the age of the man who was working for me. The young guy had a westerner's contempt for effete easterners, and it was all too clear that he thought I was a typical effeminate literature professor who did not know a hammer from a nail, and there was something personal in these daily disputes too. We each wanted to control, natural enough for two males working on such a project, but it was more that we wanted to insist upon our personalities and identities in the confines of this two-person arena. So the matter of the argument—should the board slant this way or that? should the hammer pound down or up at this point?—mattered all too much. It was entirely funny, we were sniffing each other out, there was some kind of attraction that had nothing to do with the fence-building. I recognized that I found the kid attractive, that I would not mind jumping into bed with him, but of course I would never suggest it, because he would pound me, that was clear. His anger I just chalked up to the fact that he was that kind of person, maybe because he was from Colorado and cowboys all have that tough manner in the movies. Still, we became friends from talking during the lunch breaks I provided. It was clear that we liked each other. I told him he had beautiful eyelashes, to which he just looked glumly down at his half-eaten sandwich, and I felt silly.

Summer came, he went to special courses at Harvard Summer School, I went off to the house at the beach and the peace of my garden. One day in August when I was up in Cambridge, he stopped by to look at the fence we had built, if for no other reason than to argue that it had not exactly been a joint enterprise no matter what I thought. I asked him in for a beer, whereupon he proceeded to tell me excitedly about the great sex he had been having in the summer school dorm in Cambridge. He had never known anything like this. I reminded him that he was indeed a very sexy young man, and obviously a choice specimen for any collection of women. This was a new idea for him; clearly nothing in his Catholic boyhood and suburban school had prepared him for such a jolly summer of promiscuity. He was clearly intrigued as well as made uneasy as he heard me describe his sexual charms in my own flamboyant style. "You remind me of the newspaper editor back in Denver," he remarked without specifying, but in saying that he relaxed some kind of guard he had up. At least that was how I sensed it.

When September arrived and he went back to the university, he stopped by my office, and I invited him for the weekend to the house at the shore. On Saturday evening a former student of mine, who had transformed herself at age thirty into a singer, suddenly appeared at the door to announce that she and her rock band were performing nearby. The young man was thrilled to meet this minor celebrity, more so when she asked him to come along and sit on-stage during the performance. My other weekend guest was a graduate student, with whom I sat talking of her dissertation until she went to bed and I started doing the dishes. Eventually the young man came back, high from his experience, high from the dope they had all been smoking. He came into the kitchen, gave me a hug, touched his cheek to mine, and returned to the living room and lay down on the sofa, staring up at the ceiling and whistling some of the music he had been hearing. When I had finished the dishes, I came into the living room, and saw that his eyes met mine and stayed with me as I moved toward him. I could not resist dropping to the floor beside him and putting my hand on his chest. He turned to smile, then once again gazed at the ceiling. I moved my hand to his crotch, felt him hard there, and pressed a bit.

"Let's go upstairs," I said. And that began three wonderful years of an improbable companionship, ending only when he told me with tears on his cheeks, "Homosexuality is just not for me."

Waiting in the wings, so to speak, was a young woman with whom he had been working, whose interest in him was so palpable that I was amazed he had not noticed long since. It was the truth, and I had to admit they looked beautiful together, and I tried as best I could to keep a smile on my face watching them walk down the garden path, hand in hand, and stand under the chuppah at their wedding in the summer of the following year. I was often amused when I thought that his two bêtes noires, gay men and Jewish girls, had ended up in his bed one after the other. We had lived together, had fought again and again, just like father and son, on many more building projects, and when we went hiking we were like brothers, exploring the trails of Massachusetts, one of his great passions. In the afternoons when we were in bed together we were lovers, but he did not talk of this except when saying goodbye. Years later he invited me to join him in Mexico to show me all the favorite places that he and his wife visited. (It was the impetus for the many trips I have made there, including one six-week stay when I learned the language.) He was just as great a guy in his forties as he had been early on, and I was so happy that our friendship had progressed to this new stage. We steered clear of anything physical on our trip in Mexico, except at the end when we were saying goodbye in the airport. "Well, this it," he said, as he prepared to see me go off in the direction of what passes for security there and on to my gate. He took me in his arms, we embraced warmly, and then he kissed me on the lips, for not too long a time, but enough to seal into it all that great emotion and passion of the days gone by.

The saga of the boyfriends ends with the young man who had been the first of the four, the young married Englishman. He returned to my erotic life from time to time in England, in the Norfolk countryside where he was born and in London, then again in New York City off Tompkins Square when he had been divorced. He was always introducing me to another new girlfriend, a habit also of Boyfriend Number Two, and which so clearly unsettled the young ladies. They understood only too well whom they were meeting and how they were being vetted by him. Eventually I myself introduced him to a young woman, who became his second wife. I was best man at their wedding and then their nearby neighbor in Cambridge. And so our affair finally ended, this time forever, as I made clear to his new bride so that she would not have to be uncertain and unhappy when he walked the dog and stopped by for a chat.

# SEVEN

# SOMEDAY MY PRINCE WILL COME

*"With this ring I thee wed," words spoken before the altar of the Swedenborg Chapel, Cambridge, Massachusetts, May 10, 2008, eighteen years and one hundred forty-four days after we met* (Kent Johnson)

Before the prince arrived, however, I lay around for some time asleep with the apple in my mouth. Which is to say, in the landscape of life I was trudging a lot more down in the valleys than looking out joyously from the peaks. Teaching at Boston University was so disagreeable to me that I grew depressed whenever I had to think about going to the campus, let alone actually entering the place. Imagine my joy, therefore, in the autumn of 1981 when I got a call from the chair at Vassar College, a guy I had met when I was in Athens, inviting me to come to the college for the academic year 1982–83 as the Blegen Professor of Classics. This, he explained, was an endowed chair for scholarly research given annually, in which the holder's main obligation, apart from being a "presence" on campus, was to give a lecture course in the spring semester. It was only four years after my year at the American School. Some academics would have trouble getting leaves in such close succession, but the administration of Boston University, having tried and failed to get me to resign, evidently saw their next best option was to let me take as many leaves as I liked to get me off campus. So I was off to Poughkeepsie for what turned out to be nothing but fun for nine months. The Blegen Professor was housed in a fully furnished little house on the edge of the campus. ("Rather twee, but it will serve," was the description of one of the previous holders of the Blegen chair.) The campus itself was a miniature park, elegant in its proportion and its plantings, having been designed by the firm of Frederick Law Olmsted, the designer who cocreated New York's Central Park. Vassar's faculty and its president welcomed me so warmly that I felt I was in another universe after the coldness, suspicion, spying, and treachery that was daily fare at Boston University. The faculty meetings were an absolute delight, in which one could step over to a sideboard set out with hors d'oeuvres and wine as the debates and discussions grew long.

As the Blegen Professor I gave an inaugural lecture on Berlioz's opera *Les Troyens*, which is based on Virgil's *Aeneid*. Because the Metropolitan Opera was opening its season with *Les Troyens*, and since Berlioz was a fervent Latinist whose opera closely follows Virgil's text with interesting variations, the topic was a perfect fit for a classicist who wanted to talk to a general audience of educated people. It went over very well, as the discussion that evening and random encounters in the subsequent weeks made clear. Not since my Stanford days had I been able to socialize so easily and well, as one can in a confined population with common interests, incomes, and intellects. The inherent insularity was offset by New York City only an hour and half away on a train line that ran along the wide scope of the Hudson River, endlessly beautiful, intimations of Frederick Church at every turn.

My arrival at Vassar coincided with the publication of my Apollonius book. It was a bittersweet moment for me, since my editor, John Gardner, died in a motorcycle accident on the very day of its publication. That was John, doing the sort of crazy and dangerous thing that matched his brilliance and literary daring. Typically, he had begun the series for Southern Illinois only to showcase his favorite authors, and because it would be fun for him to edit critical works on them. John was a novelist, but also an inventive critic and careful reader. He was also eccentric and a prima donna. Other than our initial lunch meeting the day he proposed the book, we were in contact only through the written word. Because his novel *Jason and Medeia* (1973), was based on the same material used by

Apollonius, he had a certain proprietary take on the poem, which sometimes caused us much anguish. But I owe him so much. His initial reaction to what I had written was harsh and dismissive; he objected strongly to the timid, stiff style of academic circumlocution and evasion. I had been guilty of writing as though for Sterling Dow, I realized, wanting to make sure that nothing I said would raise the scholarly eyebrow. Gardner gave me permission—he was the editor, after all—to write what I really meant, go all the way, take risks. It changed me forever, and I could never again write with that scholarly distance. I well remember under his influence describing Augustus Caesar in the Apollonius book as "the man who made the trains run on time," which seemed like an innocuous way to indicate his affinities with the ruling style of Il Duce, only to have some critic complain, "They did not have trains in ancient Rome." I wish I had saved the letters from the next two or three years, John's either berating me for my style or for surrendering to stodginess, mine exasperatedly pointing out where he erred in matters of fact, he apologizing for his angry outbursts, claiming late-night drunkenness, I thanking him for pushing me further. It was a great collaboration, and I grew to love him. But when I arrived at Vassar I was tired, the book was out, and I had postpartum depression and could do little more than lie on the sofa of my twee little cottage and read in a completely desultory fashion various titles that caught my eye in random sweeps of the shelves of the college library. Slowly I began the more concentrated reading that I needed to do for what I wanted to write next, a book on the Apollonian element in Virgil's *Aeneid*. Sad to say, by the time I retired I had only managed to write four chapters, which I then summarized in a longish essay, "Virgil's Apollonian *Aeneid*," which was published in a variorum collection on Virgil.

Into the swamp of my despond came cheery reminders of the good things of life: my younger son, working at the Ritz, had the funniest stories of life in that kitchen; my younger daughter, who had recently spent a year in Kenya and was now studying geology at Boston University, had endless stories of life in the bush alternating with days in Nairobi; a former Stanford student on his way to becoming a major ancient historian sent me a book that he had dedicated to me and Ted Doyle (who had died of a heart attack in 1966); a woman who had been a member of my seminar in Athens wrote to tell me that she was turning her exquisite dissertation on Apollonius into a controversial and interesting book on Apollonius and Callimachus and wanted to dedicate it to me along with her father; another member of that seminar, who was curating the Greek vase collection for the Joslyn Museum in Omaha, invited me to write a contribution for the catalogue she was preparing, and got me a gig at the museum to lecture.

It was about this time when I thought up the idea of taking each one of my children on a trip of their choosing, when we would have the chance in their early maturity to reconnect. For one it was theater in Manhattan, for another restaurants in London and Paris, for the third a week in Maui, and finally the fourth chose geology in Iceland. This kind of concentrated dose makes up as best it can for the geographic separation so endemic to the American family.

In the summer of 1983 I came back to prepare for another academic year; ah, more of the same old dreary same, I reckoned, and metaphorically bent my head, like a peasant heading into a strong rain—at least that is how I would have translated my feelings into art. One drizzly winter day I was stumbling through mounds of broken ice to reach my home, when I slipped and fell— nothing hurt but my dignity, that and sensing right away that I was now wet through. Then I was home and in and out of a hot shower, sitting moodily in front of the fire when the phone rang. It was the head of the classics program at Lehman College, one of the liberal arts colleges that make up the City University of New York, this one being in the Bronx. He was an old friend who had often invited me to lecture in his humanities program at Lehman. His wife and colleague I had known since she was a freshman at Stanford, always recalling the sweet moment when the dear seventeen-year-old had excitedly informed me at the end of her first semester that she was going to major in Latin.

"Charlie," he demanded in his heavy Bronx accent, "how would you like to get a chair, become Distinguished Professor of Classics out here at Lehman?"

He explained that the New York state legislature had mandated a sum of money to endow each one of the branches of the City University with a super-salaried professor in one of the disciplines taught at the place. One might imagine that in this modern world a professor of some branch of science would be the immediate first choice. But my friend was a power with the college president who was in any case predisposed to favor the humanities. "Think it over," he counseled, "and let me know."

"I have, and I am letting you know," I replied. "I would like to be considered."

"Well, when can you come down for an interview?"

"Tomorrow"—I laughed—"if that does not sound too crude and pushy."

"We thought you'd be in a hurry to get out of there."

The next fall I was installed at Lehman College and the Graduate Center of the City University of New York as the Distinguished Professor of Classics with a salary more than double what I was making at Boston University. Those who invited me were candid enough to admit that I had not been their first choice, and I did not have ego enough to imagine that I was in any way the equal of the candidate who declined them. They also shared the gist of the letters of recommendation, including one from a very sour martinet of a man who had survived the camps, who declared that appointing me would be a "travesty." Still and all, a later friendship with a man in the central office of the provost, through whom these appointments were processed, gave me the chance to learn that they were all very impressed "at Eightieth Street" with my previous accomplishments. We all need our doubts satisfied from time to time.

They say that when I called my dean at Boston University to announce my resignation, he called President Silber, who called Bill Arrowsmith, who had left the university a few years earlier in despair of my ever going, and within hours Bill had accepted another appointment as professor at BU. God moves in mysterious ways.

When I came to New York to rent an apartment I discovered that Natasha, a former student from Boston University who, last I had seen her, was off to her native land and London University for an advanced degree, had returned to the States to study for a PhD at the Graduate Center. "Couldn't really stand England anymore; wanted New York," was her explanation. I immediately enlisted her to house-sit for me so that I could spend the three summer months in Cambridge. This transaction caused us to become very good friends, an important detail in the ongoing saga of the arrival of my future prince. When I returned at the end of August, I had a solitary dinner at a nearby Chinese restaurant, where my fortune cookie read, "You are going to be happy for the rest of your life." True enough, so far—I add a caveat thinking of Solon's well-known dictum that no man can be called happy until he is dead, when there is no longer a chance for disaster. After a year I bought a co-op apartment on West Fifty-seventh Street, a busy enough street to ensure that there would be people around when I came back from the theater, since this was the mid-eighties and the city was still considerably crime-ridden.

My initial experience of Lehman College was from the seventies, when, as I said, I lectured on classical literature in their humanities program. The course was popular; the two hundred people filling the auditorium were always a serious audience. It seemed that they were all earnest young Jews whose ambition to move into the professional class was as obvious as their belief that a knowledge of classical antiquity was the sine qua non for bourgeois society. I loved talking to these youngsters; they were so dedicated and intense that once I even flew back from Rome for a couple weeks of lectures at Lehman.

Over the years people in classics at Lehman saw their enrollments dramatically falling; certainly the audience for these lectures declined. There was dramatic, swift change in the ethnicity of the students at the college as much of its Jewish enrollment was replaced by Hispanics. This reflected the changing demographic of the borough as the original Irish American, Italian American, and Jewish American populations began to leave the borough or concentrate themselves in the giant Co-op City designed in one small island of land to hold sixty thousand people. The Dominicans and Puerto Ricans who replaced them were from rural backgrounds, much poorer people with fewer resources for economic advancement, and the once-elegant Bronx became remarkably changed. The art deco Grand Concourse remained, but the walls of the buildings were covered in graffiti. The construction of the hateful Cross Bronx Expressway and other systems of moving automobiles cut through the borough, which was a tragic blow to its physical and social integrity. Landlords confronted with an unstable and poor population began to empty their buildings and torch them to collect the insurance. The Bronx grew to resemble a bombed-out city. Tour operators ran buses of Europeans through the Bronx, so they could marvel at the irony of ruins not unlike what they remembered of their own immediately after the Second World War.

The faculty of Lehman were predominantly Jewish, a first generation up from an immigrant working class. Many of them were bitter or in despair at the change in their student population, but just as many were political liberals who welcomed the chance to display the fruits of education to a hitherto unsuspecting population. I who am so conscious of my WASPiness was startled at being asked all the time, "You Jewish?" and I realized it was simply because I was white. Bronx shopkeepers and landlords were Jewish. I well remember visiting a clothing store owned and operated by Orthodox Jews, where the clerks were all young African American boys perfectly attuned to the African American clientele. The delightful oddity of the place was that customers had to inquire about prices, as none were displayed, and the boys turned to the owners and spoke to them in Yiddish, whereupon a discussion of what the customer could possibly pay took place. Black teenagers speaking fluent Yiddish is not only a delightful curiosity but is also a lesson to those tiresome people who fault blacks for their limited intellectual attainments. If there is a need and an interest the student will respond. The greatest problem to my mind was that so many of the students arrived with a high school diploma from one of New York's public schools, where they had been so poorly and minimally instructed that they could scarcely read and write, and yet they proudly thought of themselves as "college students." How often I thought, *If these poor kids could know what their counterparts in other parts of the country are achieving.* I never finished the sentence, because they were not going to know.

But then I started teaching in the Honors Program, a kind of oasis of excellence where the bright and ambitious could refresh themselves. In my second year at Lehman I had the fourth of my four extraordinary moments in my forty-two years of teaching. It was my honors course in American film, something completely different from my usual experience. Since I was the holder of a chair, I could offer whatever I chose, and I determined to do something with film. I had been surprised in another course when at every reference I made to films in black-and-white—almost the only kind that a cineaste snob like myself would mention—my students drew a blank. Just saying "black-and-white film" made my students shy away as though I were offering broccoli to my children. It turned out that no one in the class had ever seen a film in black-and-white! I determined to offer a course entitled American Film 1930–1950 and rounded up the usual suspects—*Stagecoach* and *Notorious*, for example. I asked them to write a short paper on each film, giving their critique of what they had seen. I wanted them to think of them as "film" rather than simply entertaining "movies." How pretentious can you get!

The experience was extraordinary for me, both for the interesting students who enrolled and for the ideas they expressed. The fact that the films were in black-and-white distanced them for these students, as though they were looking at a remote and unknown culture. They brought an almost anthropological analysis to their viewing, which made for acute observations of a society that they did not for one minute associate with the world they knew from the Bronx. They did not know they were watching what nowadays many critics call a Jewish Hollywood version of the United States. Those movie men, all immigrants, imagined what goyish Middle America wanted to see of themselves in the movies. This added another level of irony to the interpretation, my students being another alien audience doing their imagining of the first set of aliens, the filmmakers.

Whatever it was, I found the papers as stimulating as the classroom comments, always a minefield of ignorance, prejudice, and crudity, as well as sharp, shrewd perceptions, perspectives that skewed my traditional understanding of the film in question. I would have been happy to teach this course on and on forever. I began to question why it seemed to be different from other classes, and I found my answer in a course I offered on ancient epic and its derivatives in contemporary film. I started with the *Iliad*, obviously enough, with bits of *War and Peace* thrown in, and then later on showing the students *Il Gattopardo* and *Gone With the Wind*. I wanted to demonstrate the tragedy of the overthrow of a great city or civilization (Troy, the South [Atlanta], Sicilian Bourbon aristocracy [Palermo]), set into the drama of a love interest that was either comic (Tancredi Falconeri and Angelica Sedara) or tragic (Ashley

Wilkes and Melanie Hamilton, Hector and Andromache). *Gone With the Wind* turned out to be an embarrassment that had not occurred to me when I was planning the course. Many of my black students were offended or uncomfortable with the depictions of Mammy and Pork and Prissy in the film, and were understandably offended by my focus solely on the tragic theme of white supremacy destroyed. I began to extrapolate from that to a general listlessness I had noticed in the last decade, perhaps, toward the literature I had on offer, to wit, the masterpieces of ancient Greek culture, as well as some highlights of Roman, like the *Aeneid*. A lightbulb went off in my head, stupid me. The literature of antiquity is all seen from the perspective of the ruling class; its characters are exploiters, controllers, conquerors. There is where the sympathies of the narrator invariably lies and it is the elite audience for whom the author is playing. The victims by and large have walk-on parts; they do not matter. That is the truth of the slaves in *Gone With the Wind*, no matter that Hattie McDaniel won an Oscar for her forceful portrayal of Mammy in the film. The slaves are so unrealistically portrayed that no one with the slightest knowledge of the sociology of the antebellum American South could possibly consider the characters identifiable. Think of Theresienstadt, the so-called model concentration camp.

Then it was that I began unconsciously to find my lifetime's subject matter unpalatable. The glorification of cruelty, the self-pity of the exploiter and despoiler, these were the stuff of ancient literature, and adopted easily by ruling classes throughout history. Our obvious spiritual ancestors, the English aristocracy at their Greek and Latin at Eton and Oxford, the German Junker class, were then embraced by the bourgeoisie in both those countries and in the United States as a means of empowerment. Children of this class could reinforce their notions of superiority by recourse to identifying with Aeneas or Achilles or Hector and their consorts. Historians have often noticed that our earliest forefathers on these shores established schools to teach the young the legends and culture of Greece and Rome while absolutely ignoring the myths and culture of the Native American peoples who surrounded them. Nowadays, when the American people are so polyglot, products of so many backgrounds, so many of them tortured, poor, and desperate, classical literature courses increasingly grow unpopular unless they are tarted up to pretend to be something about the women or gays or slaves and their struggles for independence, better yet "identity," when in fact those literatures record a very definite effort to push these marginal figures right off the stage.

About the time I left Boston University most everyone with whom I worked knew that I was gay, and I sensed that most of the students knew that or learned quickly enough. The growing political consciousness of gays and lesbians meant that a gay identity did not make one uncomfortable at the university. It was very different at Lehman College, where the predominantly Latino presence brought the macho sensibility with it: women wore spike heels, and the guys were butch, and gays were nowhere to be seen. I was always struck with the extraordinary femininity of the Hispanic gays one saw on the subway in dress and manner, and I ached for them having to act out what they thought of themselves, or rather what their culture demanded that they think of themselves. So at Lehman I was just as closeted as I ever had been thirty or so years earlier, when Mary and I moved to Cambridge.

None of my students ever seemed to be gay, or so it appeared. One of my students was a police officer, who startled me during one evening's lecture by laughing when I made a witticism pretty much for myself, since only someone with a gay sensibility would laugh. During the next student-teacher conference he told me that after police academy and before he had enrolled at Lehman he spent a couple years in San Francisco "to see what it was like." So I worked the fact that I was gay into the conference, and he acknowledged the same, and we became quite good friends. He was always a surprise, just because I have my stereotypes like everyone else. One time we were walking to the Cloisters through Fort Tryon Park, and he surveyed the greenery, this big burly butch, butch guy, and exclaimed, "Wow, I spent a lot of time on my knees here when I was in my teens." Another time, when he was driving me home to Manhattan, he took a route through Central Park and, as the light changed to red in the very darkest middle of the park and he idled the car, I looked out the window and asked, "Isn't this a little bit scary?" "Not with these," he replied, opening the glove compartment to show me two loaded pistols sitting there. No fag, he. It surprised me to hear him insist firmly that he would never come out to his fellow officers, not because they might reject him, but because in the locker room and shower room of the precinct headquarters half-nude male horsing around and sex jokes with gay themes were central to their bonding process as men who are always at risk, and he was not going to spoil their fun. A few years later he surprised me again when, as I was confessing to him my performance anxiety at the prospect of having sex for the first time in years, he offered to go to bed with me a few times to "get the equipment working again."

Since I held a position of such prominence, and hence power, and was a "real American," a "gringo," I could get away with vamping it up quite a bit. I well remember one night talking to a woman during a break in the three-hour class who was introducing me to her husband. She was Hispanic, maybe thirty-three or -four (already a grandmother!), and he was Arab, nervously exuding a possessiveness as to make one wilt. Suddenly another woman student shouted a greeting to me across the hall, and I went over and gave her a kiss on the cheek—we had that kind of relationship. When I resumed my previous conversation, the Hispanic woman asked jokingly, "Aren't you going to give me a kiss too?" and so I did, at which her husband was clearly incensed, although he tried to hide it by smiling in a most peculiar way. Suddenly I was infuriated, so I asked in the sweetest way possible, "What's the matter? Do you want a kiss too?" and all he could do was grin as the crowd in the corridor hooted with laughter: *"El profesor está haciendo el gracioso de nuevo!"*

I was decidedly put off by the vociferous and frequent expressions of hostility and contempt for gay males that emanated from my African American male students. Nothing was directed at me, but they never missed a chance to make a negative comment about male homosexuality real or inferred anytime it cropped up in the discussion of whatever was the subject matter of the course. They insisted, of course, that AIDS was God's punishment for gay men. Since we were not having a class on the idea of god, or god's vengeance, or anything to do with the Christian religion, I held my tongue, although one time, following news reports of the fatal destruction of a bus full of children coming from a Christian camp, I insisted that if the same reasoning were applied here, one would have to say that God punished these children for going to a Christian camp. The idea was so shocking and heretical, my students digested it in silence, and no discussion ensued. On another occasion it was all I could do to hold my tongue from saying that perhaps these black males were thinking of relatives of theirs in prison who either submitted to or aggressively pursued male-to-male sex, which made them prejudiced against males genetically homosexual.

It was during this time that I had an amusing moment of opening the closet door a crack when I was invited to give a prestigious endowed lecture at a university in the American South, after which there was the usual elaborate drinks reception at someone's grand mansion. The bar table was manned by a number of exceedingly nice-looking young African American males, impeccable in their white jackets. I was suddenly in a private conversation with a grotesquely drunk writer of some national celebrity who observed in a voice loud enough for the nearby servers to hear him, "We shoot niggers like these down here." Shocked, angered, and humiliated for those young men, who could do nothing about this, I could only respond in an equally audible voice, "Really? Well, I would prefer to go down on them." The line of servers could hardly control themselves for their laughter.

About this time I discovered the kitchen of God's Love We Deliver, an organization set up to provide nourishing hot lunchtime meals for people with AIDS who were no longer regularly ambulatory. With the assistance of three professionals, volunteers manned the kitchen and cooked, boxed, and delivered the meals throughout all the boroughs. What began with thirty lunches was up to a thousand by the time I left the place. I worked there three mornings a week from six to nine, and it was one of the most satisfying jobs I have ever had, partly for the delightful mix of people who were attracted to the kitchen, needless to say, most of them being the most outrageous, theatrical funny men one could ever meet, but here and there sad parents of now dead or dying young men. When I moved back to Boston I naturally sought out the equivalent organization. It was, however, principally staffed by men on a stipend who were parolees, most of them black, and essentially hostile or at least grudging to the gay male volunteers like myself. So fuck them, was all I could think.

At the time of the catastrophe of September 11 the so-called religious leader Jerry Falwell announced that the collapse of the Twin Towers was God's vengeance for the United States's sin of homosexuality. I was interested to note that not one religious leader, or political leader, for that matter, took to a national forum to refute or speak out against him. One could think back to the early days of the rise of the Nazi party when no leader spoke against their vicious anti-Semitism. If I were given to speaking in a national forum, I would not be able to stress strongly enough to my fellow gay males that they are living in a fool's paradise if they believe they are not totally vulnerable to the Christians. Some of the current politicians with their strategy based on an anti-gay agenda may seem to be a joke, but it is a dangerous one. Think back to the laughter directed at Hitler in the very earliest days. Democracies are so vulnerable to politicians who work to focus the voters' instinct for hatred. It is hard to believe that the tolerance won with such a struggle through the fifties to the nineties is being so quickly eroded in so many parts of the country, gradually surrendering to the perverted thinking of evangelical Christians. How far removed from hate and psychic murder was the wonderful, loving world of God's Love We Deliver.

In my other life as a professor I decided that Natasha, with whom I was on the most cordial and intimate terms, needed some romance. She was at loose ends after a failed relationship, and when I surveyed the males who were in the graduate program at the Graduate Center, I saw that they were either gay or rather dismal, except for one Greek guy in my Aeschylus seminar, who was not only good-looking but bright and very funny. *Aha*, thought I, and planned a dinner party. In order not to rouse suspicion, I also invited a kind of sidekick of the Greek, a Pakistani student who I could see was clearly gay. The party was for Washington's birthday, and the theme was a kind of campy Americanism for three foreigners. That would be the pretext. I even made a cherry pie. Everything went as I had hoped. While the Pakistani and I compared notes on hair gel and other gay ephemera, the other two sat at their end of the table, staring into each other's face, talking non-stop. Before too long they were in a relationship, and, a little later still, moved in together.

Two major events occurred in the next six months that turned my life around. First, I became the director of the Classics Program at the Graduate Center, where I not only taught a seminar but oversaw the formation of a consortium of the classics graduate programs at Fordham University, New York University, and the Graduate Center. It meant going to work on the fifty-second floor of the Grace Building, which fronts Bryant Park on Forty-second Street. It was amusing to ride up in the elevator with all the suits, lawyers, accountants, financial people, almost all of them male, whom in three years of shared rides I never heard speaking of anything but baseball scores. The offices and seminar rooms opened onto breathtaking views of midtown architecture. When I used our seminar room at gloaming I would always enter, stop everything by turning the lights off, and command the students to gaze at the incredible beauty only Manhattan can give at that height. There was the Chrysler Building, its art deco pinnacle shimmering in the sunset or twilight or night lights, whatever the time dictated. My God, it was gorgeous!

Forming the consortium meant hours of discussion, which went slowly or fast depending on the principals in various days of negotiation. Academics are attuned to the sounds of their own voices; some never seem to get over the ecstasy of listening to themselves, while others can move along with brief statements. I am not a patient man and was not at all so good in the role of mediator and administrator as I might have been. Proof of it all is that the day I stepped down from the position of director, and two years later the evening when I left the building after teaching my last class ever as a professor, no colleague said goodbye. I am sure they were opening champagne later in the evening in the Classics Program at the Graduate Center. It doesn't matter in retrospect. The fact is the mission was accomplished, but more important was that I met some wonderful students, many of them friends for life.

And still more than that, I met my future husband at the graduate school. That was the second major change, more than a change, of course, but a dramatic rearrangement of my entire existence. He arrived in my life about two years before I moved into the executive officer's position at the Graduate Center, actually at a Christmas party for students and faculty, which I attended because after Christmas I was going to be teaching a seminar in Virgil's *Aeneid*. Richard was in his forties when he came to the graduate program, just another guy trying to resolve the midlife crisis we all go through. His career of teacher and administrator in a foreign language program of a private school in New Jersey was coming apart as he and the head tangled over goals and achievements. It seemed a perfect time to step back, go on half-pay, and try to earn a PhD in classics, since Greek and Latin were both well-known to him and the literature was something he had already studied. He was born gifted with that special something that allows some people to learn, retain, and speak foreign languages securely and easily. I am still amazed that Germans and Italians, when they hear him speak their language, ask him where in their country he was born; his Spanish is also first-rate, and, though he pooh-poohs it, so is his French.

He had met Natasha at the Graduate Center, and she related to me with some amusement his announcing, in order to forestall invitations for a date or for a drink, that he was a "homosexual and a recovering alcoholic." That anecdote was delivered in the midst of a gossipy conversation about the graduate school in which she also described the pleasure she was having with her new beau, which motivated us to ponder how I had no one in my life, and from that, well, it is obvious I am sure, she mentioned this Richard Deppe, for that was his name, as a possible lover for me. She had grown to know him better, and they had gone from discussing classics to their love lives, and he had told her of his recent breakup. We thought up a scheme in which she and her beau could get Richard together with me. It was early December and the Classics Program was going to be having their annual Christmas party. They would invite Richard for a supper after the party, and then that very evening I would, as it were, be invited as a last-minute idea, so he would not suspect that there was a setup. Richard is such a guileless person, and by nature so optimistic that he never, ever suspects plots, schemes, and subterfuges.

Everything went as planned. We had a spirited meeting at their house, talking of, among other things, the course I was to teach on the *Aeneid*, which Richard himself was taking. If he had been a youngster I might have thought twice about pursuing a relationship with someone who was about to become my student; there is too great an imbalance of power. But since we were, as I saw it, both of us professionals, already ensconced in careers, there did not seem to be any serious conflict of interest. I have always wondered if the gossipmongers and scandal-bearers in the department had wanted to make something of this as well, but I guess by the time they realized that Richard and I were an item the course was long since over, and he had decided not to pursue the PhD. At the dinner party I was the first to leave, and after the Greek boyfriend kissed me as Greek males do, and then his girlfriend did as well, Richard stepped forward and deposited his own lips upon my cheek. Aha, thought I, and departed.

I returned to Boston for Christmas, from where I wrote Richard a letter ostensibly to continue an argument we had begun at the dinner, but in fact to invite him to go with me to a fund-raising dance for a gay seniors organization in mid-January. He countered by saying that he would if he could bring me earlier in that same evening to a party that the foreign-language teachers in his New Jersey school were holding. The evening went perfectly. He arrived to pick me up five minutes early, foreshadowing a life of bliss for two people always anxious, always early, and aggressively intolerant of tardiness. The foreign-language party in New Jersey was amusing, as each one of the participants drew me separately into a side room to tell me how wonderful Richard was, just like any church group promoting one of their own as husband material. The dance was a revelation of the fact that Richard and I dance the foxtrot very well together, and can take turns leading and following with equanimity—remarkable in two such controlling males. In the middle of the evening the organization paused to auction off a week trip, airfare/hotels for two, to Puerto Rico. Richard immediately put in a bid, and stayed in as the dollar amount rose. I knew perfectly well that he was on half pay and not much of that in any case, so I insisted he stop this romantic foolishness. Then I suddenly thought that I was going to be sixty in March, had been thinking of something celebratory, had even thought of hiring a hustler to take on a trip. Now, much, much better, there on the dance floor I invited Richard to come as my guest for a week in Paris. It would be his school's spring vacation, the Graduate Center would be on break as well, and off we would go. He accepted.

Since we had met in circumstances where men do not necessarily rip off their clothes directly thereafter—unless they possess the raging hormones of the very young—we had continued on our progress of getting acquainted in similar social situations. Before the trip to Paris, however, we had to sleep together. At last he invited me over to his apartment in New Jersey for dinner and the night. I was understandably nervous, since I had been away from male companionship for several years, and had said, "Thanks, but no thanks," to the gay cop who had wanted to help. Richard and I both had to confront a sexual experience unique to each of us: neither had been to bed with another man who was older than thirty, and now a naked male age fifty-nine was face-to-face with a naked male age forty-six. You know the advice to the novice swimmer? Just shut your eyes and jump in. I think the equivalent is avert your eyes and start hugging.

My sixtieth birthday in Paris with Richard, ah, well, it was a dream. He had arranged by letter from the United States a dinner in the three-star restaurant of Michel Rostang, ending in a trolley brought out from the kitchen with a cake on the side of which was written in chocolate *Bon Anniversaire, Charlie.* Sophisticated Parisians in the restaurant collectively drew in a breath of joy, witnessing this sixty-year-old male treated to the loving attention of his beau. Richard was so handsome, gallant, and charming, and I was besotted. At our hotel, when the young man at the front desk asked if everything was all right, I had the temerity to say that as a rule I found the French difficult, but not on this visit, to which he replied with a smile, "You and Monsieur give off such an aura of happiness, how could we in this hotel not respond?" To which I must append that as we sat on a bench at the edge of the Seine and embraced with a long kiss we suddenly heard loud applause, only to discover that we had an enthusiastic audience on the decks of one of the Bateaux Mouches passing by. At Richard's suggestion we had already gone to rural British Columbia to see my older son perform as Lord Evelyn Oakleigh; in the summer we would set out on a three-thousand-mile drive across the United States, giving Richard a chance to meet up with my past, and before that we went to London for the wedding of Natasha and her beau, our dear friends who had brought us together. To my mind one of the great tests of true love—whatever that word is supposed to mean—is the ease with which the lovers travel together, and over the years we have tested ourselves with high passing grades again and again, from Saint Petersburg to Tokyo.

The details of our twenty-odd years together, which are endlessly fascinating to us both, can easily make our auditors' eyes glaze over in the telling and retelling. The most significant is certainly the struggle from the beginning for two alpha males to live together in harmony. Richard still laughs over my disinclination to cede him space for his toiletries in my master bedroom bathroom in Cambridge. To this day we both pull out the grocery list when we are off to the market, and until a few years ago there was always a tussle over who would drive. They talk about Ginger Rogers dancing backward in high heels. With alpha males we are dealing with two Fred Astaires. I remember years ago complaining to my children that Richard was a very "controlling, overbearing person" and all four of them hooting, "And you aren't?" After our flight back from Paris in March when he first slept over in my bed in Cambridge, he ran his hand over the sheets and asked when they had last been washed, to which I replied, "Oh, I don't know, maybe

September," and ever after he has washed all our personal clothing and the bedding in whatever house we are in every week, always. So fussy, is all I have to say. Over the years Richard's stern observance of a weekly laundry day has made him seem to be the unofficial "housekeeper" of the ménage, and I sometimes feel that I am playing Joan Fontaine's second Mrs. de Winter to his version of Judith Anderson's Mrs. Danvers.

Richard grew up in a working-class family; his father was a carpenter. When Richard was working he used to come home with the attitude of one who puts his lunch bucket down on the table, takes his paper to the living room sofa, and waits for the woman to put the meal on the table. That was his family home, whereas my childhood memory was of one of the kitchen help coming to open the door that separated the dining room from the living room where we were all assembled to announce, "Dinner is served." Because I was a college professor and Richard a schoolteacher, I was amazed at how hard and long he worked—from early morning until late five days a week, week in and week out. I felt like Marie Antoinette among the citizens of Paris. I had no idea. The result was that for twenty years until he retired I cooked dinner every night, and because I am a good cook, I varied the menu, dreamed up interesting items. He was always tremendously appreciative and mentions it now in his retirement to everyone we meet. A peculiar feature of our relationship is that Richard, who has been completely easy and open with his sexuality from the time he came out in Berlin in 1963, is also the most conventionally masculine gay male I have ever encountered. I did not realize this in the heady days of our early romance; but there he is, not the least bit interested in girly gossip, clothes, decor, oh, the list is endless, and most of all he disdains small talk. My older daughter once sent a comic strip of two dumpy old people on the sofa with the wife saying, "Why don't we try some witty banter with each other?" to which he stops to ponder, then says, "I like cheese," and she, reaching for the television control, says, "Never mind, let's turn on the TV." She labeled it *Charlie and Richard.*

People who want to assign acculturated gender roles to a gay couple will have trouble here. He does the washing, I do the cooking, anybody near the sink washes the dishes, we have a cleaning person for the house, he does the home repair, I do the decorating, we both invite people to dinner, and he often cooks then, he always cooks the fish, I make pies. He served me rusted lettuce without demur the first time he asked me for dinner, and thinks that the sell-by date on packaging is just part of the design, whereas I used to toss the refrigerator leftovers after he had left for work every day. And so it goes. Since I did not grow up in a home where housework was the natural responsibility of any of my family, I have an inclination to let it slide always. Our friend Natasha says she still expects that when she takes off her clothes and drops them on the floor, someone will come by to put them away sooner or later. *Where are the maids of yesteryear?* is sort of my François Villon moment.

When I retired I wanted a project. Richard was willing to go in financially with me on another house in the seashore town where my former house, which I had sold in 1985, was. We planned that the new place would have space for a large garden, and so it has developed over the ten years since we bought it. The property originally had not one single planting. Now there is an elaborate formal Italianate garden of raised beds geometrically arranged and centered on a large fountain. The borders of the property have been planted with a variety of trees, shrubs, and vines, so that one has the sense of complete privacy when sitting out in the yard. Behind the house the previous owners had put in a twenty-by-twenty-foot sandbox with children's equipment. Richard bricked this over to create a very Italianate terrazzo, and put over it a wooden trellis on which we have trained wisteria, so that in the heat of the summer sun there is constant shade and cool in that lovely spot. He had already built a superb deck on the side of our house in Cambridge. He sometimes crows about his many great projects, although I will not let him lord it over me too much, since I want to say that Mary and I built all our furniture in our first Cambridge apartment even if, I must confess it, we used decorator nails for everything.

Our house is in a town inhabited predominantly by Italian American and Irish American working-class families who tend not to move away. When I lived there before, the various young men in my life were assumed by my neighbors to be nephews or some other family member. Now I was returning with a man who was clearly a "partner," as the parlance had it, and if it was not clear, then the very gossipy real estate agent would pave the way with the news. I wondered what kind of reception we would get from the people around us. In the very first summer, Richard got out his tools and bought lumber to fix a rotting step in the front porch stairs. Instantly every male in the nearby houses stopped by to comment on his progress, uniformly changing their mode of address to "Richie." When he set to work on the grand project of the terrazzo behind the house, our next-door neighbor and his buddies would monitor the developments from his side porch, until one day one of the men came over to suggest that Richard might want to install lateral rods to contain the outward pressure of the bricked area. And so we were launched, or at least Richard was, as guy-guys.

This town is extraordinary. When there came the first day on which it was legal for same-sex couples to apply for wedding licenses, there were greeters at the town hall to bestow a rose upon each couple who came up to the counter. The local paper, an enthusiastic supporter of the local Roman Catholic church, the principal religious affiliation of the townspeople, published photos of every one of these couples and added enthusiastic human interest accounts. It was an unexpected development that in fact reminded us of the basic live-and-let-live philosophy of the town, which is, as it should be, the true fallout of the humanistic implications of the Christian religion, rather than shooting employees of abortion clinics and other so-called Christian calls to action.

One day we decided to get married. We were contemplating moving to New Jersey to live in a retirement community and learned that unmarried couples in New Jersey must pay a surtax of 15 percent when inheriting from each other. Forget about love; it's all about money. When I went to the Cambridge town hall to apply for a wedding license, I thought, *I shall be the thrice-wed Iowa City beauty*, just as they used to style the Baltimore-born Wallis Warfield Simpson when she married King Edward VIII. Once we got interested in the idea of the wedding, our take-charge personalities managed to work up a rather grand wedding day. We arranged to rent the Swedenborg Chapel located on the edge of the Harvard campus, which has a marvelous ersatz Gothic interior. The minister of my older daughter's church in New Hampshire agreed to come to Boston for the service. I had some hesitation in arranging all this, since only two years before I had suggested to the children that they rent this very same space for their mother's memorial service. I talked it over with them, and was happy to hear them all agree that time moves on, and so it was thoroughly appropriate for Richard and me to hold our wedding there with the very same minister. Our darling friend Sally put all her time and effort into flowers and other details, and her beautiful daughters poured champagne at the reception, while my wonderful teetotaling son-in-law dramatically popped cork after cork. A friend promised to bring her delicious spanakopita. The night before, Richard and I made bowls of ingredients for sandwiches and other reception treats, which we then assembled before the wedding in the church basement. The space was a little bare, but Sally's flower arrangements helped immensely. It was very cramped, and that we could not change.

We invited about 140 people, all but two of whom accepted, much to our surprise. But, as someone who came up from New York on the train and afterward went right back because he had so little time remarked, "I could not miss seeing this moment, two men getting married, it is so special." We had to dissuade parents from bringing their children to watch this "historic occasion," there just was not room. The minister in her remarks during the service quoted from the preamble to the decision by the Massachusetts Supreme Judicial Court, words that are an eloquent defense of the human right and need to gather into relationships. She also had interviewed the both of us and quoted from our remarks to her, such as Richard's saying that "living with Charles is like a perpetual AA meeting." That brought down the house, plus her words of advice for two alpha males living under the same roof. At the end, when the pastor presented us to the congregation as a married couple, there was not a dry eye in the place, and we received a standing ovation, which, ham that I am, I treasure to this day.

Recently, to mark my eightieth birthday, I told my children and grandchildren that I would pay their airfare, car rentals, hotel bills, and restaurant meals if they would settle on four days or so when they could all assemble at the seashore for a family get-together. We had sold the Cambridge house, given up the idea of New Jersey because of the financial crisis, bought a condo for the winter in Florida instead. But the house at the seashore was, I suppose, to be considered the family manse. We are not a compulsively close family, so this was an undertaking, but on the fourth of August they duly arrived, one after another, and registered at the hotel where the management in an access of goodwill and sympathy had assigned to them rooms overlooking the ocean. For some of the grandchildren this was the first time they'd met. The first night Richard had a barbecue on our terrazzo; the second night I hosted a buffet dinner on a balcony of a restaurant overlooking the beach; and the third night, again on the terrazzo, we made sushi and pizza. There were four children and six grandchildren, some spouses, Richard, and myself—Papa Richard and Papa Charlie, as my younger son's children call us. Not exactly *Dynasty* or *The Forsyte Saga*, but a family, nonetheless.

*Gathered in our garden at Hull, Massachusetts, August 5, 2010. Standing, left to right: my son Howard; his daughter, Jasmine, and son, Jesse; my daughter Gile; her fiancé, Kent; my son Willis; his wife, Sheree, and their son Zachary; my daughter Helen (whose husband could not be there). Seated on the bench are Willis's daughter Olivia; myself; Richard; and Willis's daughter Rebekah, with Willis's son Noah occupying the foreground.*
(Howard Beye)